PRESIDENTS AND THE PEOPLE

PRESIDENTS
and the People

THE PARTISAN STORY OF GOING PUBLIC

Mel Laracey

TEXAS A&M UNIVERSITY PRESS
College Station

For a complete list of books in this series, see the back of the book.

The paper used in this book meets the minimum requirements
of the American National Standard for Permanence
of Paper for Printed Library Materials, z39.48-1984.
Binding materials have been chosen for durability.

Library of Congress Cataloging-in-Publication Data

Laracey, Melvin C., 1951–
      Presidents and the people : the partisan story of going public/
Melvin C. Laracey.—1st ed.
            p. cm.—(Joseph V. Hughes, Jr., and Holly O. Hughes series
in the presidency and leadership studies ; no. 10)
      Includes bibliographical references and index.
      ISBN 1-58544-180-5
      1. Presidents—United States—Public opinion—History.
2. Public opinion—United States—History.   3. Communication
in politics—United States—History.   I. Title.   II. Series.
JK511.L37   2002
302.2'24'0883510973—dc21   2001005190

CONTENTS

TABLES

ACKNOWLEDGMENTS

I have had a very fortunate intellectual life. At Notre Dame I encountered two wonderful professors, Walter Nicgorski and Edward Cronin. Dr. Nicgorski was my first mentor and the first to encourage my interest in American history and government. Dr. Cronin inspired me with his dedication to teaching and good writing.

At Harvard, where this book began as a research paper in Mark Peterson's course on the presidency, I was introduced to the graduate study of American politics by Mark, Morris Fiorina, Richard Neustadt, H. W. Perry, and Paul Peterson. Mark Peterson was my second mentor, a strong source of encouragement and ideas for my work, and another inspiration as a teacher.

At the University of Michigan, where I wrote the dissertation that served as the starting point for this book, I enjoyed learning from and working with Mark Brandon, Richard Cohen, John Kingdon, Kent Jennings, Kim Scheppele, Tom Green, and Stephen Smith, who visited for a semester. Mark Brandon in particular has always been there to encourage me as I worked through this project (and many other matters). I am also indebted to fellow graduate students Scott Allard, Susan Ellis, and Glenn Beamer for their help and encouragement at Michigan.

Near the end of my dissertation work, I had the pleasure of contributing a chapter to *Speaking to the People*, a collection of essays on the history of the rhetorical presidency conceived and edited by Richard J. Ellis. Some of the material in chapters 2, 3, and 4 of this book appeared in that chapter. The University of Massachusetts Press has granted me permission to incorporate this material here, which I gratefully acknowledge.

Stephen Wayne and George Edwards then encouraged me to turn my dissertation into a book, Martin Medhurst and another anonymous reviewer provided extensive commentaries on the initial manuscript that helped greatly, and Dale Wilson improved the manuscript with his thorough and thoughtful editing.

I would also like to thank the George Bush Center for Presidential Studies at Texas A&M University, the Texas A&M University Press, and my institution, the University of Texas at San Antonio, for their support in making the publication of this book possible.

Finally, I owe my deepest thanks to my wife (and first editor), Marian Aitches, and our son, Nick, who not only put up with all my late-night and weekend labors, but also brought such happiness into my life.

PRESIDENTS AND THE PEOPLE

Introduction

IN THIS ERA OF MASS COMMUNICATIONS when presidents go over the heads of Congress and speak directly to the American people on an almost daily basis, it is hard to imagine a time when presidents did not engage in the practice of "going public."[1] According to the currently accepted wisdom in the field of presidential studies, though, going public is a twentieth-century phenomenon. This conclusion is based on some seemingly compelling facts: Although a few presidents before the twentieth century gave policy speeches, many hardly spoke at all—and those who did generally restricted their remarks to noncontroversial, nonpolicy-specific subjects.

Why did presidents of old supposedly avoid going public? The only answer ever proposed is that these presidents did not want to express their positions on policy matters directly to the American people because of a universally felt understanding—a common-law constitutional norm—of what constituted legitimate presidential involvement in the public policy process. This theory was first advanced in "The Rise of the Rhetorical Presidency," an article by James W. Ceaser, Glen E. Thurow, Jeffrey K. Tulis, and Joseph M. Bessette, and then elaborated on in Jeffrey Tulis's *The Rhetorical Presidency.* Pre-twentieth-century presidents and politicians, we are told, were constrained by a powerful political norm against direct appeals to the people on policy matters. According to this theory, the sole proper avenue for such public persuasion "led through Congress, not to the people directly," because of the central role played by the legislative branch in the deliberative process by which public policy was to be developed under our constitutional system. To facilitate the deliberative process, the norm held that presidential communications on matters of public policy were to be addressed principally to Congress, in writing. While some presidents might be tempted to "speak to the people through these messages," they would be restrained rhetorically by having to address them in writing to Congress. "To the extent" that the people might read these messages, "they would be called upon to raise their understanding" of them "to the level of deliberative speech."[2]

Influenced by this powerful norm, presidents "only rarely" employed oral or written techniques of "popular or mass rhetoric." Presidential communications to the people instead were couched in general terms and avoided policy specifics. This "political importance of formality" even "extended to 'unofficial' or 'informal' speech and behavior by presidents."[3]

This is an attractive argument, seemingly unassailable from the empirical record and buttressed by enough citations to the *Federalist Papers* to overawe most scholars. If the argument stopped there, it might well be left alone as a sort of historical curiosity. Instead, the assertion that pre-twentieth-century presidents behaved differently out of deference to a now-superseded conception of our constitutional order has led Tulis, Samuel Kernell, and others to advance sweeping normative claims about our current political system that are based on its supposed deviation from the "original" constitutional order.

The first important normative claim rests on the unassailable and well-documented fact that policy-oriented speechmaking by presidents increased dramatically in the twentieth century. Somehow, it is said, the old norm against going public withered away in the twentieth century. With the demise of this proscription, presidents have been free to go "over the heads" of Congress and appeal directly to the people on policy matters.

Now we are said to be in a new era, the era of the "rhetorical" or "plebiscitary" presidency, in which presidents' efforts to mobilize public support for their policies are a routine part of the public policy process.[4] Previously, the public was, in effect, an interested bystander as Congress, and sometimes the president, carefully debated and produced public policy that reflected the distilled, reasoned will of the people. Today, the president is expected to be both the leader and the follower of public opinion, with Congress serving as the ratifier of the public's will that has been discovered and/or stimulated by the president.

This is a drastic and unfortunate change, we are told by the proponents of this theory, because with it the careful, deliberative public policy process intended by the Founders has been lost.[5] The assumption of a publicly reserved presidency before the twentieth century is even cited by political and legal philosophers as evidence that the nature of modern political discourse has changed significantly.[6]

In *Going Public*, Samuel Kernell draws a different but also serious conclusion from his assertion that the technique of "going public" has only "lately come into vogue at the White House." He concludes that when presidents invoke the technique of going public in a policy dispute with Congress, bargaining and compromise suffer because publicized issues become "stylized in ways that frequently reduce choices to black-and-white alternatives and to principles that are difficult to modify."[7] Again, the implication is that our system of government operates differently than it used to, and that this change has detrimentally affected public policy making and also altered the institution of the presidency.

This book constitutes a hard second look at these normative claims and the empirical claims upon which they rest. As I will show, both kinds of claims rest on fundamental misconceptions. These misconceptions are essentially due to scholars having employed such narrow views of terms such as "going public" and "original intent" that they basically eliminated from consideration any evidence or factors that might have contradicted their hypotheses.

Since the empirical claims are the foundation for the normative claims, let us begin with a reconsideration of the facts. The prior scholarship in this area focused mainly on whether pre-twentieth-century presidents gave policy speeches. Since few did, the conclusion that these presidents did not go public seemed obvious. This study, however, takes a broader view of going public to include *any* means—rather than just speech-making—by which a president conveyed his policy positions to the American people.

Furthermore, the analysis in this study moves beyond the single dimension of whether or not presidents communicated with the public on policy matters. Instead, in analyzing the public communications activity of pre-twentieth-century presidents, I employ two dimensions. They are: (1) if a president was active in the public policy-making process in any way (ranging from going public to exercising the veto power); and (2) if a president still communicated with the people even if he did not involve himself significantly in the public policy-making process.

The use of two dimensions is important because there were strong partisan divisions throughout the nineteenth century over the proper role of the president in the policy-making process. One conception held that the people, and thus their presidents, were legitimate participants in the public policy-making process. The other competing conception held that policy making was the exclusive province of Congress, and that presidents should not become involved in the process in any way, including communicating with the public on policy issues. Nevertheless, some presidents who followed the reserved conception of the presidency still spoke to the public quite a bit about nonpolicy matters (such as the need for national unity), whereas others said little about anything.

This more nuanced look at pre-twentieth century presidents reveals a remarkable finding: half of the nineteenth century presidents managed to engage in a form of going public—communicating their policy positions rather clearly to the American public—even though only a few made many policy speeches. That so many presidents *did* engage in direct communications with the public on policy matters calls into question the validity of the empirical and normative claims previously made about the supposed absence of policy communications to the public by nineteenth century chief executives. Among other things, it means that there could not have been a universally felt, constitutionally based norm against going public, as has been asserted.

The use of a two dimensional analysis of pre-twentieth century presidential behavior yields the following typology:

TABLE I
Two Dimensions of Presidential Activity

President Communicates with Public	President Active in Policy Making	
	Yes	*No*
Yes	[1] Mobilizer Model (Goes Public)	[3] Celebrator Model (National Cheerleader)
No	[2] Deliberator Model (Works only with Congress)	[4] Reserved Model (Silent Figurehead)

As Table 1 suggests, there are, in fact, four institutional models of presidential behavior. The first of these is the Mobilizer Model, in which a president is actively involved in the public policy process and, to enhance his or her influence, communicates directly with the American people over the heads of Congress. This is the classic model for contemporary presidents, exemplified by the title of Kernell's book, *Going Public: New Strategies of Presidential Leadership.* The second is the Deliberator Model, in which a president participates in the public policy process but keeps a low public profile, working through Congress and avoiding direct communications with the people on policy matters. This model is set forth in great detail in Tulis's book, *The Rhetorical Presidency.*

The other two models describe the two ways presidents may behave publicly even if they are not active in the policy-making process. The third is the Celebrator (or National Cheerleader) Model, in which presidents use public events to communicate with the people but only on policy-neutral themes such as patriotism or the nation's character and progress. The fourth is the Reserved (or Silent Figurehead) Model, in which a president avoids public communications almost entirely. (For a description of the criteria employed for determining which presidents fit into which model, see Appendix A.)

As is shown in this study, the use of this two-dimensional typology reveals that the previous one-dimensional way of gauging public communication activities by pre-twentieth century presidents is inadequate. It improperly conflates two aspects of presidential behavior—public communications and involvement in the public policy process—leading to the erroneous conclusion that virtually all presidents before the twentieth century behaved the same way for the same reason.

Furthermore, the focus on presidential speechmaking is an over-specified indicator of presidential communication that improperly excludes other potential means of communication. As I show in this study, a major deficiency of the empirical claim that pre-twentieth-century presidents were different because they avoided public communications is that it does not take into account presidents' extensive use of newspapers throughout the nineteenth century as a means of communicating with the American people. Indeed, there was almost no such thing as a "nonpartisan" newspaper in the first half of the nineteenth century. Rather, papers were aligned with, supported, and even created by political parties and senior party officials for the express purpose of generating support for chosen political viewpoints and individuals.

From 1800 to 1860, every president supported a newspaper that was regarded as at least the semiofficial voice of his administration. This phenomenon reached its high points in the presidencies of Andrew Jackson and James Polk with what can only be called "presidential newspapers:" newspapers established and heavily subsidized by the presidents as a venue to attack their opponents and announce and defend their public policy positions. Both Jackson and Polk felt so strongly about the importance of this weapon that they met daily with the papers' editors to plot their media strategies and hone their messages.

Somehow, the presidential newspaper has become the forgotten way of going public. As Tulis recognized, public communication can be accomplished through more means than just formal speechmaking. However, the only other means he considered were presidential proclamations and "informal" speeches by presidents. There is no consideration of how presidents might have sought to appeal to the people through the newspapers of the time or other means.[8] This is a serious oversight, because getting messages to a mass public through speeches was a difficult process before the twentieth century. There was no voice amplification or transmission, so only a limited number of people could hear the speech or even see the speaker. Moreover, although the newspapers of the time (most of which were rabidly partisan) might convey a speech's content, the speechmaker had little control over how accurately and fairly its message was conveyed.

The explanation for this oversight may be that modern scholars have almost automatically equated "going public" with speechmaking, since that is essentially the only way presidents communicate with the public today.[9] In studying the development of presidential communications, it is important to avoid imposing our current, technologically colored conception of public policy rhetoric on the past. The term rhetoric, after all, encompasses more than just speech. It is conventionally defined as "public persuasion on significant public issues," including "all forms of persuasive discourse—both written and spoken."[10] The biased way in which scholars have approached "going public" means they may well have not fully considered whether presidents might have used other ways to communicate with the public at other times in our history. Until that possibility is considered, as it is here, conclusions about the office of the presidency and our system of government that are based on incomplete, time-bound studies and one-dimensional analyses must be treated with caution.

This study employs a more comprehensive definition of going public as any identifiable means by which a president appeals to the public for support or understanding of his policies. Consequently, it produces a radically different conclusion than previous studies. While earlier studies concluded that going public was a twentieth-century presidential phenomenon, this study shows that the presidency has, virtually from its inception, contained a component of "going public." This more historically accurate view of the presidency casts serious doubt on the normative claims of scholars that rest ultimately on the notion that going public is a twentieth century permutation of the original constitutional order. Going public is not an illegitimate or ill-advised modern replacement for the congressionally dominated "deliberative" and "bargaining" processes for making public policy that were established by "original consensus" by the Founding Fathers. Rather, I argue, "going public" is a legitimate mass mobilization tool that is (1) the modern manifestation of a philosophy that was present at the founding, represented most visibly in aspects of the "Antifederalist" and Jeffersonian "Democratic-Republican" movements, and (2) the logical product of a presidency that is constitutionally involved in the public policy-making process.

The characterization of pre-twentieth-century presidents as relatively passive figures who distanced themselves from the public has never really been seriously questioned by scholars, although it has been described as "an unusual portrait of nineteenth century politics which, after all, was a period, especially at its close, of intense political participation and partisan organization." Moreover, if it is true, as Richard Neustadt observed, that "presidential power is the power to persuade," is it really plausible that all the presidents during the first century of our government's existence made no effort at public persuasion on policy matters? Under Neustadt's schema, going public enhances presidential power by increasing a president's prestige. The greater a president's prestige, the less likely members of Congress will be to resist that president's policy initiatives because they anticipate there will be public support for the initiatives resulting in pressure on them to provide enabling legislation.[11] Therefore, even before the twentieth century, presidents who desired to take the lead in setting national public policy might be expected to have tried going public.

Despite these apparent anomalies, the characterization that pre-twentieth-century presidents did not go public has been almost automatically accepted and has come to dominate the common conception of the modern presidency. Indeed, many scholarly works on presidential communications today begin with a discussion of how the relationship of presidents to the public is different now than it used to be.[12] The distinction between pre-twentieth-century presidents and their successors also permeates the literature on the development of the American presidency.[13]

Such assertions leave students of American politics, constitutional law, and political communication with the unsettling impression that the presidency has evolved in ways that conflict with the Founders' "original intent," and also serve to foreclose the eighteenth and nineteenth centuries as relevant sources of information on the development of the presidency. The area of presidential studies already labors under the problem, perceived or real, that, because there are so few cases (i.e., individual presidencies) to study, sound research is impossible. This problem is then exacerbated by the perception that there were basic differences between "modern" presidents (those after Theodore Roosevelt in 1901 or even post–Franklin Roosevelt) and predecessors, because scholars then exclude from their study the "premodern" presidencies, leaving an even smaller number of cases for analysis and comparison.

Stephen Skowronek's *The Politics Presidents Make* represents a notable attempt to rescue presidential studies from this predicament. Skowronek argues that it is possible to group presidents across time into various "ordering principles," or "reference sets," according to the common political environments and "leadership dilemmas" they faced. By focusing on whether a president takes office as a dismantler, affirmer, or creator of the political order, Skowronek is then able to compare presidents from widely varying time periods.[14]

By surveying the approaches toward public communications of all presidents before the twentieth century, my research develops yet another "ordering principle" for the study of the presidency: how pre-twentieth-century presidents approached the common question of whether to communicate with American people and, if so, by what means. I have limited my study to this "premodern" period because it has been so neglected by scholars in comparison to the "modern" era of presidential communications that most scholars believe began with the "bully pulpit" media tactics of Teddy Roosevelt, who became president in 1901 after the assassination of William McKinley.

This study involves a two-pronged critical reexamination of the conventional wisdom that pre-twentieth century presidents avoided public communications on policy matters. The first is a careful study of the public communication philosophy and actions of every president from George Washington to William McKinley. Its purpose is to develop an accurate historical record of how those presidents did or did not go about communicating their policy positions to the public, so that theoretical inferences about their behavior can be tested and justified.

The second is the development of an overall theoretical framework for understanding the differing presidential approaches toward public communications uncovered in the first part of the research project. Such a framework will deepen our understanding of the development of the presidency as an institution that has both shaped and been shaped by social and political expectations. Several recent studies have pursued this line of inquiry. Herbert Stein has argued that presidents were constrained for forty years after the Great Depression by an overwhelming academic preference for Keynesian economic theory. In *The Symbolic Presidency*, Barbara Hinckley asserts that common understandings of presidents as national symbols have shaped the development of the presidency. Finally, Stephen Skowronek argues that in exercising their powers, presidents react explicitly "to perceptions of what is appropriate for a given president to do."[15] In a similar vein, this study shows how differing perceptions of the place of the presidency in the constitutional order affected the policy making and public communications activities of presidents in the nineteenth century and beyond, resulting in no fewer than four models of presidential behavior in these fields.

As noted earlier, an important aspect of this reassessment of public communication activities by pre-twentieth century presidents is a deeper look at their widespread use of newspapers to communicate with the public on policy matters. The use of subsidized newspapers by presidents to influence public opinion is discussed, often only briefly, in works of journalistic history.[16] The use of presidential newspapers is also discussed in some political histories, but usually without focusing on its institutional implications.[17] Finally, the numerous books about the development of the institution of the presidency either ignore the widespread use of presidential newspapers, note the fact without analyzing the theoretical significance of the phenomenon, or treat presidential newspapers more as quasi-independent partisan echoes of the president rather than the primary presidential communications tools they actually were.[18] There has been no critical study from a political science perspective of what the existence of presidential newspapers for more than half of the nineteenth century tells us about the institutional development of the presidency and its relationship to Congress and the American people.

Works that assert a difference in the public communications activities of pre-twentieth century presidents ignore more than just the presidential newspaper. They also ignore the use of other nineteenth-century presidential communications tools, such as the interview, the press release, and letters written by presidents to be read in public or published in newspapers. They also slight the use of presidential messages to Congress as tools of popular communication. Because these messages were published in newspapers, sometimes even before their delivery to Congress, it is clear that some presidents aimed their messages as much or more at the public as at Congress. Also glossed over or misinterpreted is the fact that some presidents went on extensive speaking tours to arouse public opinion in favor of their positions. These other forms of communication were used by a significant number of nineteenth-century presidents, and provide further evidence that not all of them avoided public communications on policy matters.

On the other hand, as this study also shows, a significant number of presidents, especially in the last third of the nineteenth century, did indeed avoid most public communications. It is the mistaken assumption that *all* presidents behaved in this reserved manner that led to the hypothesis that there must have been a norm against going public in the nineteenth century. In reality, though, there is an even split in the numbers (see table 2 in chapter 6), with eleven nineteenth-century presidents going public, either through their administration newspapers or speechmaking, and eleven remaining largely silent on policy matters.

What, then, explains this split in presidential approaches? The literature on the history and development of presidential communications either ignores the differences in behavior or simply explains the differences in terms of the presidents' personalities. One notable exception is the thesis put forth by the proponents of the "Rise of the Rhetorical Presidency" school of thought. Although the thesis grows out of an erroneous perception that almost all pre-twentieth-century presidents avoided going public, it does provide an explanation for why some early presidents might have avoided doing so. That explanation is simple: they shared a common philosophy that going public was constitutionally inappropriate. On the other hand, half of the nineteenth century presidents did go public and so obviously did not share this philosophy.

What is the source of the philosophy of those presidents who did go public? It is the populist, direct democracy, "voice of the people" philosophy that sprang up in America at the time of the Revolution and that found its simplest expression in the bold assertion in the Declaration of Independence that all men are created equal. Adherents of this philosophy took these words literally, and took from them the conclusion that all (free white) men were entitled to have their voices considered equally in the affairs of government.[19] The role of elected government officials was simply to carry out the majority will of the people on key political decisions. I call this the Democratist philosophy for obvious reasons.

This was indeed a very different conclusion than the one reached by another important segment of American society. This group thought that, whatever the Declaration of Independence said, not all men were created equal in many important ways, including intelligence and character, and so it was clear that not all men were fit to have their voices considered in the affairs of government. It was, rather, the civic duty, privilege, and, perhaps, even destiny of those relative few of suitable talent and background to rule on behalf of the many, filtering out in the legislative arena the inappropriate demands and passions of the "many" to discern and implement the true "public good."[20] I call this the Classicist philosophy because it is based on the classical idea of a representative republic in Western political thought.

During the battle over the ratification of the Constitution, these two competing philosophies became core components of the political thought of many Antifederalists and Federalists. The philosophies eventually came to comprise some of the fundamental tenets of the Democratic and Republican Parties in the nineteenth century.

It is the continuing influence of these two radically different views of the meaning of representative democracy throughout the nineteenth century that explains the variance one sees in presidential behavior in the area of going public. This fundamental disagreement over the meaning of a "republican form of government" underlay the competing conceptions of going public among presidents, and thus determined whether presidents chose to try to go public or not. Each partisan-based philosophy had different implications for presidents going public. Therefore, presidents who followed one philosophy would have been open to going public, whereas those who followed the other philosophy would not have been. Not surprisingly, then, one sees a century-long fluctuation in the approaches presidents took toward going public.

Democratist views found their way, via the Jeffersonian Republicans/ Democratic-Republicans, into the Democratic Party orthodoxy of the nineteenth century. Similarly, the Classicist views found their way into nineteenth-century Republican orthodoxy via the Whig Party. Most Democratic presidents, consistent with their party's direct representational, populist view of democracy inherited from the Antifederalists, went public. Most Republican presidents, consistent with their party's indirect representational, congressionally dominant view of democracy, avoided the practice.

Chapter 1 uses the window of George Washington's presidency to introduce another central point of this book: that there was, at the time of the founding of our national system of government, fundamental disagreement among Americans about many basic concepts of the presidency, the Constitution, and the nature of government itself. This chapter assesses the early level of overall consensus about the institution of the presidency by examining some of the controversial actions taken by Washington and the reactions to them by the other most prominent Founding Fathers: Alexander Hamilton and Thomas Jefferson, both of whom were in Washington's cabinet, and James Madison, who was in the House of Representatives. The results of this examination reveal a truth that is well-known to historians but largely ignored by many other scholars: there was surprising disagreement among these men over many early aspects of the presidency and even the Constitution itself. Once the magnitude and expanse of the disagreements is glimpsed through this window, chapter 1 turns to a brief survey of the fundamental disagreement over the meaning of "republicanism," or representative democracy, that divided Americans in the 1780s.

Chapter 1 then moves on to an examination of the claim that the source of the "limited norm" against going public is the *Federalist Papers*. Even though the philosophy of the Federalists was undoubtedly the basis for the "limited norm" against going public that was followed by half of the presidents in the nineteenth century, a literal reading of the *Federalist*

Papers themselves, I argue, reveals only tenuous references at best to any such norm. Once the *Federalist Papers* are placed in their historical context, this ambiguity can be seen as a reflection of two discomforting realities for the Federalists. First, there was the necessity for the main authors, Alexander Hamilton and James Madison, to accommodate as much as possible the views of the Antifederalists who, after all, were the ones the authors were trying to win over. Second, Hamilton's and Madison's own conflicted and still-evolving attitudes toward the role of the "people" in government would have deterred them from espousing in the *Federalist Papers* ideas that they themselves did not necessarily share. Chapter 1 then concludes with a brief survey of how significant elements of the Antifederalist and Federalist philosophies evolved into the Democratic and Republican orthodoxies of the nineteenth century.

Chapters 2–5 present the results of a close examination of the public communication philosophies of every president from Washington to McKinley. Interwoven with this inquiry is the story of how each of these presidents did or did not communicate their policy positions to the public.

As will be shown, the group of presidents who avoided or minimized their public communications can be divided further into two categories. The first category consists of presidents such as Ulysses Grant and Chester Arthur, who remained publicly silent because their conception of the presidency in the constitutional order demanded it. Under this conservative conception of the presidency, Congress was the only legitimate participant in the public policy process. Presidents who adhered to this view therefore quite understandably did not go public.

The second category consists of presidents such as Rutherford Hayes and Benjamin Harrison, who explained their reticence on nonconstitutional grounds (such as politeness or lack of preparation) but were clearly following the Whig-Republican notion of a reserved presidency.

Another conception of the presidency, one held mostly by Democrats— including Andrew Jackson, James Polk, and Andrew Johnson—held that the president was a perfectly legitimate participant in the national policy-making process. For these presidents, going public was part of their job, perhaps even a responsibility.

These differing views have their roots in the constitutional ambiguity and philosophical disagreements that underlay the founding of the American republic, and with it the creation of the presidency. On one hand, many Americans quickly came to believe that the president should be an independent, vigorous participant in the public policy-making process as the representative of the *direct* will of the people. On the other hand, many other Americans quickly came to believe that the executive should be just that, subserviently executing the *deliberative* will of the people as determined by the legislature, while not getting involved in the legislative process which was, after all, reserved for legislators.

The former, presidentially active view had its roots in the radically populist ideals that swept over America and France in the late 1700s and in the ambiguous structure of the Constitution, which set Congress and the president up as potentially coequal participants in the public policy process. Perceiving themselves as equally if not more capable as Congress at representing and mobilizing the will of the people, presidents who adhered to this view would have perceived direct contact with the people on matters of public policy as fundamentally *legitimate.*

The latter, presidentially reserved view would be a logical manifestation of the classic conception of a "republic," in which the "few" ruled on behalf of the "many" through the legislature. Under this older view, grounded in the example of the British Parliament, the legislative body in a republic was considered the only institution capable of filtering out the "passions of the people" and determining, through careful, personally disinterested deliberation, the true "public good."[21] Therefore, direct contact with the people on matters of public policy was fundamentally *illegitimate.* This principle, of course, would have extended to the presidency, as the first president, George Washington, clearly recognized. As described by Harry Jaffa, Washington's understanding of classical republicanism was that "the holders of [high] office should, and could, work out their differences behind closed doors, much as the Constitutional Convention had done, and then present to the country a standard to which the wise and good had already repaired, and which the rest of the country would certainly follow."[22] Under this conception, there is no place for direct public communications by presidents on policy matters.

One can see both views at work in the nineteenth century. Indeed, for a long time in American political history, the presidency sat squarely on a fundamental political fault line. Democracy literally means government by the people, which in a large community simply is not feasible. Representatives therefore had to be involved to make the system of popularly based, or republican, government function. However, there was fundamental disagreement over the *nature* of that representation. Should it be indirect or direct, with representatives following the trustee or the delegate model of representation?[23]

On one side of the line were American politicians and political thinkers who believed that democracy could only be made to work through the device of refined, indirect representation, in which the desires and passions of the people could be passed through the deliberative public policy filter of Congress. Representatives would act as trustees, employing their best judgment on policy matters, and the president's job would be to carry out congressional decisions.

On the other side were politicians and thinkers who trusted in the masses, saw no need for any filtering processes, and so wanted direct popular control of the government. They envisioned the national government as a direct democracy in which the role of elected representatives, especially the president, was simply to ascertain, advocate, and carry out the "will of the people" on policy matters.[24] Representatives would act as instructed delegates.

The remarkable aspect of this political division is that it rarely manifested itself as a serious problem in the nineteenth century. Most of the time, the fundamental division on the meaning of representative democracy and the role of the president in it seems to have bubbled below the surface of American politics or at least been barely visible, with some presidents following one conception of the presidency and some following the other without much notice either way.

Several historians have noted this phenomenon of hidden political conflict, including Joyce Appleby, who observes: "The link between belief and action in politics is usually left implicit. Understandings do the work of open declarations. When intellectual disputes do bubble up to the surface of public life the provocation is usually temporary. Calm returns without too much digging among tacit assumptions."[25]

Just once, as we shall see, did the disagreement over the appropriate role of the president in the public policy process surface in a sustained way in the nineteenth century. When it did, it resulted in the equivalent of political civil war. This happened in 1868, when Andrew Johnson was impeached and almost convicted by Republicans and Whigs in Congress for, among other things, daring to have made an "inflammatory" public policy speaking tour.

The parallel existence of these two strains of thought about the presidency even provides an explanation for the thinly veiled way that many early presidents went public through their own newspapers. Their concealment would be evidence of the transition time, when some presidents were doing one thing, "going public," while also trying not to look too much like they were doing so, out of deference to the other conception of our representative institutions.

One can see these competing conceptions or paradigms in play throughout the nineteenth century, coloring the actions of presidents as well as other politicians and actors in the political system. In the twentieth century, with the dynamic presidencies of Theodore Roosevelt, Woodrow Wilson, and Franklin Roosevelt, this constitutionally based debate essentially was settled in favor of the principle that it is perfectly appropriate for the president to be involved in direct public appeals and all other aspects of the public policy-making process.

Thus, as discussed in chapter 6, going public is not a modern manifestation, but rather the modern triumph of one view of the proper place of the presidency and the people in the constitutional order over another very different view. In broader terms, it is also a graphic illustration of how, rather than producing consensus when it was adopted, the Constitution actually served as a framework that was expansive enough for differing views of democratic government and of an important institution, the presidency, to coexist throughout the first century of our government. Ultimately, spurred by changes in the electorate, social expectations, and the mass media, the view that more closely matched the inherent institutional logic of the presidency prevailed.

From this revised historical perspective, some of the normative claims that have been made about going public seem dubious. The most prominent of those claims are critiqued in chapter 7. Rather than being of questionable legitimacy, the practice of presidents going public is and always has been, for many Americans, an essential aspect of a truly democratic republic.

CHAPTER 1

Just Whose Constitution Is It, Anyway?

THE CLAIM THAT THERE WAS ONCE a presidential norm against going public is based on the premise that there was an early consensus among the Founders regarding the character of the presidency. Is this premise correct? Just how much consensus was there among the Founders over the presidency, or, for that matter, the Constitution itself? If there was, in fact, a great deal of consensus about such matters, then the idea that there was a consensus that presidents should avoid going public on policy matters would seem quite plausible. If, on the other hand, there were many disagreements over the early presidency or other constitutional matters, then the idea that there might have been a consensus on such an important aspect of the presidency as communicating with the people becomes less plausible.

A survey of George Washington's presidency is an appropriate test of this notion. That first presidency, being the closest in time to America's founding and comprising some of the most distinguished Founders in its administration, should be a good reflection of the level of consensus regarding the institutions of their new government. This survey reveals that there were, in fact, rampant disagreements over all sorts of issues during the Washington administration, hardly manifesting a spirit of constitutional consensus.

The flowering of scholarship on the founding period in the past few decades has revealed the fundamental disagreement over the meaning of representative government that divided Americans in the 1780s. As will be seen, this disagreement was an important factor in the debate over whether the proposed Constitution of 1787 should even be ratified. The existence of the disagreement raises the question of whose understanding of the Constitution should be consulted when interpreting it.

Another significant question, especially in light of the fact that the *Federalist Papers* were written to convert Antifederalist opponents of the Constitution, is whether the *Federalist Papers* really do say that presidents should avoid going public, as proponents of the concept of the modern rhetorical presidency assert.[1] A reanalysis of all the *Federalist Papers* cited by proponents of the concept casts doubt on this assertion. Rather than clearly saying so, the *Federalist Papers* seem curiously ambiguous on this point. The ambiguity arguably reflects the purpose of the essays, which was to convert or at least neutralize opponents of the proposed Constitution. Those opponents would have been generally much more open to the idea of direct public communications from presidents and other elected officials, and the authors of the *Federalist Papers* may have shaped their arguments accordingly.

Differences of opinion over the true nature of "republicanism," or representative democracy, continued long after the ratification battle ended. This chapter concludes by tracing the persistence of these conflicting views in the party orthodoxies of the Whig, Republican, and Democratic Parties throughout the nineteenth century.

George Washington's Presidency and the New Government

The American presidency is, in reality, a remarkably ambiguous office. The Constitution provides only the barest of outlines for the office, stating in Article II that "the executive power shall be vested in the president," and then listing several of the president's powers and duties. "The executive article fairly bristles with contentious matter," says Charles Thach, "and, until it is seen what decision was given to these contentions, it is impossible to say just what the national executive meant."[2] As Ralph Ketcham puts it, "when Washington took his oath of office in April 1789, then, far from everything being settled, virtually nothing was." The problem was that "there was very little plainly given, very little clearly withheld;" the Constitution "did not define: it deferred." On the key point of whether the drafters themselves intended the enumeration of presidential powers to be an exhaustive description of those powers, for example, there seems to be little or no evidence.[3]

Rather than bequeathing the nation a detailed blueprint for its government, the Founders left a "spider's web of words" over which there was a surprising lack of consensus. Those who attended the Constitutional Convention and participated in the drafting of the Constitution "thought about the executive in notably divergent ways," that became a "potent source of constitutional controversy in the 1790s" and beyond.[4] This situation left those elected to serve as president of the United States with a wide range of choice in determining how they would govern. Most importantly, the vagueness of the Constitution on the office of the president left room for two conceptions of the presidency to flourish practically side by side throughout the nineteenth century, with many presidents deciding whether or not to "go public" based on which conception they held.

This lack of constitutional consensus can be seen in the disagreements over the character of the office that began during George Washington's first term. The architect of Washington's program and his chief adviser was Alexander Hamilton, who has been described as a virtual prime minister for the administration. Between them, Washington and Hamilton laid the groundwork for a good part of the modern presidency by resolving many of the most important questions about the character and breadth of presidential authority. As one of Hamilton's biographers put it, "the political, financial, diplomatic, and personal battles he fought as Secretary of the Treasury with the leaders of the opposition, notably Jefferson and Madison, . . . added up to a decisive five-year war over the meaning of the Constitution of 1787, and . . . out of it Hamilton emerged the undoubted victor." Much of the credit for this victory can be attributed to Hamilton's skillful "exploitation of the ambiguity of Article II."[5]

That there were so many battles over the presidency is perhaps the most convincing proof that there was no consensus over what the presidency should be. There was not even agreement over how the holder of the office should be addressed. Almost immediately after Washington's election, the question was first referred to a committee in the House of Representatives. The committee chose the simple title "President of the United States," but the Senate chose "His Highness the President of the

United States and protector of their Liberties." At Washington's and Madison's urging, the former title was eventually settled upon. Significantly, Lance Banning notes that this "debate over the tone of the new government raged on in the press and among the people for months and years to come."[6]

That there was disagreement over even how to address the president is early evidence of the existence of competing conceptions of the office. The Senate's preference for an address fit for a king indicates a conception of the presidency as a sort of royal national figurehead, an English model with which colonial Americans were quite well acquainted. Significantly, that model calls for the titular head of the government to be that in name only, with real policy-making power reserved to the legislature. Another aspect of that model is one of public reserve. Even today, the British king or queen hardly ever speaks publicly, a practice that proved quite controversial in England after the death of Princess Diana.[7] In its idealized form, this is the model of the "patriot-king" to which Washington aspired as president.

More fundamentally for the future of the presidential office, Washington, advised and supported by Hamilton, staked out a claim to an independent institution with broad powers. This was made manifest in his opposition to a bill in the first Congress which provided that Senate approval was required before the president could dismiss an executive official. The argument was a simple one: since the Senate clearly had the power under the Constitution to approve presidential appointments, it must have the power to approve dismissals also. Interestingly, two of the eight members of the House who had been delegates to the Constitutional Convention supported the legislation, while the other six, led by James Madison, opposed it. With the aid of a tie-breaking vote in the Senate by Vice President John Adams, Washington's position prevailed. From then on, in passing laws to establish the major departments of the government, Congress usually steered clear of much involvement in the internal workings of the executive branch.[8]

There were other clashes over the propriety of presidential actions. The problem was that "in the eyes of Jefferson, Madison and many others, Hamilton's policies were ultra-Federalist, viciously so." From their much narrower perspective on the proper powers of the national government, Madison and Jefferson raised concerns about matters that we now take for granted. One example is the criticism they levied when Washington, at Hamilton's urging, personally led militia troops to put down a rebellion in western Pennsylvania against excise taxes on whiskey. Madison and Jefferson interpreted the action as proof that Hamilton was planning to subvert the Constitution by establishing a standing army. They even disapproved of Hamilton making legislative proposals to Congress as treasury secretary. If the president assumed a principal role in policy formulation, they argued, Congress and the states would eventually be subordinated to the executive, which would undermine popular sovereignty and result in an American-style monarchy.[9] (As will be seen, Jefferson's attitude on this point changed when he became president.)

As with domestic policy, there were also conflicts over foreign affairs in the Washington administration. Once again, these conflicts involved contradictory opinions concerning the appropriate extent of presidential power. What is noteworthy is that the disagreements involved the very men one would expect to have the best understanding of what the Founding Fathers meant when they wrote the Constitution: Washington, Madison, Hamilton, and Jefferson. Their disagreements came to a head when Washington issued the Neutrality Proclamation of 1793, which declared that the United States would stay neutral in the war between France and Britain. Jefferson and Madison were convinced that, since only Congress could declare war, only Congress could declare American neutrality in time of war. Hamilton, as usual, believed that the president could issue a proclamation of neutrality on his own authority.[10] As described in the next chapter, the disagreement spilled over into a monumental newspaper war in which both sides presented their cases to the public in articles written by prominent anonymous authors.

There was not just a lack of consensus over the presidency. The Founders disagreed about many things, including the basic powers of the new national government itself. For example, in 1791, after Hamilton proposed the creation of a national bank, Madison, to Hamilton's amazement, rose and spoke for a whole day on the House floor in opposition to the legislation. Madison insisted the law was unconstitutional because the Constitution did not give the federal government the power necessary to incorporate a bank. He noted that giving Congress the power to incorporate institutions had been discussed at the Constitutional Convention and laid aside.[11] Nevertheless, the legislation passed the House by a vote of thirty-nine to twenty, and would become law unless Washington vetoed it.

Concerned about the constitutionality question, Washington consulted Thomas Jefferson and Attorney General Edmund Randolph, who had been an influential member of the Committee of Detail at the Constitutional Convention. They both backed Madison's main contention that powers not specifically granted to Congress were forbidden to it. Madison's position, incidentally, was seemingly at odds with his argument in *Federalist Paper no. 44* that granting Congress the power to make all "necessary and proper" laws had been the only reasonable way to "accommodate all the possible changes which futurity may produce."[12]

Turning to Hamilton, Washington gave him the opportunity to defend his legislation against these substantial attacks. Hamilton responded with his famous "Opinion on the Constitutionality of the Bank," which persuasively argued that Congress, as the legislature of a nation, must be considered to have, under the "necessary and proper" clause of the Constitution, implied powers that surely included the power to incorporate a national bank. This opinion not only persuaded Washington to not veto the legislation, but also provided the argument which Chief Justice John Marshall later relied on to sustain a broad interpretation of federal powers in *McCulloch v Maryland*.[13]

Later, as presidents themselves, Jefferson and Madison continued to express a different view of the federal government's constitutional powers. Because they thought that a constitutional amendment was needed first, both men refused to support funding for public education, a national university (which was Washington's lifelong goal), or internal improvements such as roads and canals.[14]

Over twenty-five years after Hamilton's death, Madison was still carrying on his disagreement with his old collaborator and nemesis. In 1831, he gave Hamilton credit for having cooperated "faithfully in maturing and supporting a system which was not his choice," but then added that Hamilton had tried to give to the Constitution "a constructive and practical bearing not warranted by its true and intended character."[15]

Against this backdrop, it is hard to see much consensus among the most prominent of the Founders about what the provisions of the Constitution meant, especially those concerning the presidency. Instead, we see squabbling over many key aspects of the new government. While such squabbling does not mean there could not have been consensus on other fundamental questions, such as the constitutional legitimacy of direct appeals to the public on policy issues, the breadth of disagreement suggests that the Founders could have had differing views among themselves on that point as well.

The Federalists vs. the Antifederalists

There is an even bigger problem for the argument that the norm against going public was based on a universally felt, constitutionally based consensus. The problem is that a significant proportion (perhaps even a majority) of Americans did not support the Constitution when it was proposed. These Americans, who opposed ratification for a variety of reasons, came to be known as the Antifederalists. In general, Antifederalists opposed the Constitution because their philosophical views about two important aspects of government were fundamentally different from the views of most supporters of the Constitution. The two main areas of disagreement were over the extent of powers to be given the new national government, and over the directness of representation that the American people should be afforded in the new government. Antifederalists typically believed that the federal government would be a threat to liberty and so should be kept small and constrained. Many also believed that popular representation and participation in the new government should be as immediate and direct as possible.

Few non-Federalists attended the Constitutional Convention, partly out of suspicion that a vast strengthening of the national government was planned (Patrick Henry said he "smelt a rat"), and partly because Federalists had managed to pack most state delegations with their sympathizers.[16] Furthermore, those who did attend either walked out before the convention was over, or refused to sign the completed document. During the state-by-state ratification process that followed, Antifederalists put up a spirited battle that the Federalists barely won.[17]

As we shall see, this disagreement did not end with the ratification of the Constitution. Instead, those who had been on the losing end of that battle kept on fighting the bigger battle over the true nature of the American republic and representative democracy. Moreover, this battle was carried on *within* the confines of the narrowly adopted new Constitution. That is, even though many Americans had opposed ratification because, in their opinion, it did not reflect their fundamental conception of democratic government, once the Constitution had been ratified and a new government formed, most opponents did not attempt to undo the ratification (although many did push for clarifications and limitations, which resulted in the first ten amendments).[18]

As Lance Banning explains, the objections of the Antifederalists "never reached as far as the underlying principles of government structure around which the convention had ordered its plan." Instead, taking advantage of the vaguely worded nature of the Constitution, which really ruled *out* very little (especially in terms of the presidency), they simply continued to pursue their own vision of democratic government within the institutional framework that had been created.[19] In pursuing this vision, they "would claim to be more loyal to the Constitution than the [Federalist] government itself."[20]

Consequently, a major deficiency in the argument that there was a universally felt consensus is that the supposed "universe" only includes the expressed thought of the Federalists and not of their opponents. We are shown only one dimension of constitutional thought, instead of the two that actually existed and influenced political behavior at the time.

This fact raises an important question: Just who were the "architects of the American constitutional order" that supposedly proscribed the rhetorical presidency? Or, to put it another way, "Just whose Constitution are we talking about, anyway?" Were the architects only those involved in the actual writing of the language, plus perhaps those who voted to approve the document (with no Bill of Rights) at the convention?[21] Once the question is asked, the problem in answering it becomes apparent. The Constitution, because it was so vaguely worded, was hardly a completed work when it was (contentiously) ratified. Instead, the document was just a starting point, and an ambiguous one at that. Because the document truly was not much more than an "invitation to struggle" over its meaning, any persons or groups who joined in the struggle and had an impact on the development of our "constitutional order," logically must be considered to have been architects of the Constitution as well.[22] In particular, it can be argued that, "since the Constitution would not have been ratified without recommendatory amendments, the will of the community was neither Federalist nor Anti-Federalist, but some combination of the two." More broadly, as Jack Rakove has observed: "since 1789 Americans have always possessed two constitutions, not one: the formal document adopted in 1787–88, with its amendments; and the working constitution comprising the body of precedents, habits, understandings, and attitudes that shape how the federal system operates at any historical moment."[23]

Any claims about what the Constitution meant, therefore, must be considered incomplete if they do not take into account *all* of the significant conceptions of what the Constitution meant—or should mean—that existed among Americans at or around the time of its ratification, and which continued to influence political actors (especially presidents) into the nineteenth century. After all, how can we privilege only one professed understanding of the proper constitutional order when another equally vibrant understanding existed at the time? Specifically, why are we to assume that all nineteenth-century presidents, whatever their partisan philosophy, followed only one of two traditions in American political thought on how a "republican" or "representative" government should operate?

The two traditions were starkly different. Many Americans took literally the assertion in the Declaration of Independence that "all men are created equal," whereas many others thought just the opposite—that "all men were created unequal."[24] Members of both groups fought together in the Revolution, but they came out of that struggle with very different conceptions of the extent to which Americans should be able to participate in their government. After all, if men either were or were not essentially equal in ability, then they arguably either were or were not all equally suited to participate fully in the affairs of government. Which was it? As Linda Kerber puts it, "the revolutionary generation had left an ambiguous legacy."[25]

Echoing the classic English Whig conceptions of society and government, most Federalists thought that there were "two orders of men—the talented few and the ordinary many," who many thought actually "represented two orders of being." Because the "blind ignorant herd," also known as the "unthinking multitude," was incapable of rational behavior in the political sphere, "classical republicanism gave the talented few a critical function as the brains of the body politic." Without this control over the baser impulses of the common people, government would degenerate into anarchy, demagoguery, and tyranny.[26]

There was a strong strain of economic and social elitism in the Federalist philosophy because classical republicanism presumed that only those who had achieved economic independence and high social status could be expected to deliberate in a disinterested way toward the "public good."[27] Indeed, because legislators in a republic were there to rise above personal and local interests, they were not expected to be bound by, or even to consult, the views of their constituents.[28] Similarly, once they had performed their function of electing the legislature, the people had no right to try to influence their representatives or even to debate what they had done.[29]

In contrast, many other Americans believed there were no fundamental differences among men, because, in the final analysis, all human behavior, even in the arena of republican (representative) government, came down to the pursuit of personal interests. All men, they asserted, even the "patrician elite," pursue their own economic interests in an equally rational way. This meant that "liberally educated gentlemen were no more capable than ordinary people of classical republic disinterestedness and virtue and that consequently there was no one in the society equipped to promote an exclusive public interest that was distinguishable from the private interests of people."[30]

There thus was no logical basis for the "common folk"—the great mass of Americans—to defer to their "betters" in any aspect of government, from elections to legislating to running government offices. Indeed, the best representatives for the various classes and interests in society would be persons from those classes and interests, because they would best understand the views and needs of their constituents.[31]

In this populist view, since everyone was entitled to pursue their private interests within the governmental sphere, they logically were entitled to an equal voice in the affairs of government. Representation was to become actual and direct, with representatives ascertaining and implementing the private interests and majority will of their constituents rather than trying to divine the "public good." To these Americans, a republic meant an "egalitarian democracy" that "granted to citizens a large measure of direct political power." They therefore "rejected the need for any mediating class of political leaders," looked "to the press for information" needed by the polity, and "counted on direct action by the people as the best means for discerning the will of the people." The process of governance would be one of "jarring individuals and interests," with "no disinterested umpires" from the patrician class and, for that matter, "no mechanisms at all for reconciling and harmonizing these clashing selfish interests."[32]

In Thomas Jefferson's distillation of the philosophy that he had himself adopted, the "rights of the whole" were to be "no more than the sum of the rights of individuals." Consequently, all government representatives were to be "mere agents or tools of the people." The actions of elected representatives should, in the words of prominent Anti-federalist Samuel Chase, reflect the will of the people "like the reflected light of the moon." These early American populists envisioned a government under the direct control of the people, with representatives operating as delegates and not trustees to implement the majority's will. It thus was critical that "the men entrusted with power had to be kept responsive to public opinion," which itself became a communal creation based upon the participation of "thousands upon thousands of obscure ordinary people" rather than the social elites.[33] Significantly, this radically different definition of representation did not mean there would be no deliberation in the polity over public policy. It just meant that the deliberation would occur in a different setting: "Federalists regarded representation as a device to facilitate deliberation. Anti-Federalists, on the other hand, conceived of the deliberation pre-requisite to sound governing as primarily social; that is, taking place within the body of the people."[34]

During the fight for independence, the revolutionary generation of Federalists "had endorsed popular participation in government because it expected that the citizenry would continue to accept the leadership of an educated and generally conservative elite." Instead, the democratic, egalitarian ideals of the revolution had then swept through American society, changing the character of many state governments. Men from the "lower class" began to dominate the state legislatures, which in turn began adopting legislation, such as debtor relief provisions, that favored their constituencies.[35]

Alarmed, the Federalists determined that something had to be done to prevent these local excesses of democracy from destroying the social foundation of hierarchy on which classical republicanism was based. Their first steps were to push through changes in many state constitutions that cut back the unfettered authority of state legislatures by strengthening governors and the judiciary. However, their ultimate solution was a drastic strengthening of the powers and protections of the federal government, to enable it to resist the leveling forces that had been unleashed in the states by the Revolution.[36]

As Gordon Wood puts it, the Founder-Federalists planned to use the Constitution as a political device to control these discomforting social forces.[37] To place the control in the proper hands,

The new federal Constitution was designed to ensure that government leadership would be entrusted as much as possible to just those kinds of disinterested gentlemen who had neither occupations nor narrow mercantile interests to promote; "men who," in Madison's words, "possess most wisdom to discern and most virtue to pursue the common good of society." In an interest-ridden society the secret of good government was to enlarge and elevate the national government, . . . and thus screen out the kind of interested men who had dominated the state legislatures in the 1780s—"men of factious tempers, of local prejudices, or of sinister designs"—and replace them with classically educated gentlemen "whose enlightened views and virtuous sentiments render them superior to local prejudices, and to schemes of injustice."[38]

In other words, elected government officials were to be detached as much as possible from local concerns. The classic British concept of a republic had been the model for most of the drafters.[39]

Those who came to be known as Antifederalists perceived exactly what the Federalists had in mind, and began attacking the proposed Constitution. The new federal system, they charged, had been "aristocratically designed to 'raise the fortunes and respectability of the well-born few, and oppress the plebeians.'" The sheer size of the government, the comparatively few national representatives who would be elected to it, and the indirect methods of electing senators and the president, guaranteed in the minds of the Antifederalists an aristocratic government uninfluenced by and unresponsible to the people.[40]

The Antifederalists thus came to oppose the new national government for the same reason the Federalists favored it: because its very structure and detachment from the people would work to exclude any kind of actual and local interest representation and prevent those who were not rich, well born, or prominent from exercising political power. Both sides fully appreciated the central issue the Constitution posed and grappled with it throughout the debates [on ratification]: whether a professedly popular government should actually be in the hands of, rather than simply derived from, common ordinary people.

Out of the division in 1787–88 over this issue, an issue which was as conspicuously social as any in American history, the Antifederalists emerged as the spokesman for the growing American antagonism to aristocracy and as the defenders of the most intimate participation in politics of the widest variety of people possible. . . . Whatever else may be said about the Antifederalists, their populism cannot be impugned. They were true champions of the most extreme kind of democratic and egalitarian politics expressed in the Revolutionary era.[41]

This assessment by Gordon Wood is confirmed by James Ceaser in his discussion of the role that Federalists envisioned for the presidency under the new Constitution: "it was generally believed that the principal threat to constitutional government would come from the popular side— from *disruptive currents of public opinion* or from the House, in particular from certain demagogues who might win its confidence. It was ultimately for the president to make use of his independence to restrain these influences *and to prevent constitutional government from dissolving into representative democracy.*"[42]

The Antifederalists lost the battle over ratification of the Constitution, but just barely.[43] Moreover, the direct-representation arguments many of them articulated during the battle would have a profound influence on America's future political development. In particular, Antifederalist calls for the "most explicit form of representation possible" led naturally to the idea that presidents, linked to the public via national, popular elections, could be the best representatives of the people in the national government.[44]

The Federalist Papers and Going Public

Madison and Hamilton were the principal authors of the *Federalist Papers.* Since they were also two of the main combatants in the early wars over the powers of the presidency and the meaning of the Constitution, it would seem that statements extracted from their essays (which some have labeled opportunistic propaganda) cannot so easily be said to represent a "generally agreed upon" articulation of the principles of the Constitution, as the proponents of the "rhetorical presidency" claim.[45] Indeed, when one hears from Jefferson that Hamilton had later referred to the Constitution as a "shilly-shally thing of milk and water which could not last and was good only as a step to something better," how much confidence can we have in the supposed definitiveness of the pronouncements found in the *Federalist Papers?*[46]

At the very least, Madison's and Hamilton's later disagreements indicate that there was less real consensus among the Founders than a casual reading of the *Federalist Papers* alone might indicate. Thus, claims that are based not on direct statements in the *Federalist Papers*, but rather on interpretations of such statements, are liable to the criticism that not all Founders or even the authors themselves would have necessarily agreed with the interpretation. Indeed, Madison himself disavowed the notion that the *Federalist Papers* could be said to reflect the Founders' intentions: "He never hinted, for example, that the *Federalist* was in any way a direct digest of the leading ideas he had recorded in Philadelphia. Nor did he feel that either those essays or those recorded debates could fairly represent the meaning of the Constitution."[47]

A similar criticism has been made of the *Federalist Papers* as they pertained to other issues that would have been of even more immediate interest to most Americans in the late 1790s. The judgment of Stanley Elkins and Eric McKitrick in *The Age of Federalism* is that "as with any exposition of first principles, these were essentially abstractions. There was little if anything in *The Federalist* that gave any real hint of the specific shape and detail Federalism would shortly take on with the issuance of Hamilton's Treasury papers on public credit, taxation, a national bank, and a program of government-encouraged manufactures."[48]

An even more fundamental problem for the proponents of the idea that there was a nineteenth-century norm against presidents going public is that an objective reading of the *Papers* said to stand for this proposition reveals no clear, explicit statement of the claimed prohibition or, indeed, of any understanding regarding the president in particular. Of the six *Federalist Papers* cited by Tulis, only one uses language that can be loosely read as referring to the inappropriateness of government leaders in general making appeals to the "public passion." The discussion occurs in *Federalist Paper no. 49*, which addressed Jefferson's suggestion that whenever two of the branches of the government concurred, a constitutional convention would be called. Madison, the paper's author, thought Jefferson's idea was dangerous because in such conventions, the "passions therefore not the reason, of the public, would sit in judgment. But it is the reason of the public alone that ought to control and regulate the government. The passions ought to be controlled and regulated by the government."[49]

This is the *Federalist Paper* that comes closest to providing some explicit support for the contention that appeals to the public by government officials were not regarded as proper. Note, however, that such a conclusion can only be inferred with some effort. After all, the actual words say only that the government ought to control public passion. Saying that the government should control public passion is quite different from saying that it is improper for the president or other government officials to make appeals to the public on matters of public interest.

In fact, Madison in this paper explicitly recognizes that presidents and other members of the government would be expected to make appeals to the public. For Madison, the "greatest objection of all" to Jefferson's proposal is that most of the time, such constitutional conventions would be called at the behest of the executive and judicial branches in an attempt to resist the "aggrandizement of the legislative at the expense of the other departments." In such an "appeal to the people," which he also called a "trial," Madison argued that the executive and judiciary branches would be hopelessly outclassed. The president, he said, would normally be disadvantaged in the public's eye because "members of the executive . . . are usually the objects of jealousy and their administration is always liable to be discolored and rendered unpopular." In Madison's view, even when "the executive power might be in the hands of a particular favorite of the people" whose arguments might carry more weight with the public, the legislature would still prevail at the constitutional convention because the outcome would become the product of political passion, not reason.[50] Whether Madison was right or not, the important point for this discussion is that, instead of proscribing appeals to the public by the president on policy issues, Madison freely anticipates them.

Tulis cites five other *Federalist Papers*—numbers 1, 10, 63, 71, and 85—in his discussion of the Founders' fear of demagoguery. These papers do refer in general terms to the dangers of demagogues inflaming the public in a democracy. This concern was no doubt heightened by the debtors' rebellion in Massachusetts led by Daniel Shay, which is referred to in *Federalist Paper no. 43* as that "recent and well-known event among ourselves."[51] However, these five papers reserve their condemnation for demagogues. Nothing in any of these papers says it is wrong for government leaders, let alone presidents, to speak to the public about matters of public interest. In fact, the subject is not even addressed.

The reference to demagoguery in *Federalist Paper no. 1* comes in the context of a warning by Hamilton for citizens to beware of those opponents of the proposed Constitution who portray themselves as defenders of civil rights. "History will teach us," he says, that such zeal more often masks a "dangerous ambition," and "that of those men who have overturned the liberties of republics, the greatest number have begun their career by paying an obsequious court to the people, commencing demagogues and ending tyrants."[52]

Federalist Paper no. 10, famous for its discussion of "factions" and how they will be controlled under the new government, does not even mention the word demagogue. There are, however, some disparaging references to popular leaders. In some cases, factions may be encouraged by "different leaders ambitiously contending for pre-eminence and power." In others, "men of factious tempers, of local prejudices, or of sinister designs, may, by intrigue, by corruption, or by other means, first obtain the suffrages, and then betray the interests of the people." Obviously, Madison observes, "enlightened statesmen will not always be at the helm."[53] There is nothing in this paper about presidents, or about appeals to the public on policy matters.

Federalist Paper no. 63, probably written by Madison, is mostly about the virtues of the proposed U.S. Senate. One of those virtues, according to Madison, is that the Senate would ensure that the "cool and deliberate sense of the community" would be maintained even in those "particular moments in public affairs, when the people stimulated by some irregular passion, or some illicit advantage, or misled by the artful misrepresentations of interested men, may call for measures" they will later regret.[54] Again, there is nothing specific in this paper about presidents or politicians going public.

Hamilton's Federalist Paper no. 71 considers the appropriateness of a four-year term for the president. Ironically, Hamilton justifies the length as necessary to give the holder of the office enough of a stake in it to be willing to defend it against demagogues. The presidency must be institutionally strong, argues Hamilton, to protect the people against "the wiles of parasites and sycophants" and "the snares of the ambitious, the avaricious, the desperate," who may "flatter their prejudices to betray their interests." After all, he says, "The republican principle . . . does not require an unqualified complaisance to every sudden breeze of passion, or to every transient impulse which the people may receive from the arts of men, who flatter their prejudices to betray their interests."[55] Thus, while this paper clearly disparages demagogic leadership, it actually casts the president not as someone liable of *becoming* a demagogue, but as an institutional leader sufficiently fortified to be capable of *resisting* one.

Federalist Paper no. 85 by Hamilton is an example of an old trick of lawyers and politicians: the scare tactic. Hamilton acknowledges, as had others before, that the proposed Constitution was a compromise and therefore not perfect. But, he warns, the creation of a new republic is such a delicate undertaking that the proposed union might fall apart if the Constitution were not ratified. This possibility, he wrote, ought to put the "sincere lovers of the Union . . . upon their guard against hazarding anarchy, civil war, a perpetual alienation of the states from each other, and perhaps the military despotism of a victorious demagogue."[56] Again, there is nothing in the paper about the presidency.

The essay by Ceaser, Thurow, Tulis, and Bessette that introduced the concept of the "rhetorical presidency" cited *Federalist Paper no. 58* as being an example of the supposed connection between the presidency and demagoguery. Madison's purpose in writing this paper was to justify the number of members chosen for the House of Representatives. He argues that the larger legislative bodies become, the "fewer will be the men who actually direct their proceedings." As proof of this rule, he notes that "in the ancient republics, where the whole body of the people assembled in person, a single orator, or an artful statesman, was generally seen to rule with as complete a sway, as if a scepter had been placed in his single hands."[57]

While all of these *Federalist Papers* refer in one way or another to the hazards of demagoguery, none of them actually say anything specifically about proscribing appeals to the public by the president or any other government leaders.[58] This omission should not be surprising. After all, as some of these papers recognize, appeals to the public—especially to the "public reason"—might well be a necessary part of the fight by government leaders *against* demagoguery.

The reach of the supposed norm against "popular rhetoric" becomes even more uncertain when we learn from Tulis (and Ceaser) that, under the norm, demagoguery actually "might be good if it were a means to a good end," and that demagoguery should be permitted "when appeals to passion are needed" for good ends, such as the "preservation of a decent nation or successful prosecution of a just war," but "proscribe[d] . . . for normal politics."[59] Significantly, neither this statement nor similar ones in the essay by Ceaser et al., are supported by any citations to the *Federalist Papers*.

It is hard to find in the words of the *Federalist Papers* much evidence of a consensus against public appeals by presidents or other politicians. In fact, the papers examined here can, if anything, be interpreted as anticipating such appeals. Even in the earliest days of our republic, any government official given power that depended on public opinion might well have been expected to find ways of appealing to or influencing it. After all, it has always been true that someone elected to a high position in government could only have gotten there by in some way appealing to the public for support.

At least one of the authors of the *Federalist Papers* seems to have recognized this necessity. Alexander Hamilton touched on this point in his defense of the four-year term for the president. He argued that a term of that length would give the president a period of time before the next election in which he would feel free to act with the "firmness and independence" of a judge. There would be still be enough time before the next election for the president to "make the community sensible of the propriety of the measures he might incline to pursue, . . . [thereby] establishing himself in the esteem and good will of his constituents."[60]

Clearly, Hamilton is recognizing here that some form of "going public" is expected from presidents, at least in his view. Furthermore, such an effort to marshal public support for a president's initiatives seems to be part of the Hamiltonian concept of the presidency, which posits a fundamental independence from the other branches.[61] As will be seen, several nineteenth-century presidents followed Hamilton's lead, while an equal number did not.

A final problem with relying on the *Federalist Papers* is that not even their primary authors, Hamilton and Madison, hesitated to disavow the positions they had taken when circumstances dictated doing so. For example, during the very first session of Congress in 1789, the question arose of whether the consent of the Senate was required for the removal of a presidential appointee, as was the case for appointments. To prove that it was, Rep. William L. Smith cited *Federalist Paper no. 77*, which plainly stated that the Senate's consent would be "necessary to displace as well as appoint." The next day, however, Smith received a note from another congressman telling him that he had just been informed by Hamilton that, "upon mature reflection, [Hamilton] had changed his opinion and was now convinced that the President alone should have the power of removal at pleasure." This example highlights the general approach to the *Federalist Papers* that, in the judgment of Jack Rakove, Hamilton took after ratification had been secured: "Once the government was launched, Hamilton did not allow the rhetoric of 1788 [in the *Federalist Papers*] to constrain his sense of the possible uses of the formal power and informal political initiative of the executive."[62]

How are we to know which position was the position of the Founders in this case—or, for that matter, any other one? If there had been some kind of vetting process in which draft *Federalist Papers* had been reviewed and approved by a group of Founders, then we could be confident that the papers indeed represented the positions of at least that group. In fact, however, there was no such review process. On the contrary, Hamilton and Madison dashed the papers off quickly, often with no time to even consult with each other. Consequently, the best judgment of the significance of the *Federalist Papers* seems to be that of Albert Furtwangler: "The *Federalist* does not represent the fixed intentions of the framers of the Constitution. But it does embody the *developing* intentions of two of them—two of the most active, articulate, reflective, and well-informed men who ever joined forces or crossed each other in American politics."[63]

Despite the foregoing critique of just how much can be read from the *Federalist Papers* themselves, there can be no doubt that Federalist theory was indeed based on concepts that were ultimately inimical to appeals to the public by anyone, including presidents, on public policy matters. This critique has been offered not to disagree with the basic limited premise of what the Founder-Federalists thought, but to draw attention to the ambiguity of publicized Federalist thought on the concept of going public.[64]

The central thesis of this book is based on the fact that the Founders-Who-Were-Federalists reflect only *one* of the two important lines of thought underlying the making of our constitutional republic. Because the writers of the *Federalist Papers* were well aware of that other, non-Federalist line of populist thought, their need to accommodate that thought in their public arguments may explain what at best can be called the indirect and ambiguous way that going public was actually addressed in those essays.[65]

The existence of this other fundamental conception of American constitutionalism and its impact on the authority of the *Federalist Papers* was recognized by none other than James Madison himself toward the end of his life. In 1825, Jefferson asked Madison to comment on the proposed plan of the Board of Visitors of the University of Virginia to mandate the use of the *Federalist Papers* in the government curriculum as one of the "best guides" to general principles of government in America. Madison qualified his endorsement of them in a very significant way. "What equally deserves remark," he pointed out, was that "neither of the great rival parties [by then, the Federalist-Republicans and the Democratic-Republicans] have acquiesced in all its comments."[66] Here is proof in the words of one of the preeminent Founders himself that there were not one but two constitutional orthodoxies whose views had to be considered in the study and application of principles of American constitutionalism.

Nineteenth Century Partisan Philosophies and Implications for the Presidency

The strong intellectual divisions between many Antifederalists and the Federalists over what I call the Democratist and Classicist views of representative democracy did not fade away after 1789. Instead of being the end of the battle between the two philosophies, the ratification of the Constitution was just the beginning of a long process of "constitutional contestation." The different philosophies carried on into the nineteenth century, and were eventually subsumed into the core principles of the Democratic and Republican Parties as they developed in that century.[67]

The Federalists, of course, captured the first national elections under the new Constitution. Almost immediately, the Washington administration's actions in both domestic and foreign matters began to cause discontent among Antifederalists. To them, actions such as the refunding of the national debt and the establishment of a national bank proved that the Federalists were indeed bent on instituting a form of elitist, aristocratic government in this country modeled after England's. At the state level, the attempts by Federalists to have the states' congressional representatives elected at large rather than by district was taken as further proof of the aristocratic, nationalistic intentions of the Federalists. Opposition to the Federalists began to coalesce around Thomas Jefferson after his return to the United States from France in 1790. James Madison was soon on board as well.[68]

As what came at first to be called the Jeffersonian Republican Party began to take shape in the 1790s, it was strongly influenced by the same populist philosophy that had motivated many Antifederalists. In fact, many Antifederalists became Jeffersonian Republicans, providing the movement with "important spokesmen who reshaped many ideas from the original debate over the Constitution and adapted them to the struggle against Hamilton and his Federalist allies."[69] Moreover, many Jeffersonian Republicans, including Jefferson himself, evolved in their political thinking to positions much closer to the populist revolutionary ideals of many Antifederalists.[70]

The Jeffersonian Republican vision was grounded on basic populist democratic principles: opposition to the aristocratic, elitist society envisioned by the Federalists and a corresponding emphasis upon the literal political equality of "the people" and the primacy of their will in political affairs. Jeffersonian Republicans envisioned an open, directly representative government "clearly responsive to public opinion, in contrast to the refined, largely indirect representation envisioned by Federalists." Among Republicans, there was increasing recourse to citizen petitions, resolutions adopted at open meetings, and other such "spontaneous" expressions as ways of identifying the direct "will of the people."[71]

As the Jeffersonian Republicans became more populist in their orientation—influenced not only by populist Antifederalist thought but also by the inspiring spectacle of the French Revolution in 1789—the term *democrat* came to be applied to them. Their enemies, the Federalists, originally intended for the name to denigrate the Jeffersonian Republicans, because democracy, to the Federalists, was the lowest form of government, equivalent to uncontrolled mob rule. However, Jeffersonian Republicans soon began to enthusiastically call themselves Republican-Democrats, Democratic-Republicans, and, increasingly, just plain Democrats as they realized that the term conveyed precisely what they stood for, which was indeed direct control of the government by the people as a whole.[72]

With the continuing democratic upheavals in France serving as the catalyst, the differences between the two parties were fought out in the newspapers of the time, sharpening as the 1790s progressed. By 1800, according to Joyce Appleby, "two opposing conceptions of society had emerged to polarize the voters' sympathies." In contrast to the Federalists, the Republican-Democrats conceptualized popular sovereignty "to justify active, intrusive participation from the body of voters" in the affairs of government. Political power and legitimacy were to be derived "from the will of the majority, not merely in some remote way, but as directly as possible." In this popular spirit, "Democratic-Republicans made a concerted effort to create a network of newspapers and political societies to help spread their message and increase public awareness about political matters."[73] The "deferential quality of elections " advocated by Federalists was countered by a Republican-Democrat conception of elections as "connecting more with issues instead of personal character."[74]

These differences culminated in the epic battle between the Federalists and the Republican-Democrats for control of the presidency and Congress in 1800. The sweeping victory of Jefferson and the Republican-Democrats was the "first major transfer of power in the life of the Federal Republic, momentous enough in many minds for it to be thought of as a revolution."[75] Jefferson called it "the revolution of 1800," saying it had been "as real a revolution in the principles of our government as that of 1776 was in its form."[76] With that victory in what Jefferson said had been a "contest of opinion," allegiance to party became a fixed characteristic of American political life.[77] Gordon Wood sees the role of public opinion in government as having been transformed: "By the early years of the nineteenth century, Americans had come to realize that public opinion . . . had become 'the vital principle' underlying American government, society, and culture. It became the resolving force not only of political truth but of all truth. . . . In the end it became America's nineteenth-century popular substitute for the elitist intellectual leadership of the Revolutionary generation."[78]

These attitudes formed a coherent view of representative democracy that can be called the Democratist paradigm. Democratists viewed government's role as one of carrying out the national will as expressed through "public opinion." There was no place for Congress to engage in any mediation or refinement of that public opinion, and therefore no need for any institutional deliberation.[79] The deliberation necessary would have already taken place among citizens at the local level, drawing their information mainly from the newspapers that had become so readily accessible. As the *Democratic Review* explained, the legislature was "but a . . . convenient labor-saving machinery, to supersede the necessity for the assemblage of the great masses of the people themselves." A representative should only be a "delegate" with "no will of his own which is independent of that of his constituents."[80]

For Democratists, the national sphere of public discourse had both a real and a virtual locus: in hometown communities and in the web of newspapers that covered America. By the time of Andrew Jackson, the party of these principles was known simply as the Democratic Party. The party's first official national platform in 1840 stated that elected officials were "responsible to the people for the performance of their duties," and that "this responsibility should be as direct and immediate as possible." Expressions of "public opinion" were of course entitled to the highest consideration by those in the government. While classic republican theory viewed representatives as trustees, "Democrats insisted upon an unmediated, *delegatory* relationship."[81]

The implications for the presidency were obvious. Democratists viewed the presidency as at least coequal with—if not superior to—Congress in terms of legislative power and popular representational legitimacy.[82] Therefore, in the national government, whoever could claim to be acting with the support of public opinion could also claim to be the true representative of the national political will. Presidents imbued with this populist attitude would see communications with the public on policy matters not only as proper but also as necessary. Such communications would be necessary to first solidify popular support for the president's position, and then to mobilize that support to pressure Congress to go along with the popular will as expressed through the president.

Ideally, Congress, with all of its institutional processes and checkpoints, was simply "not in the loop" of the Democratist policy process, except as a device to effectuate the public's will or as an obstacle to be overcome if it was seen as thwarting the public's will. The president's role as the only (except for the vice president) nationally elected representative of the people was to see that their will was carried out, mobilizing them as necessary to pressure Congress to follow the lead of the president and the people. This concept of the presidency was in full flower by the time of Andrew Jackson's presidency: "Jacksonians, again like the Anti-Federalists, looked for leaders who would resemble those they represented. The successful Democratic leader had to have the ability to lead people and yet simultaneously appear as one of the people. In Jacksonian thought, . . . 'the vertical distance that separates the leader from the led must be denied.'"[83]

On the other side, what can be called the Classicist notion of indirect representative democracy became a core part of Republican Party orthodoxy in the nineteenth century.[84] It was transmitted via an intermediary, the Whig Party, which sprang up in the 1830s as the new standard-bearer for opponents of the forces of democracy that seemed to be overrunning the country.[85] The American Whigs took their name and inspiration from the great English Whig Party, which championed the classic concept of a republic based on a very limited notion of popular sovereignty. This notion, identical to that espoused by the Federalists a century later in America, held that the people (or at least those allowed to vote) were sovereign in the sense that all political power flowed from them to the legislature, via regular elections.

The critical point here for both English Whigs and American Federalists, though, was that elections were the only direct involvement of the ordinary people in the process of government. Once the legislature had been elected, ideally out of the "natural aristocracy," popular involvement ended. After all, in its original formulation, only the higher order of citizens had the level of personal disinterestedness that was critical to the deliberative process in the legislature by which public opinion would be refined and the "public good" determined.[86] Whigs and then Republicans throughout the nineteenth century believed that "good government occurred when the voice of the masses was properly channeled through institutions, rather than directly expressed. It was only through the *representative*, deliberative processes of Congress that the "crystallized intelligence" and "enlightened conscience" of the majority could be determined: "Viewing the public as a generally passive body, National Republicans looked to parties, legislatures, bureaucracies, and courts to provide the political leadership necessary to conduct the affairs of government in a rational and considered manner. . . . National Republicans believed that public servants, once chosen, served as trustees, not delegates of the people, that their responsibility was to the good of the community, not to a particular constituency; and that, to this end, legislatures were to be deliberative bodies, not conveyor belts for public opinion."[87]

This conception was a staple of Whig-Republican thought for over a century. In his recent study of "presidential election rhetoric," John Gerring states that "virtually no statements in support of a majority-rule interpretation of democracy can be found in Whig-Republican rhetoric until the 1920s."[88]

The other cornerstone principle of the English Whigs was that "popular sovereignty in England was to be exercised, as from its inception, by Parliament." Thus, as "representatives of the people," Parliament was superior to the king. Lawmaking was to be done by Parliament, without interference from or involvement by the king. In the Whig-Republican American constitutional system, therefore, Congress, as the true representative of the people in their sovereign capacity, was the only appropriate institution to make national policy.[89]

The classic Whig-Republican attitude toward the presidency is perhaps best conveyed by the words of the most famous ex-Whig, Abraham Lincoln. In a campaign speech for Whig presidential candidate Zachary Taylor in 1848, Lincoln asserted that "the will of the people should produce its own result without executive influence. This principle that the people should do what—under the Constitution—they pleased, is a Whig principle. . . . It was the platform on which they had fought all their battles, *the resistance of executive influence* and the principle of enabling the people to frame the government according to their will."[90] Later, on the House floor, Lincoln, as a Whig representative, declared: "Were I President, I should desire the legislation of the country to rest with Congress, uninfluenced in its origin or progress, and undisturbed by the veto unless in very special and clear cases."[91] (Lincoln's attitude changed some by the time he became president, but that is another story.)

A major fear of Whigs and Republicans throughout the nineteenth century was the "specter of a radical, plebiscitarian executive, on the model of 'King Andrew' Jackson, in tandem with a directly elected, nondeliberative House of Representatives." Not only had Jackson explicitly claimed to be representing the voice and will of the "common people," but he also had asserted the right to intrude upon and even direct the legislative process as the only elected representative of all the people.[92] Jackson's dominance led to this classic Whig complaint from Henry Clay in 1833: "Are we not governed now, and have we not been for some time past, pretty much by the will of one man? And do not large masses of the people, perhaps a majority, seem disposed to follow him wherever he leads, through all his inconsistencies? . . . If that single man were an enlightened philosopher, and a true patriot, the popular sanction which is given to all his acts, however inconsistent or extravagant, might find some justification."[93] To Whigs, the radical egalitarianism of the Jacksonian Democrats had "threatened the very foundations of society and substituted impulse for deliberation." With the demise of their party in the 1850s, most Whigs migrated to the new Republican Party, which became the home for the Federalist/Whig understandings of republican government and a constitutionally reserved presidency.[94]

These conceptions had significant implications for presidential behavior and rhetoric. They are embodied in the British ideal of the nonpartisan, patriotic king or leader that greatly influenced early American presidents such as George Washington and John Adams and then served as a powerful model for many presidents throughout the nineteenth century.

The concept of the patriot-leader embodied fundamental aspects of classical republicanism with rhetorical roots that reached back to Greek and Roman times.[95] The ideal leader of a country would be the promoter and protector of national unity, possessing a "disinterested commitment to the national welfare" that was above "parties and factions." The leader's actions would convey to the people the "calm dignity" of a man of classic civic virtue who, without seeking public office or any private benefit from it, had nevertheless been called to the service of his country and would, in Washington's words, pursue "the great line of my duty . . . as pointedly as the needle to the pole." Despite his potential for overarching political power, the patriot-leader would resist the temptation to co-opt the powers of the legislature. According to the radical British Whig philosophy adopted by Washington and most Revolutionary War leaders, this corruption of the legislature by the executive would ultimately lead to the total loss of the citizens' independence and liberties.[96]

For Washington and many of the other Federalist Founders, the Roman orator and statesman Cicero was their constant "reference and inspiration." In their public speaking appearances, these patriot leaders would follow Cicero's injunction that "It is the particular responsibility of the magistrate to realize that he represents the character of the state and that he ought to maintain its dignity and distinction." Moreover, according to Cicero, the "universal rule, in oratory as in life," was to "consider propriety."[97] Propriety included speaking respectfully of one's opponents in public.

The Ciceronian "rich conception of public address" had several components. Because it was ultimately based on popular consent to a system of government that essentially excluded most of the people from direct participation in governmental affairs, a republic was an inherently fragile creation. The purpose of public oratory, therefore, was to reinforce support for classic republicanism. Popular respect and deference to our system of government, in which the polity is "rationally regulated" rather than blindly served, was to be cultivated. Disinterested civic virtue that rose above base private (especially commercial) interests, was to be celebrated.[98] In short, Classicist presidents were to aim at consensus, not controversy.

There was an alternative to this "gentlemanly mode" of public address. It was the "popular mode" of address, and public communications in general, employed by those who believed in truly direct, popular democracy. For them, controversy was just part of the process. In fact, to these Democratists, the decorous, formal, withdrawn public manners exhibited by Classicist leaders "embodied the mores of those who deliberately distanced themselves from the many, thus creating dissonance between the theory of democracy and its practice."[99]

A major theme of this book is that the Democratist and Classicist paradigms sketched out here strongly influenced the behavior of many presidents in the nineteenth century. In general, presidents with Democratist leanings went public in speeches and through newspapers, promoting themselves and their policies to the public "over the heads" of Congress. Presidents of the Classicist persuasion did not go public, although a number of them did make public speeches, sometimes quite frequently. Consistent with the rhetorical conventions of classical republicanism, however, these speeches avoided policy matters. Instead, the speeches of Classicist presidents focused on patriotic, uplifting, consensus-building themes aimed at reinforcing popular support for the nation's political institutions and processes. The story of going public is the story of these two conceptions of the presidency.

CHAPTER 2

The Presidential Newspaper

The Forgotten Way of Going Public

Only a newspaper can put the same thought at the same time before a thousand readers. A newspaper is an adviser that need not be sought out, but comes of its own accord and talks to you briefly every day about the commonweal, without distracting you from your private affairs.

—ALEXIS DE TOCQUEVILLE
Democracy in America

ALEXIS DE TOCQUEVILLE made this observation about the power of newspapers after seeing politics at work in America in the 1830s.[1] Long before then, government officials had been using newspapers as a way to communicate with the people on political matters. As will be demonstrated in this chapter, the value of newspapers for political communication was recognized by all the major figures in early American government. Both Alexander Hamilton and Thomas Jefferson, for example, were instrumental in establishing newspapers to spread their particular partisan political philosophies. According to journalism historian Willard Bleyer, "Both men, as keen students of government and politics, recognized the importance of the press in a republic. Each sought to use newspapers to shape public opinion in support of the theories of government that he believed to be vital to the success of the first great experiment in democracy. Thus political party organs became inevitable. . . . Out of this situation grew a new era in American journalism."[2]

Indeed, there was almost no such thing as a "nonpartisan" newspaper in the first half of the nineteenth century. Instead, papers were aligned with, supported, and even created by political parties and top party officials for the express purpose of generating support for chosen political viewpoints and individuals.[3]

Moreover, from 1800 to 1860, every American president supported a newspaper that was regarded as at least the semiofficial voice of his administration. This phenomenon reached its high points in the presidencies of Andrew Jackson and James Polk with what can only be called "presidential newspapers:" newspapers established and heavily subsidized—via subscriptions from supporters and profits from lucrative government printing contracts—by the presidents to attack their opponents and announce and defend their public policy positions. Both Jackson and Polk felt so strongly about the importance of this weapon that they met daily with the papers' editors to plot their media strategies and messages. This extensive use of newspapers by presidents and other politicians to influence public opinion on policy matters indicates that "going public" is as old as the republic itself, and that the practice was, for many nineteenth-century presidents, an integral part of their office.

A Brief History of the Political Newspaper

Newspapers began being used extensively for partisan political purposes in eighteenth-century England. The model is remarkably similar to the one that was to develop later in America in the first half of the nineteenth century. Papers in England were primarily used to mold public opinion along the lines desired by the papers' sponsors. The papers were connected to English government at the highest level; most important eighteenth-century politicians coached or even wrote for the press.[4] In 1831, Lord Chancellor Henry Brougham said: "Indeed, no one ever knows or cares who or what the editor is. The print is read solely to learn what is thought by the best-informed men of that particular party of which it happens, for the time being, to be considered as the organ. It is the express business of the editor to find out what are generally held to be the soundest opinions of the sensible men of that party to which his subscribers are attached, and to put *their* actual views in a distinct and forcible shape before the public."[5]

Most readers could not afford to purchase newspapers, so circulation was limited. However, the papers could always be found in the coffeehouses and other public places where people congregated, and there were even "subscription reading rooms" where, for an annual membership fee, one could go to read the latest papers from around the country. Because of this availability, the papers' influence was magnified far beyond their meager circulation. They would often be read by one person to the rest of the patrons, and the discussions that were spawned reverberated throughout the community. In 1829, a London newspaper calculated that, on average, a single copy in that city was read by thirty people.[6]

American newspapers at first had similarly limited circulation. Newspapers probably went into fewer than forty thousand homes at the outbreak of the Revolution, but in America, too, copies were passed from hand to hand and often read aloud in coffeehouses, inns, and taverns. Philip Freneau, a famous poet of the American Revolution who later served as editor of a newspaper sponsored by Thomas Jefferson, once said that the main activities in America's taverns were "drinking, smoking, spitting, and reading the news."[7]

Originally kept impartial in tone and devoid of editorial comment by the threat of British censorship, newspapers after 1765 rapidly moved into the realm of political commentary as the events of the Revolutionary War unfolded. By war's end, the power of the press to influence political events had been amply demonstrated through such achievements as the repeal of the Stamp Act, which was attributed in large part to the united opposition of newspapers. Such results, as Frank Luther Mott points out in his classic history of American journalism, "taught the political organizers and the manipulators of public opinion how useful newspapers could be to them. From this time forward the press was recognized as a strong arm of the Patriot movement. . . . The leaders all respected this new power. Washington repeatedly encouraged the Patriot press; he aided in the establishment of the *New Jersey Gazette* that his army might have a newspaper to read in the winter of 1777; he consigned quantities of worn-out tenting to the paper mills to be made into printing-paper."[8]

The power of the press was further demonstrated during the debate over ratification of the new Constitution, when the country's papers were filled with discussions of the issue including the series of articles now known as the *Federalist Papers*. By the 1790s, most Americans had access to newspapers one way or another, whether by subscription or by reading shared copies at inns and taverns, and the party press had become the chief conduit of information between party leaders and their followers.

Newspapers soon became plentiful in America. By 1810, the country had "more journals in proportion to its population than had ever been known anywhere in the world." This high demand was probably due to the fact that 95 percent of Americans lived in rural areas and so relied mainly on newspapers for information about governmental affairs. In 1800, Pierre Dupont de Nemours observed that, while "a large part of the nation reads the Bible, all of it assiduously peruse the newspapers. The fathers read them aloud to their children while the mothers are preparing the breakfast."[9]

War: The Political Newspapers of Hamilton and Jefferson

Alexander Hamilton, the first treasury secretary and, according to some, a virtual prime minister for the Washington administration, took the first step toward the presidential newspaper. When the federal government established its capital in New York, there were no strongly politically oriented papers in the city. Hamilton and other prominent Federalists, seeing the need for a "reliable political organ" to further their interests, moved quickly to establish the *Federal Gazette of the United States*, which began publishing on April 15, 1789.[10]

Wealthy Federalists put up the money to start the paper, and Hamilton fed it the printing business from the Treasury Department and the Senate. Hamilton and others wrote political editorials for the *Gazette*, signed with such pseudonyms as Publicola, Fact, Amicus, Scourge, and Plain Facts. The *Gazette* became the Federalists' flagship paper, from which Federalist supporters and party newspapers throughout the country took their cues. Political historian Richard L. Rubin describes the paper as "the court journal" of the Washington administration, "an officially sanctioned organ of incumbent political opinion." The paper was well on the way to accomplishing Hamilton's purposes. As he put it, "the first thing in all great operations of such a government as ours is to secure the opinion of the people."[11]

The Federalists' opponents soon noted the paper's success. Jefferson and his allies, James Madison and Henry Lee, decided they needed a newspaper to mobilize democratically inclined Americans around the country. Returning to the United States in 1790 after serving as ambassador to France, Jefferson by his own account had been "much astonished, indeed, at the mimicry I found established of royal forms and ceremonies, and . . . by the monarchical sentiments I heard expressed and openly maintained in every company, and among others by the high members of the government, executive and judiciary, (General Washington alone excepted), and by a great part of the legislature."[12] In 1791, Jefferson, describing the *Federal Gazette* as "a paper of pure Toryism, disseminating the doctrines of monarchy, aristocracy, and the exclusion of the influence of the people," wrote that he was "trying to get another weekly or half-weekly paper set up . . . , so that it might go through the states, and furnish a whig vehicle of intelligence."[13]

Jefferson, Madison, and Lee settled on Philip Freneau, who was known as the "Poet of the Revolution" for his stirring writings in favor of independence, as editor of their new paper. Lee agreed to finance the establishment of the paper in Philadelphia, where the national government had relocated. Jefferson arranged for Freneau to get a job in the State Department that would require so little of his time "as not to interfere with any other calling." He also arranged for Freneau to receive all of the State Department's printing business. When Washington later questioned him about his involvement with Freneau's paper, Jefferson claimed to have had no knowledge of Freneau's plans for a newspaper when he offered him the State Department clerkship.[14]

The new paper began publishing on October 31, 1791, spreading the Jeffersonian Party's message. One of the leading Boston newspapers reported that "'a great number of gentlemen in this and neighboring towns have subscribed for the *National Gazette* published by Mr. Philip Freneau . . . , which is said to be printed under the eye of that established patriot, Thomas Jefferson.'"[15] There were by then two nationally circulated, partisan newspapers identified as the organs of two of the nation's most powerful political leaders, one of whom was viewed as speaking for the administration. The papers quickly became the "journalistic leaders of the nation's political press," with their messages being reprinted in other newspapers throughout the country.[16]

For the next two years, the two papers fought a fierce war over the policies of the Washington administration. The words of the *Federal Gazette* were usually those of Alexander Hamilton, while the *National Gazette* relied on a coalition of pseudonymous writers including Madison, Monroe, Attorney General Edmund Randolph, and Jefferson himself. Hamilton attacked under a series of aliases, including: Catullus, Fact, Amicus, Scourge, and Metellus. At various times, he described Jefferson as "an 'intriguing incendiary' whose tenets tended to promote 'national disunion, national insignificance, public disorder and discredit'," and who was the "perpetrator of 'the most wanton and flagitious acts that ever stained the annals of a civilized nation.'" The Jeffersonian team used the pseudonym Aristides, and responded that Hamilton's accusations against Jefferson were "founded in the basest calumny and falsehood."[17]

The battling reached a peak in 1793, when Washington issued his famous Neutrality Proclamation, declaring that the United States would stay out of the war between France and Britain. The controversy over the proclamation led Hamilton to write a series of seven newspaper articles, this time under the pseudonym Pacificus, defending the administration's action. The articles appeared in the *Federal Gazette* and were widely reprinted. In them, Hamilton argued that foreign policy was practically the exclusive domain of the president, limited only by Congress's right to declare war and the Senate's to ratify treaties.[18] This expansive interpretation of presidential powers appalled Jefferson, who wrote to Madison: "'For God's sake, my dear Sir, take up your pen, select the most striking heresies and cut him to pieces in face of the public.'"[19] With Jefferson's editorial assistance, Madison, writing in the *National Gazette* as Helvidius, produced several long editorials denying Hamilton's "vicious" claim and attacking many other aspects of Hamiltonian national policy.[20]

Washington was concerned over the public fighting. He commented in a letter to Gouverneur Morris that, "from the complexion of some of our newspapers, foreigners would be led to believe that inveterate political dissensions existed among us, and that we were on the very verge of disunion, but the fact is otherwise."[21] In letters to both Hamilton and Jefferson, he sought to negotiate a cease-fire. He wrote that the "irritating charges" flying about in the press would, if continued, "tear the machine asunder" with "fatal consequences." Hamilton responded that the "attacks on Treasury policy were so dangerous to government that replies must be risked, though they added to the discord."[22] Jefferson replied that Hamilton was a monarchist bent on overthrowing the government, a charge which Washington dismissed.[23] No rapprochement between the two men occurred, but their public quarreling—at least in the newspapers—finally died out at the end of 1792. Later, in response to what he took to be a suggestion from Washington that he "interpose in some way with Freneau," Jefferson recorded in his diary: "But I will not do it! His paper has saved our Constitution which was galloping fast into monarchy."[24]

These statements by Hamilton and Jefferson constitute their clear affirmations of the value and propriety of direct communications to the public on policy matters. Even at the very beginning of the republic there were two avenues for public discourse on policy issues, one running directly to the people and one running through Congress in the legislative process. The Founders recognized this and freely employed both avenues in seeking to influence the new nation's public policy process.

Although there is as yet no evidence that Washington was ever personally involved in the use of newspapers for political purposes, he clearly benefited from Hamilton's strenuous editorial exertions on behalf of his administration. An intriguing story in Broadus Mitchell's *Alexander Hamilton, The National Adventure* suggests that Washington was open to the possibility of using the press to generate public support for his actions. In 1793, Washington and his cabinet were debating whether to demand the recall of France's new ambassador, Edmond Genet, because of his attempts to spread the French Revolution to America through direct appeals to the American people to turn against their government. Hamilton argued in favor of publishing "to the world" the whole account of Genet's activities in America, and Washington said he liked the idea. When the president was then reminded of a recent newspaper cartoon portraying him as a king on a guillotine, he flew into a rage. Referring to Philip Freneau, Washington complained that the "rascal Freneau sent him 3 of his papers every day, . . . an impudent design to insult him." In the month following this meeting, a series of nine articles by Hamilton attacking Genet appeared in the newspapers. Interestingly, one of the main thrusts of Hamilton's attack was that Genet had insulted the president "by threatening to appeal over Washington's head to the nation's voters." Although Freneau's *Gazette* and a number of other Democratic-

Republican, pro-Jeffersonian newspapers defended Genet's actions, public opinion ultimately turned against Genet and France recalled him when Washington demanded it.[25]

The newspaper war between the Federalists and the Jeffersonians ended when the *National Gazette* closed due to a common malady of the time: economic starvation. The final blow came late in 1793, when Jefferson resigned as secretary of state, causing the loss of the State Department printing business that had been funneled to the paper. The Federalist Party's paper ceased publication in 1798 with the death of its editor.[26]

In light of this amazing public battling by the some of the most prominent Founders, it is hard to accept the claim that there was a consensus among them that appeals to the public were proscribed by the Constitution. There is, to be sure, the calm counsel of *Federalist Paper No. 49* that public passions "ought to be controlled and regulated by the government." On the other hand, we have Thomas Jefferson testifying that the *National Gazette* "had saved our Constitution" and beseeching James Madison to join the newspaper battle against Alexander Hamilton with these strong words: "Take up your pen, select the most striking heresies and *cut him to pieces in face of the public.*" That Madison, the author of this and many other *Federalist Papers*, promptly sought to do what Jefferson urged indicates strongly that, at least as a matter of original constitutional theory, direct appeals to the public on policy matters were considered a legitimate part of the early American political process.

Anonymity: The Use of Pseudonyms in Early Newspapers

Early politicians signed their newspaper commentaries with pseudonyms rather than their own names. Might that be evidence of an attempt to disguise their authorship out of deference (or at least lip service) to a norm against direct appeals to the public on policy matters? The first problem with this idea is that even if the use of pen names could be construed as evidence of such a norm, it was an extraordinarily weak one because it did not deter politicians from making the appeals. More significantly, the contributors' identities were often well known, which suggests that, for many, the use of pen names was little more than a journalistic or societal convention. Referring to the pseudonyms used by Hamilton and his opponents during their newspaper war in the 1790s, for example, Marcus Cunliffe describes them as a "clandestine means that deceived nobody."[27]

In fact, not only politicians used pseudonyms in newspapers in early America. Just about everyone else did, too—including the publishers and editors of the papers themselves. Moreover, the practice was followed in colonial papers for at least a century before the nation's independence, and even earlier in Europe. Describing the earliest American papers in the period of 1690 to 1765, journalism historian Frank Mott wrote: "Though formal editorials were rare, discussion of public affairs was by no means neglected. It was carried on through contributed letters or essays addressed to the editors (some of them written by the editors themselves) and signed by fanciful pen names, as well as by extracts from published books and pamphlets."[28]

The reasons behind the common practice of using pen names are murky and lie mainly outside the realm of this book. They included such utterly pragmatic considerations as the desire to avoid government prosecution for sedition or private lawsuits for libel, guard against political retribution, and protect one's life, property, and family from brute retaliation. Intellectual considerations included the use of well-known pseudonyms as signals to readers, and the populist attitude that all political writings in the public discourse sphere should be judged solely on their merits and not on their authors' identities.[29] In any event, because the practice predates the nation's founding and was followed by virtually all contributors of journalistic opinion, its origins cannot readily be attributed to any universally felt, constitutionally based understanding.

Historian George Payne suggests that pen names may have been a manifestation of the low status that journalism was accorded before the twentieth century. Payne writes that men such as Alexander Hamilton would have "indignantly resented" the suggestion that they were actively involved in the practice of journalism. "With the prejudices against the trade—prejudices inherited from England, the social ideas of which still dominated the nation," wrote Payne in 1926, "it was understandable that men who prided themselves on being 'gentlemen' should disown too close an association with a calling such as 'Printing,' which had yet to live down its early stigma. What is today regarded as the very strength of the press was then a great cause of its being held in some contempt—it actually represented the people, the 'rabble;' it came from the people, its mechanical artificers were of the people, and therefore, except when it was properly 'led,' it was not considered a power for good." As such notables as Thomas Jefferson would attest, not everyone thought this way.[30] Nevertheless, the supposed anonymity of pen names might have been a way for some distinguished citizens to take advantage of the public forum afforded by newspapers while still preserving an illusion of separation from the real world of politics or, at least, democracy. It is not that such involvement in appeals to the public would necessarily have been considered inappropriate—many prominent citizens were known to be making such appeals—but that a pen name might in some way, real or contrived, preserve the writer's social dignity as being "above" or at least removed from the fray. There is, after all, a difference between just having one's ideas introduced into a political fray and in having one's identity trumpeted as well.

From this perspective, the use of surrogates as journalistic "attack dogs" for their patrons becomes more understandable as well: "As gentlemen maintained a posture of cool detachment, they subsidized or otherwise supported men of lower social rank to fling themselves into the contests of character defamation, rumor-mongering, and generalized vitriol . . . . Of all these surrogate warriors, the most coveted were the skilled pamphleteers and newspaper editors, the professional assassins of gentry politics who could reach the widest audience with the fewest restraints and the least personal jeopardy to their sponsors. . . . Like fighting cocks, the partisan editors were set in the pit to draw blood for their gentlemanly sponsors." Of course, another advantage of employing these surrogates is that any of them who became an embarrassment to their sponsors could be promptly abandoned.[31]

In any event, such a social style is not to be confused with a constitutionally based, universal social norm against direct appeals to the public on policy matters. During the earliest years of the American republic there was, in fact, a rich mix of such appeals being made by politicians, and those appeals were formally concealed, if at all, by only the thinnest of veneers.

George Washington (1789–97): The First Reserved Presidency

While George Washington's presidency spurred the newspaper's development as a political communications weapon, Washington himself stayed out of the fray. Modeling his presidency after the British ideal of the nonpartisan patriot-king or leader, Washington adopted a very reserved tone in his public behavior and rhetoric that was followed by many of his successors.[32]

Notwithstanding this somewhat removed conception of his role as the nation's leader, Washington did have periodic informal contacts with the American people. As president-elect, he rode from Virginia to his inauguration ceremony in New York. During this trek he was the recipient of extraordinary displays of honor and affection, including escorts of tens of thousands of citizens and grand public banquets. Once in New York and installed as president, however, Washington found he had little time to himself. He wrote that "'from the time I had done breakfast and thence till dinner and afterwards till bedtime I could not get relieved from the ceremony of one visit before I had to attend to another.'" Two days after his inauguration he attempted to deal with the crush by publishing a newspaper notice stating that he would henceforth "receive 'visits of compliment' only between the hours of two and three on Tuesdays and Fridays." This prompted a protest from a senator from western Pennsylvania that it would be offensive for the president "to be seen only in public on stated times, like an eastern Lama."[33]

Washington also went on three tours of the new country. In 1789 he visited New England, traveling as far as Maine, spending the night in taverns along the way and presiding on horseback over the interminable welcoming ceremonies held for him. Two years later he toured the South for two months, visiting battlefields and cities in North Carolina, South Carolina, Georgia, and Virginia. The third trip was to Rhode Island after it joined the Union.[34] Washington typically would be greeted with festivities and formal welcoming addresses to which he would briefly respond. The forty-three speeches Washington made on these three tours were reserved, almost ceremonial in nature: "In keeping with eighteenth century rhetorical conventions, Washington's replies were staunchly formal. . . . [H]is speeches during the regional tours often praised his auditors for traits and actions he wanted them to adopt: industry, virtue, love of country, and, above all, attachment to the Constitution. Almost invariably he concluded by expressing his hope for the prosperity and happiness of the group addressing him."[35] The speeches were short (usually just a few paragraphs) and did not refer to current events or issues.[36] Washington was so cautious in his rhetorical practice that, if not given an advance copy of a town's welcoming address, he would say only a few words and send a formal written reply later. Usually, though, both the welcome and Washington's reply were printed in the local newspapers.[37]

Washington did, however, publish what has come to be known as his Farewell Address in a newspaper instead of sending it to Congress or delivering it as a speech.[38] This apparently was the only time he used a newspaper to communicate directly with the people on public affairs. While there are aspects of national celebration in the short addresses he made to groups of citizens, Washington overall seems to best fit the Reserved Model of the presidency because of the sporadic and limited nature of his public communication efforts.

John Adams (1797–1801): Another Reserved President

John Adams, a man steeped in the classical republican attitudes of the Federalists, succeeded Washington. Consequently, to the extent he had opinions on policy matters, he sent Congress written messages, most of which seem to have fallen on deaf ears. Operating from the ideal of the president as the virtuous and vigorous nonpartisan patriot leader of the country, he avoided popular communications on policy matters.[39]

In the spring and summer of 1798, however, Adams engaged in a public patriotic dialogue with citizen groups from across the country that had been organized by Federalists to express support for the administration in its dealings with France. Anti-French sentiment had soared in America when Adams released the details of what came to be known as the XYZ Affair, in which French diplomats had demanded bribes before agreeing to negotiate with American emissaries over the return of American ships and crews seized by the French. Many of these groups sent Adams letters pledging their willingness to fight if it became necessary to redeem America's honor. The language Adams used in his replies to these letters ranged from elevated and patriotic to quite inflamed rhetoric against the French and their supporters in America.[40] Madison told Jefferson he thought some of Adams's statements were "the most abominable and degrading that could fall from the lips of the first magistrate of an independent people." The citizens' letters and Adams's replies were usually printed in local newspapers and then reprinted in other newspapers.[41]

Except for this one aberration, the record of Adams's administration is one of silence toward the public. Overall, his presidency seems to best fit the Deliberator Model, in which presidents avoid public communications on policy matters and instead communicate directly with Congress in an attempt to influence the policy-making process.

Thomas Jefferson (1801–1809) and the First Presidential Newspaper

The next stage in the development of the presidential newspaper occurred with Thomas Jefferson's election in 1800. Newspapers had played a crucial role during the campaign, in which he defeated the Federalist incumbent, John Adams. Connecticut senator Uriah Tracy reported in the summer of 1800 that Republicans were setting up newspapers "in almost every town and county in the country" to help their election effort.[42]

Although the Jeffersonians' first paper, Freneau's *National Gazette,* folded in 1793, it was succeeded by the Philadelphia *Aurora,* published first by Benjamin Franklin Bache, the grandson of Benjamin Franklin, and then by William Duane. The nationally circulated *Aurora* was "commonly called 'the bible of democracy,'" and "set the standard for the Republican Press." Jefferson, of course, subscribed to the *Aurora* and read it regularly, frequently enlisting friends to write articles for the paper.[43] With the election approaching, he stepped up his efforts on the paper's behalf. In 1799 he wrote to Madison and others, asking that they write daily for the paper and reminding them, "The engine is the press."[44]

The *Aurora* led the press campaign for Jefferson, in the process making its columns "'an uninterrupted stream of slander of the American Government,'" in the eyes of the Federalists. Despite being one of the main targets of prosecution under the Alien and Sedition Acts, Duane courageously refused to abate his criticism of the Adams government.[45] In terms that convey vividly how partisan newspapers of the time were used as tools of national political communication, the Federalist editor of the *Connecticut Courant* in 1800 credited the *Aurora* with the central role in spreading Jeffersonian Republicanism throughout the country:

> What ever appeared in that [paper] was faithfully copied into the others; and tho' but a few were to be found in many parts of the country who would pay for such papers, they were sent round the country *gratis.* They were read by those few, the main sentiments were repeated to others, and in this way the sentiments were not only scattered, but a perfect union of opinion was established. Whoever has been careful enough to watch the progress of Jacobinism [Jeffersonian Democratic-Republicanism] in the country, must have observed, that on every important subject, the sentiments to be inculcated among the democrats, has been first put into the Aurora. This was the heart, the seat of

life. From thence the blood has flowed to the extremities by a sure and rapid circulation, and the life and strength of the paper have thus been supported and nourished. It is even astonishing to remark, with how much punctuality and rapidity, *the same opinion* has been circulated and repeated by these people, from the highest to the lowest.

By means like these, the greatest part of the mischief which we now experience has been occasioned. A constant publication, and repetition of falsehood, which, to a great part of the people, is never contradicted, will eventually produce mischief; because the conclusion which they will draw, will be, that if these things are not true they would be contradicted.[46]

For his efforts, Duane expected to be rewarded by being asked to move the *Aurora* to the new capital in Washington, where he could receive government printing patronage if Jefferson won.[47] Apparently uncomfortable with Duane's rabid journalistic style, however, Jefferson spurned Duane and the *Aurora*. Instead, he invited a Philadelphia editor, Samuel Harrison Smith, to come to Washington and establish a paper there. In a bold step, Smith moved to Washington several months before the election results were known. On October 31, 1800, he published the first edition of the *National Intelligencer,* the newspaper that became known as the "faithful, though not servile, supporter of President Jefferson and his two Virginia successors. It was often called the "'official gazette,' the 'court paper,' and the 'government organ.'"[48]

The special character of the paper—and Jefferson's appreciation for the way that a newspaper could magnify his ability to communicate with the public—was made clear from the beginning of his administration. Although Jefferson delivered his inaugural address in a barely audible voice, his audience and Americans around the country were able to read the speech in the *National Intelligencer.* Smith had printed the address from a copy given to him by Jefferson before the inauguration. Jefferson's plan was to make the presidency "more popular" in orientation, and Smith's paper was obviously part of that plan.[49]

On March 27, 1801, within the first month of his administration, Jefferson advised: "I recommend to you to pay not the least credit to pretended appointments in any paper, till you see it in Smith's. . . . He is at hand to enquire at the offices, and is careful not to publish them on any other authority." In October, 1801, Vice President Aaron Burr wrote: "The

Washington paper edited by Smith has the countenance and support of the administration. His explanations of the Measures of Government and of the Motives which produce them are, I believe, the result of information and advice from high Authority." This assessment was echoed by James Bayard, a prominent Federalist and Smith's brother-in-law, who regarded the *Intelligencer* as the "official administrative organ . . . unquestionably under the direction of Mr. Jefferson and his party." In 1807, a Boston Federalist newspaper described the *National Intelligencer* as the "Index of the Executive mind."[50]

The *Intelligencer* carried all of the federal government's official notices, proclamations, and advertisements. Smith also became the self-appointed semiofficial reporter of congressional proceedings. The *Intelligencer* was thus virtually the only reliable source of information about the executive and legislative branches, which meant that all papers in the country based their government news on *National Intelligencer* reports, a practice that continued throughout the first quarter of the nineteenth century.[51]

Thanks to the healthy Jeffersonian majorities in the House and Senate, Smith also became the government's official printer. He received an average of several thousand dollars a year in large printing orders from the State and other executive departments, and both Houses of Congress. This provided enough support to allow the *Intelligencer* to escape the common experience of papers in that period of failing for lack of subscriptions, because outside the few larger cities, a newspaper had difficulty getting even a thousand paying subscribers. It also allowed Smith to place the prestigious notation "By Authority" on the paper's masthead, which must have been good for business.[52]

In exchange for his financial support of Smith's paper, Jefferson acquired a tool for presenting the public with information on national affairs and his administration's policies, which historians say he did on a number of occasions. For example, when the administration was having some difficulty enforcing the embargo against Great Britain, Jefferson wrote Smith and asked him to publish a notice that a certain customs officer had been removed by the president "'for not using due diligence in the execution of the embargo laws.'" Jefferson thought that such a notice published in Smith's paper "'would do some good.'" Shortly after passage of the Embargo Act, the *Intelligencer* carried a series of articles later attributed to Madison defending Jefferson's policy.[53]

Another time, Jefferson sent Smith a brief analysis of a recent Connecticut election. The analysis showed that although Republicans had elected fewer representatives to the state legislature than in 1802, the party had actually increased its percentage of the vote from 29 percent to 35 percent. "'Would it not be worth presenting to the public . . . this concise view?'" Jefferson asked Smith. Two days later, the *Intelligencer* carried the analysis as its lead story, headlined: "Plain View of the Politics of Connecticut." On another occasion, Jefferson sent Madison a pamphlet that supported his proposal to reorganize the militia and asked: "'Could S. H. Smith put better matter into his paper than the 12 pages above mentioned, and will you suggest it to him? No effort should be spared to bring the public mind to this great point.'"[54]

The newspaper also provided Jefferson with a way to spread his "official" messages quickly across the country to his popular audience. He gave Smith an advance copy of his first annual message to Congress so that copies could be distributed to all members of Congress soon after Jefferson spoke.[55] Impressed, a Federalist wrote: "[W]ith what expedition these Democrats do business! It was in the press and probably numbers struck off, before it was communicated to Congress, that numerous copies might be forwarded by this day's mail to every part of the country." Advance distribution to the *National Intelligencer* became the regular practice with all of Jefferson's presidential messages. In addition, he also had Smith print in the *National Intelligencer* many of the messages and memorials he received from groups, along with his replies. As one historian put it, "In this way statements of his were frequently before the public, despite his failure to make public speeches."[56]

Incidentally, even though Jefferson did not deliver his State of the Union messages to Congress as speeches, there still was a spoken aspect to them. That is because the House clerk read his annual addresses to Congress aloud, a practice that continued for a century thereafter. This combined written and oral method of delivery raises another difficulty for Tulis's claim that Jefferson and his nineteenth-century successors all delivered their State of the Union messages to Congress in writing out of deference to a constitutionally based norm—an understanding that somehow escaped the first two presidents, who delivered their messages in person. The real explanation for Jefferson's decision to change the practice that his predecessors had followed seems to be the one most often cited by historians (and also noted by Tulis), which is simply that Jefferson and his supporters thought the practice of presidents personally delivering their messages to Congress too closely resembled the "British 'Speech from the Throne' that opened each session of Parliament."[57]

Jefferson also used the *National Intelligencer* to communicate with Congress. On October 23, 1802, he sent the editor a piece he had received anonymously. He suggested to Smith that "The enclosed paper seems intended for the legislative as well as Executive eye; but certainly not to be laid before the former in a regular way. The only irregular one would be in the newspapers. Do with it as you may think of it worth or want of it." Members of Congress apparently read the paper closely; in one year, two-thirds of the Senate subscribed to it.[58]

Interestingly, Jefferson attempted to conceal his involvement with the press. In 1807, anxious to defuse the public uproar over an incident in which the British had attacked the American ship *Chesapeake,* Madison suggested to Jefferson that Smith be allowed to publish a report that the British had apologized for the incident. Jefferson agreed that "'it would be well for Smith to be furnished with the [British] declaration . . . only taking care that it should not appear to have been furnished by us.'" A week later, the *Intelligencer* published a story saying "it appears" that the British had disavowed any warlike intentions over the incident.[59]

On another occasion, Treasury Secretary Albert Gallatin forwarded to Jefferson an article that he thought warranted publication in the *Intelligencer*, and asked if the president would "'be good enough to look at it and to see whether it wants any additions, corrections or curtailing.'"[60] Gallatin indicated he meant for Smith to say he was republishing the piece in his paper at the "request of 'a plain citizen.'" The president approved the article, and it was published as Gallatin proposed. Another time, Jefferson sent the editor of the Richmond *Examiner* a response to some charges of old financial improprieties that had been published against him. He asked the editor to "publish it in such form, with such alterations or abridgments as you think proper, whether too as an anonymous communication, or with a feigned name, or as the editor's own observations is left to yourself, as you are sufficiently apprised of the utter impropriety of its being in any form which should engage me in that field. . . . P.S. I will thank you to destroy the original and this letter."[61] Jefferson's statement was published in the *Examiner* on June 25, 1803, under the pseudonym Timoleon.

In 1805, Jefferson wrote to Thomas Paine that "I neither have, nor ever had, any more connection with those papers than our antipodes [Federalist opponents] have; nor know what is to be in them until I see it in them, except proclamations and other documents sent for publication." In light of its ambiguous wording (his "Federalist opponents," after all, had their own political newspapers) and the evidence presented above, this protest seems at best misleading.[62]

What might have been behind Jefferson's attempts to cover up his involvement with newspapers? One historian attributes Jefferson's duplicity to the sense that "it was considered unethical, or at least undignified, for an officer of the government to be associated with political statements and actions."[63] However, the fact that so many of the Founders associated themselves with political statements under the thin veil of pseudonyms—even the *Federalist Papers* were signed with pseudonyms—indicates that such a perception received only the faintest of lip service.

There is another, more substantial explanation for Jefferson's duplicity, however. Although Jefferson, the prototypical believer in direct, full democracy, would naturally have seen the newspaper as the perfect tool of the times for public communications, he would also have been keenly aware of the other school of political thought in America (and England) that regarded direct appeals to the mass public as improper and even dangerous. By using the newspaper for communications but concealing his actions, Jefferson would have been able to accomplish his goals without needlessly opening himself up to criticism from others who were either less democratically minded or had a different view of the appropriate role of the president in the public policy process.

This indirect approach to public communications is similar to the "behind the scenes" approach Jefferson took in the legislative arena. According to historians, even though Jefferson was in fact pushing through Congress his own party agenda, he "worked behind the scenes, using Republicans in Congress as mouthpieces."[64] After all, Jefferson and the Republicans had barely triumphed in the 1800 election over the Federalists, who thought the president's role in the public policy process was purely secondary to Congress. By concealing his real involvement in the legislative process, Jefferson could avoid being seen as attempting to guide events on Capitol Hill, let alone virtually ordering them, as he seems to have done on some occasions.[65]

Just how far Jefferson did go in directing Congress can be seen from his handling of the Louisiana Purchase. For Jefferson and many other Americans, aspects of the deal with France raised some difficult constitutional questions, including whether the federal government even had the authority to acquire territory. In no mood to dwell on constitutional niceties, Jefferson called Congress into session three weeks early to ratify the treaty with France, which by its terms would lapse if not ratified within six months. He then instructed his key House leader, Albert Gallatin, to push the legislation through without delay and without debate: "Would it not be well that you should have a bill ready drawn to be offered on the first or second day of the session? It may be well to say as little as possible on the constitutional difficulty, *and that Congress should act on it without talking*."[66]

As Stephen Skowronek has noted, Jefferson sometimes hid behind the facade of "executive deference to Congress" for strategic reasons as well. When a particular initiative faltered, "he simply fell back on his official position outside the fray and avoided any personal political damage."[67] Similarly, by using close associates such as Madison to serve as "front men," Jefferson could "guard his presidential prestige by appearing as chief of state to be above the mire of political controversy. The attackers were made to appear mean, vindictive, ungentlemanly, while the president could appear the very image of the calm, benevolent statesman."[68]

Jefferson would have attempted to conceal his usage of a presidential newspaper for the same reason. His efforts to conceal his active public policy efforts are the first example of a president acting according to the active Democratist conception of the presidency, while still trying to maintain the appearance of consistency with the reserved Classicist view of indirect democracy and a deferential presidency. His was the first presidency that fits in the Mobilizer category.

James Madison (1809–17): A Classicist Presidency

Jefferson's successor, James Madison, followed the Classicist conception of the presidency and thus had no need for public communications. The *National Intelligencer* continued as the quasi-official administrative organ under his presidency, carrying official government announcements and generally supporting the administration's positions. Compared with Jefferson, though, Madison had a "far less personal relationship" with the paper's new owners and editors, Joseph Gales Jr. and William Seaton. He is known to have anonymously written at least one anti-French editorial for the paper during the War of 1812, but he apparently made no other use of the paper for his own communication purposes.[69]

Madison directed his policy communications to Congress, proposing annually a limited national legislative program. When the War of 1812 was looming, Madison left the decision to declare war up to Congress. He simply sent a message to Congress reviewing Britain's transgressions, and urged the legislators to give the matter "early deliberation."[70] His presidency fits the Deliberator Model.

James Monroe (1817–25): A Mixture of Models

James Monroe's presidency was an interesting mix of the Celebrator and Deliberator Models. Monroe made two long tours of the country during his presidency modeled after those of George Washington. Intending to promote national unity and the idea that there were no longer partisan divisions in the country, Monroe made patriotic, hortatory addresses on the tours. The speeches were printed in local newspapers, reprinted in other papers across the country, and eventually published in book form.[71]

Although there is some disagreement among historians on this point, Monroe also appears to have followed the Deliberator Model of the presidency, involving himself fairly extensively in the policy-making process via formal messages to Congress and contacts with individual members. His annual message to Congress in 1817 was reprinted in newspapers across the country, and Congress itself had seven thousand copies printed.[72]

The *National Intelligencer* continued as the semiofficial newspaper for Monroe's administration, carrying announcements and information that represented the positions of the administration. A former member of Congress told Monroe in 1819 that some foreign ambassadors "look to the *Intelligencer* as religiously official, and take it for granted that every thing in the paper proceeds directly from your Secretaries."[73]

One known example of this use of the *Intelligencer* occurred in 1818, when Monroe and his cabinet decided that the United States needed to give back to Spain the city of Pensacola in Florida. Major General Andrew Jackson had captured the city during his military expedition against the Seminole Indians. Attorney General William Wirt drafted an article explaining the decision to be published in the *Intelligencer* without attribution, and Monroe and his cabinet spent several days reviewing the piece before it was sent to the paper.[74]

John Quincy Adams, Monroe's secretary of state, contacted editor

Joseph Gales frequently in an effort to straighten out Gales's reporting on important foreign affairs issues. Monroe himself met occasionally with Gales. His relationship with the editor has been described as "formal, distant and undistinguished," and their meetings usually seem to have occurred when Monroe had a complaint about the paper's "uncertain course" in its reporting of administration matters. Except for the limited and generally indirect instances discussed here, there is no record of Monroe himself consistently using the *Intelligencer* for his own direct public communication purposes.[75] His presidency therefore can be said to have fit both the Celebrator and the Deliberator Models.

John Quincy Adams (1825–29): Last of the Federalists

John Quincy Adams had an administration newspaper, the *National Journal,* but it carried little more than the official notices of the executive branch. In reality, Adams was a "Federalist posing as a Republican," and eventually joined the Whig Party. He had an elitist disdain for populist politics, and therefore had little interest in communicating with the public.[76] For example, he wrote in his diary that as a presidential candidate he had resolved to "take no one step to advance or promote pretensions to the Presidency. If that office was to be the prize of cabal and intrigue, of purchasing newspapers, bribing by appointments, or bargaining for foreign missions, I had no ticket in that lottery. . . . I will have no stipendiary editor of newspapers to extol my talents and services and to criticize or calumniate my rivals."[77] Adams's disdainful references to "purchased newspapers" and "stipendiary editors" show how well established the politically partisan newspaper had become by the mid-1820s, and reveals his adherence to the Reserved Model of the presidency.

Andrew Jackson (1829–37) and the Presidential Newspaper

The presidential newspaper developed dramatically as a political communications tool during Andrew Jackson's presidency. In retrospect, it is easy to identify some of the contributing factors. Newspapers were circulated through the mails, and the number of post offices increased from 195 in 1792 to 2,610 in 1812 to 8,000 in 1830. By 1828, there was a post office in "virtually every locality of any consequence in the United States."[78] The combination of newspapers and the mail system was so effective that in 1817, John C. Calhoun described them as the nervous system of the "body politic." With the constant circulation of newspapers through the mails, he said, "the slightest impression made on the most remote parts is communicated to the whole system."[79]

In 1787, Thomas Jefferson wrote that all Americans should have "full information of their affairs thro' the channel of the public papers, and . . . those papers should penetrate the whole mass of people."[80] Reflecting the general sentiment that newspapers were "critical to the survival of the republic," Congress encouraged their circulation nationwide with heavily subsidized postal rates. The maximum postage for a newspaper sent anywhere in the country was only one and one-half cents, whereas it cost twice that to send a one-page letter forty miles and a dollar to send a four-page letter 450 miles. Because of these skewed rates, when Americans wanted to share public news with friends or relatives, they would often just put a newspaper in the mail rather than send a letter. Newspaper publishers had it even better: they could "exchange" papers for free. Newspapers thus began flooding the mails. In 1830, 16 million newspapers flowed through the postal system.[81]

From 1810 to 1828, the number of newspapers in the country more than doubled, going from 359 to 852, and the annual number of copies printed increased from 22 million to 68 million. The appearance of steam-powered boats and then trains in the 1830s meant that news could be moved across the country in a matter of days rather than weeks. By the mid-1830s, more than twelve hundred papers were being published, prompting Alexis de Tocqueville to observe: "There is hardly a hamlet in America without its newspaper."[82]

Similarly, the number of eligible voters increased dramatically due to population growth and the enfranchising of most white males in many states. As a result, 1,155,340 men voted in the 1828 presidential election—eight hundred thousand more than in the previous election. Also, by 1824 all but six states had made the popular vote rather than the vote of state legislators the method for selecting presidential electors.[83]

Stung by their loss of the presidency in 1824 to John Quincy Adams in the Electoral College, Jackson and his supporters realized that the next presidential campaign would have to depend heavily on newspapers to reach the newly expanded, overwhelmingly rural electorate. The Jacksonians decided they needed a newspaper network to promote the "people's candidate," and set about establishing one.[84] The usual method was for the leading politicians in the area to loan or give an editor the funds needed to start up a newspaper. Party faithful were then solicited to subscribe to it. The paper was helped along with grants of state and federal printing contracts, and editors were often appointed to minor government positions. Finally, congressmen used their unregulated franking privileges to flood the mails with party newspapers.[85]

Lacking a paper in Washington, Jackson's supporters purchased a failing publication and renamed it the *United States Telegrapher.* Duff Green, the editor, later wrote that Jackson himself had asked him to "'remove to Washington and become the organ of his party.'" At the state level, Jackson's supporters established dozens of new papers. Before the 1828 election, then, Jackson had put into place all the ingredients of the ultimate presidential newspaper.[86]

The campaign was rough, with both sides trading scurrilous charges. Adams was said to have spent lavish amounts of money on gaming and gambling furniture for the White House, and to have used a "beautiful American Girl" to seduce the Russian tsar. Jackson was branded a liar, a murderer, insane, and an adulterer for having unknowingly married his wife Rachel before she was legally divorced.[87] The Jacksonians used aggressive press techniques to counter the opposition's propaganda. In the year leading up to the election, pro-Jackson papers regularly carried long letters "by the General answering some charge brought against his public and private life."[88]

Crucial areas were blanketed with copies of newspapers containing important campaign information. In March, 1828, for example, Jackson directed that a hundred extra copies of an important newspaper edition be sent to "every printer and Jackson Committee [in] Ohio, Indiana, Illinois, Mississippi, Louisiana, and Alabama—and to the north Pennsylvania, Virginia, Maryland, New Jersey, New York and New Hampshire," adding that he would also distribute copies in Virginia and Kentucky. In a striking precursor to the "Early Response Team" employed by Bill Clinton in the 1992 campaign, Jackson established a Central Committee in Nashville for the purpose of identifying and responding to "falsehoods and calumny, by the publication of truth, and by furnishing either to the public or to individuals, whether alone or associated, full and correct information upon any matter of subject within their knowledge or power, properly connected with the fitness or qualification of Andrew Jackson to fill the office of President of the United States."[89]

The victorious Jacksonians recognized the crucial role their newspapers played in the campaign. "To Gen. Duff Green: able political standard-bearer of our great and victorious Jackson!" was one of the many toasts made on the day of victory. Green's reward was that his paper, the *United States Telegraph,* became the new presidential newspaper. It carried the administration's official announcements and devoted most of its space to praising and defending the new president. Green received all the congressional printing contracts, from which he netted a profit of over 60 percent. Jackson also rewarded more than fifty other loyal editors with government patronage jobs, such as postmaster and customs collector positions. Amos Kendall, a close Jackson aide, was given a clerkship in the Treasury Department, and was later appointed Postmaster General.[90]

When Duff Green began siding with Jackson's political rival, John C. Calhoun, the president decided, in his own words, that he needed "another organ to announce the policy and defend the Administration."[91] In 1830, Jackson's supporters established a new paper, the *Washington Globe,* to be the president's official newspaper. The editor was Francis P. Blair, a Kentucky editor who received a letter from Amos Kendall asking him: "'How would you like to be the Editor of a paper here which should have the support of the Executive, and be the *real* Administration paper?'"[92] Jackson himself told a supporter, "I expect you all to patronize the *Globe.*" Federal officers earning more than $1,000 a year were expected to subscribe, and the paper began receiving the federal government's official advertising and departmental printing jobs. Blair supposedly named the paper the *Globe* because, like the Earth, it too had been created out of nothing—with no plant, press, or subscription list. Within a year, however, it had a circulation of four thousand. It was even possible for the Jackson administration to check on who was subscribing to the *Globe.* At that time, subscribers, not the publishers, paid the postage for newspaper delivery. The U.S. Post Office kept records of the postage paid by every subscriber, and "in Jacksonian America, these lists were shipped off four times a year to Washington, where they were studied by political appointees."[93]

Less than six weeks after its establishment, it was clear the *Globe* was Jackson's new mouthpiece when it carried the announcement that the president would run for reelection. "We are permitted to say, that if it should be the will of the Nation to call on the President to serve a second term in the chief Magistracy, he will not decline the summons," declaimed the January 22, 1831, *Globe.* Word was also "passed down the line to administration papers elsewhere that the *Globe* was the official mouthpiece." The editor of the rival *National Intelligencer* was soon describing Blair as an "intimate at the palace, . . . deep in the confidence of the President's advisers," and one who "'must be believed when professing to act by *authority.*" Even Blair later described himself in the *Globe* as the "editor of the official paper in Washington."[94]

One use Jackson made of the *Globe* was as a tool for directing Democratic Party affairs. In 1831, the president and his advisers conceived of the idea of the first-ever national party convention, at which Jackson and his designee for vice president would be nominated. They arranged for Democrats in New Hampshire to call for a national convention, and then publicized the appeal in the *Globe.* Support for the idea mounted nationally, and the convention was called.[95]

In Jackson's conception of the office, the president was the "voice" of the people, ruling of, by, and for them as their "direct representative." When he began asserting this Democratist position, he encountered vociferous opposition from the many Whig Classicist members of Congress who thought that the legislature's job was to serve as an institutional intermediary, often resisting the voice of the people.[96] As the following examples show, Andrew Jackson had a very different idea of his relationship to the people. To that end, he constantly used the *Globe* as a means of communicating directly with "his" people, over the heads of Congress.

The issue that preoccupied Jackson and the country during his administration was his war against the Bank of the United States, which he regarded as the epitome of the dominance of the Eastern establishment over the lives of the common people. At the time Jackson made the decision to withdraw government deposits from the Bank in an effort to cripple it, he provided the *Globe* with a statement explaining his decision. His purpose in giving the statement to the *Globe* for publication is documented in two letters he wrote to Vice President Martin Van Buren. In Jackson's own words, he planned to "let, thro the Globe, be made unofficially, a statement of the causes and the facts that ha[d] induced" his decision.[97] He said the statement would appear in the September 23, 1833, edition, and would "give my views on, and reasons for, the removal of the deposits." The statement was needed, he said, "to counteract the gross misrepresentations that were circulated, and that the full view of the case should be made to the people and their representatives before the meeting of Congress."[98]

The statement carried in the *Globe* was a remarkable illustration of how Jackson used the press to talk directly to the public. The paper published the text of a long message Jackson had given to cabinet members the previous week explaining his decision to withdraw the deposits. How had the *Globe* gotten the statement? "As public attention has been drawn to this subject," the paper explained, "it is deemed proper, in order to prevent misunderstanding or misrepresentation, *to lay before the people the communication made by the President* as above mentioned, *and a copy has been furnished to us for that purpose,* which we now proceed to publish."[99] This statement, coupled with Jackson's own statements to Van Buren, could not be clearer manifestations of Jackson's intent to speak directly to the public, via his newspaper, regarding the most critical domestic policy issue of the day.

In his discussion of the bank withdrawal issue, however, Jeffrey Tulis simply ignores this use of the *Globe* by Jackson to communicate directly with the public on the issue. Instead, focusing solely on the written "Protest Message" that Jackson sent to the Senate in response to its censure of him for his removal of the deposits, Tulis proceeds to a very different conclusion. The fact that Jackson was "'forced' by the same doctrine to appeal to Congress in the first instance," he asserts, illustrates the power of the norm that the "sole avenue" of communications with the public by nineteenth-century presidents on policy matters "led through Congress, not to the people directly." In fact, Tulis says, "it would be hard to find a better example of a formal constraint fostering deliberation," a constraint that he says "extended to 'unofficial' or 'informal' speech and behavior by presidents" as well.[100]

These conclusions are drastically wrong. In Jackson's vigorous use of the *Globe* as a public communications tool, it is hard to find a better example of the *absence* of any such constraint.

Indeed, a few months later Jackson made it plain that, as far as he was concerned, the right of Congress to receive information from the president was *inferior* to that of the public. The Senate, which was then debating Jackson's withdrawal of deposits from the Bank, had requested a copy of the message the president had given his cabinet about the issue. Even though this was the same message that had already been published—at Jackson's instigation—in the *Globe* on September 23, Jackson refused to give the Senate a copy of it, citing executive privilege! As if to rub salt in the Senate's wounds, the *Globe* printed the message again when it carried a Senate speech by Henry Clay, Jackson's old nemesis, in which he attacked Jackson's Bank actions and berated the president for refusing to give the Senate a copy of a message "which the whole world was already in possession of."[101]

Throughout the war with the U.S. Bank, the hand of Jackson media expert Amos Kendall could be detected. Jackson was concerned that Congress might override his decision to withdraw the deposits, but Kendall believed that by going public (to use the modern term), Jackson could prevent that from happening. He proposed that Jackson make the withdrawals early enough "to give us several months to defend the measure in the *Globe,* and we will bring up the people to sustain you with a power which Congress dare not resist." Similarly, Kendall advised making a "direct issue between the Bank and President Jackson, backed by his invincible popularity."[102] That is exactly what happened.

On September 20, 1833, the *Globe* announced that federal deposits would be moved from the Bank of the United States to selected state banks by October 1. The official order, dated September 25, 1833, stated that, as of October 1, all future government deposits would be made in selected state banks and that the government would draw on its deposits in the Bank of the United States for operating expenses until the deposits were exhausted. With that order began a six-month struggle between the Jackson administration and the Bank of the United States for the heart of the American people and the support of the U.S. Congress. In the spring of 1834, public opinion began to mount in favor of the administration's position, and on April 4 Jackson prevailed in what he called a "glorious triumph" when the House of Representatives voted to sustain his removal of the deposits, thereby rejecting the Senate's earlier censure of his action.[103]

The triumph must have been aided greatly by the *Globe,* just as Amos Kendall had foreseen. During those six months, as shown in Appendix B, the paper almost daily carried long commentaries explaining the administration's position and responding to the latest attacks from the Bank's supporters. In addition, the paper carried the texts of dozens of proadministration speeches made on the House and Senate floors, excerpts from scores of favorable articles in other papers throughout the country, over forty mostly anonymous letters from "distinguished persons" in support of the administration position, and over forty resolutions of support from state legislatures and state and party conventions.[104]

Indeed, at least judging from the contents of the *Globe*, the Bank deposits issue seems to have almost totally consumed the attention of the president, Congress, most state legislatures, and many Americans for months.

The *Globe* defended Jackson's vow not to recharter the Bank of the United States as well. The very first issue of the *Globe* carried an attack on the Bank, and a series of six articles soon followed rebutting pro-Bank articles that had appeared in the *National Intelligencer* and other opposition papers.[105] Following Jackson's veto of the recharter bill in 1832, the *Globe* carried a series of sixteen articles defending the action in almost every imaginable way, ranging from Jackson's past military achievements to a point-by-point elaboration of the president's veto message.[106] While the veto message may have been addressed nominally to Congress, its content was also intended to be conveyed directly to the American public via Jackson's newspaper. In light of the extensive reprinting and explaining of the veto message that occurred in the political newspapers of the day, it becomes very difficult to say who was the real intended recipient of the message: Congress or the people. As Jackson told Martin Van Buren in 1830, he designed all of his major presidential statements "so that the people may fully understand them."[107]

Blair also helped draft Jackson's famous Nullification Proclamation of December 10, 1832, in which Jackson rejected the idea that southern states dissatisfied with newly adopted federal tariff provisions could simply declare the legislation void. The proclamation was given to Blair to publish, of course, and "a crowd of 1,500 waited outside barred doors for the first copies."[108]

According to a Blair biographer, Jackson hurried to get the proclamation out even though its language had not been fine-tuned to his satisfaction. Jackson was confident that "Blair in the columns of the Globe [could] explain away statements that might be misunderstood by the people." A few weeks later, Blair did indeed publish in the *Globe* a "Nullification Dictionary" that explained and defended Jackson's proclamation. Blair's exposition was credited with satisfying influential citizens in the key state of Virginia, who had become concerned that some of the language in Jackson's proclamation was a threat to the sacred principle of states' rights.[109]

As time went on, Blair became a daily visitor to the White House, where he and Jackson would plot out the day's media strategy. Everything in the *Globe* was quickly dispersed throughout the country because, as the official publisher of all new federal laws, the *Globe* was sent free by the federal government to all state newspapers selected to publish the laws. The editors of these state newspapers would copy and republish the new federal laws as they appeared in the *Globe*, but they were also free to use anything else in the *Globe*. Since almost all of the designated state newspapers were partisan Jackson papers, there was much in the *Globe* the editors found useful. That was the way the system was intended to work: The *Globe* gave friendly newspapers throughout the country their editorial cues, and then later published excerpts from the local editorials to prove that public opinion around the country supported the president.[110]

The *Globe*'s handling of Jackson's decision to withdraw federal deposits from the Bank of the United States illustrates how the process of public communication and mobilization worked in the days of the presidential newspaper. The outlines of that process can be seen in Appendix B, which records the approach the *Globe* took to the deposit issue over a period of six months, from the time in late September, 1833, when Jackson's decision to withdraw the deposits was announced, to early April, 1834, when the House of Representatives voted to sustain Jackson's decision and thereby repudiate the Senate's earlier censure of the action. Appendix B notes every mention of the bank controversy in every issue of the *Globe* over this six-month period. Usually, a third or more of each four-page issue of the *Globe* was devoted to the articles chronicled in the appendix, with the remainder devoted to advertisements and scraps of news and notes from around the country and world.

As noted previously, the *Globe* first announced Jackson's policy on September 20, 1833. Five days later, the first editorial explaining and defending the move appeared in the paper. Thereafter, there was an anti-Bank editorial almost every day for the next six months.

Within a week of the first *Globe* editorial, the paper also began carrying excerpts from anti-Bank editorials in state newspapers that were part of the Jacksonian chain. These editorials—from papers such as the *Richmond Enquirer*, the *Maine Democrat*, the *Boston Morning Post* and the *Hartford Times*—usually echoed themes from the *Globe*'s. In the month of October alone, seventy-eight such editorials appeared in the paper's twenty-two issues. In addition, the October 21 issue carried excerpts from ten state newspaper editorials.

In January, 1834, the *Globe* began carrying other expressions of public sentiment besides editorials. The first such expression occurred on January 9, when, in addition to reprints of excerpts from two anti-Bank editorials from state newspapers, there appeared a resolution passed by the Ohio legislature supporting Jackson's Bank policy. The next day, the first anonymous letter of support from a "citizen" appeared in the paper. Thereafter, until April, the *Globe*, in addition to its own almost daily anti-Bank editorials, carried a mixture of state editorials, mostly anonymous letters, and state and local resolutions—all of which supported Jackson's fight with the Bank. On one occasion, the paper reprinted a number of anti-Bank drinking toasts, and on another it printed a satirical anti-Bank play. By March, the *Globe*, which all along had also been carrying reports of the interminable House and Senate debates on the Bank deposits issue, was reporting that representatives and senators were referring in their speeches to the pro-Jackson letters and resolutions that were apparently pouring into Congress.

The main reach of the *Globe* nationally was through the copies of the paper delivered by mail to subscribers and newspapers in the states. In addition, Jackson also used his franking privileges to circulate important issues of the *Globe* to members of the electorate. In 1836, facing a party revolt in his home state of Tennessee against presidential-candidate Martin Van Buren, Jackson blanketed the state with issues of the *Globe* that carried abusive articles about the party rebels.[111]

The *Globe's* status was not lost on foreign governments, which read it "as an index to whatever Jackson, and therefore the United States, might be thinking and planning." Ironically, the Russian foreign minister once complained to U.S. ambassador James Buchanan, about something that had been said about Russia "'by the official paper in Washington.'" When Buchanan tried to explain that the administration had no control over the paper, the Russian minister was understandably not persuaded.[112]

Andrew Jackson, the Great Mobilizer, realized what many other presidents and politicians came to know: Public opinion can exert substantial pressure in support of an administration, and it can be used as a tool in shaping national policy and commanding (or coercing) actions from the legislature.[113] Daniel Webster recognized this power of the people when he wrote that, had it not been for the Senate's "fear of the out-door popularity of General Jackson," it would have rejected many more of Jackson's nominations of editors to government positions.[114] As Culver H. Smith puts it: "There need not be any doubt about Jackson's belief in the importance of publicity. Often at odds with Congress, his recourse was appeal to the people for support of his views. Therefore, the *Globe* was essential in making his views known."[115] Similarly, while crediting Jackson with strong party whips in Congress, Arthur M. Schlesinger Jr. notes that "in cases of doubt Jackson's appeals to the people always proved decisive."[116]

Since Jackson's public standing was so important, Richard L. Rubin writes, "his supporters had to organize instruments of mass communications to provide him with the necessary publicity. The press, the prime mass communications tool for creating public visibility, became, along with the party, critical in reaching, focusing, and solidifying a new and expanded electorate." Alexis de Tocqueville concluded during his visit to America in the Jackson era that the power of the press was "immense." The press, he said, "makes political life circulate in every corner of that vast land. . . . When many organs of the press do come to the same line, their influence in the long run is almost irresistible, and public opinion, continually struck in the same spot, ends by giving way under the blows."[117]

Andrew Jackson chose to harness this power through the device of the presidential newspaper, using it to promote himself and his policies by appealing to the American people for support in what looks like a rather modern effort at going public. As will be shown in chapters 4, 5, and 6, the rest of the nineteenth century is the story of presidents either following this activist path or refraining from going public in deference to a different conception of their office.

CHAPTER 3

The Presidential Newspaper, 1836–60

The Rest of the Story

Without a paper thus edited at Albany we may hang our harps on the willows. With it the party can survive a thousand such convulsions as those which now agitate and probably alarm most of those around you.

—MARTIN VAN BUREN

THE PRESIDENTIAL NEWSPAPER played an important role in American politics until just before the Civil War.[1] This chapter traces the story of the presidential newspaper from 1836—when Andrew Jackson's vice president and political strategist, Martin Van Buren, was elected president—to 1860, when the presidency of James Buchanan and the era of the presidential newspaper both ended. During this time, the presidential newspaper became a heavily used communications tool for several presidents. For a few presidents who held the reserved view of their office, the "official" papers of their administrations became primarily the tools of their political parties.

Martin Van Buren (1837–41): Going Public Continues

Martin Van Buren was one of Andrew Jackson's chief campaign strategists, a dominant figure in New York state politics, and, in the eyes of some historians, the founder of what eventually became the modern Democratic Party.[2] As the quotation at the beginning of this chapter indicates, Van Buren appreciated the power of the press. He was one of the owners of the Albany *Argus,* the official party newspaper in New York, and occasionally wrote articles for the paper.[3] He thus was instrumental in building up the network of Jacksonian newspapers eventually headed by the *Washington Globe.* In the words of the *National Intelligencer,* the opposition paper that served as the official presidential newspaper from Jefferson to Adams, Van Buren was a "'Master Spirit'" by whose agency "'machinery had been established to . . . control the popular election by means of organized clubs in the States, and organized presses everywhere.'"[4]

Even before he succeeded Jackson as president, Van Buren was a beneficiary of the *Globe*'s efforts. It was created as a substitute for Jackson's first presidential newspaper, the *Telegraph,* after the *Telegraph*'s editor, Duff Green, began supporting the 1832 presidential aspirations of Vice President John C. Calhoun. Jackson wrote that Green's "idol controls him as much as the showman does his puppets, and we must get another organ to announce the policy and defend the Administration."[5]

The switch to the *Globe* precipitated an all-out war between the papers, with Van Buren, Jackson's secretary of state, one of the main targets. Calhoun had published in the *Telegraph* a long diatribe in which he alleged that Van Buren had plotted to destroy his credibility with Jackson, and the angered Jackson ordered *Globe* editor Francis Blair to counterattack. Blair denounced Calhoun and defended Van Buren vociferously, and the newspaper feud carried on for weeks.[6] Jackson the old warrior won this war, too, eventually dumping Calhoun in favor of Van Buren as his running mate in the 1832 election. In 1834, having settled on Van Buren to succeed him, Jackson started a campaign in the *Globe* to assure Van Buren the Democratic nomination in 1836.[7]

When Van Buren was inaugurated on March 4, 1837, he inherited the *Globe* as the official newspaper of his administration. Unfortunately, he also took office just as a great financial panic was sweeping the country and regional differences over the slavery issue were increasingly straining the cohesiveness of the Democratic coalition. This, combined with the fact that Blair's editorials tended to focus more on defending Andrew Jackson than on his successor, meant that the *Globe* was not as powerful a weapon for Van Buren as it had been for Jackson.[8]

Nevertheless, Van Buren still made good use of the paper. In an effort to appeal to southern members of the Democratic coalition, the *Globe* assured them that the administration opposed abolitionism and favored states' rights and a strict construction of the Constitution. The *Globe* was also kept busy explaining why just about everyone except Martin Van Buren was responsible for the hard economic times caused by the financial panic of 1837. In describing the *Globe's* contents in March and April of that year, one historian observed: "A reader grows dizzy at the thrusts at banks which had over-issued, land speculators, paper money, English bankers, and varied forms of accusations against abolitionists and nullifiers, Clay and Webster, the *National Intelligencer,* and the moneyed oligarchy." The paper also featured articles by the treasury secretary on the state of the economy.[9]

As the depression deepened, Van Buren soon came under pressure to abandon the "Specie Circular" policy that had been a cornerstone of the Jackson administration's economic policies. This was a policy of requiring the speculators who were buying up surplus government lands in the West to pay with gold or silver only, and not bank notes.[10] The policy was intended to put a brake on land speculation, which was fueling inflationary pressures. When the Panic of 1837 hit, however, many bankers and politicians blamed the specie-circular policy as the cause of the crash. In their view, the policy had caused a sudden shift of gold and silver bank reserves from the eastern United States to the West, creating a liquidity problem for eastern banks and precipitating the panic.

Van Buren solicited advice from numerous political allies on whether he should abandon the policy, but the advice he received was conflicting. He received "bundles of letters" from friends urging him to abandon the policy, his cabinet was divided, and Jackson was adamantly in favor of keeping it. In April, when he finally decided to retain the policy, Van Buren used the *Globe* to disclose his decision in a way that demonstrated a highly strategic use of the paper as a public communications tool. According to historian Donald Cole, Van Buren "issued no formal announcement, but by mid-April the *Globe* made the President's position clear by publishing strong statements supporting the circular."[11]

A month later, when Van Buren decided that the federal treasury ought to be divorced from any links with private banks in the country, he again strategically used the *Globe* to further his policy goal. Although he had settled on an independent treasury, Van Buren desperately wanted to reconcile conflicting views within the Democratic Party and achieve some sort of consensus about the details of his plan. He tried to bring about this consensus through the *Globe.* While Van Buren maintained a public silence from May to September, the *Globe* ran a spectrum of articles on the issue, frequently arguing strongly for the initiative but also carrying other opinions on the issue in an attempt to moderate the effects of opposition to the plan.

Later, in a subtle display of "going public" nineteenth-century style, Van Buren used the *Globe* to indicate his willingness to compromise on the issue of an independent treasury. On December 5, 1837, he sent a special message to Congress that reiterated his basic views on the issue and made no mention of any possible compromises. However, that same day the *Globe* stated that there were, in fact, "shades of difference" among friends of the administration as to the proper "mode" of divorce, thus signaling flexibility in the president's position.[12] The bill ultimately signed into law was full of compromises and departures from the president's original proposal.[13]

His treatment of Thomas Ritchie, an old friend and editor of the highly influential Democratic Party paper in Virginia, the *Richmond Enquirer,* illustrates the value Van Buren placed on being able to go public through newspapers he controlled. When Ritchie balked at supporting the president's treasury plan, he was met with a blunt threat: Support the "divorce bill," or a new paper would be established in Richmond that would be "unequivocally committed to the administration."[14] Ritchie would have had no trouble appreciating the seriousness of the threat, since he had himself been instrumental in the creation of the *Globe* in 1830 to replace the wayward *Telegraph* as Jackson's official paper. Not surprisingly, Ritchie began supporting the administration plan in his paper.

Van Buren used the *Globe* to advance other positions as well. In 1838, border problems erupted with Canada. In the Aroostook War in Maine, the United States found itself embroiled in a border dispute with Canada and Britain. Many Americans began agitating for war after the Canadians captured the *Carolene,* a private American ship carrying arms to Canadian revolutionaries, set it on fire, and allowed it to float over Niagara

Falls. The *Globe* was used to argue for the administration's policy of restraint and to warn Americans on the border that the United States would not support them if they became involved in hostilities with Canada.[15]

Finally, the *Globe* served as one of Van Buren's main weapons in yet another scurrilous presidential campaign. For months before the 1840 election, the paper carried a wide variety of material, ranging from high-minded discussions of administration positions on states' rights, strict constructionism, and the horror of disunion, to sheer mudslinging. Van Buren's opponent, Maj. Gen. William Henry Harrison, was accused of being senile, an incompetent battlefield commander, prejudiced against Irishmen, partial to Native Americans, in favor of freeing black slaves and enslaving whites, and an advocate of whipping women who committed crimes.[16] The Whig papers responded in kind, forcing Blair to publish denials of numerous charges, including that Van Buren had opposed the war of 1812, that he was Catholic, that he was an Irishman who was secretly sending public funds to Ireland, and that the White House had been turned into a gilded palace with several pairs of hills on its grounds cleverly "designed to resemble . . . an Amazon's bosom."[17]

William Harrison (1841): The First Whig President

When the dust and stench of the 1840 presidential election campaign had dispersed, Harrison and his renegade Democrat running mate John Tyler emerged victorious. One of Harrison's first acts as president (he died after just one month in office) was to terminate the *Globe's* contract making it the printer for Congress.

Harrison was a general, not a politician, and he owed his victory to the Whig political strategists who thought that he would give the party its best chance of capturing the presidency. The Whigs ran a deliberately non issue-oriented campaign. Not even adopting a party platform, they focused instead on patriotism, Harrison's war record (which included a battle against the great Native-American warrior Tecumseh at Tippecanoe Creek), the sad state of the economy, and Van Buren's alleged monarchical airs. The Whigs saw Harrison as a reserved, figurehead leader who would preside over a government whose policy moves were determined not by the White House but by the party leaders in Congress.[18]

One of the Whigs' basic tenets was that Congress was the only legitimate policy maker under the Constitution, and that the executive had no business interfering with that process. Harrison toed the party line in his brief inaugural address, proclaiming that it was "preposterous to suppose that the President . . . could better understand the wants and wishes of the people than their own immediate representatives."[19]

Under Harrison, the *National Intelligencer,* which in the 1830s had become the voice of the Whig Party, naturally came to be regarded as the official paper of the new president. Consistent with Whig philosophy, however, the paper's first loyalty would have been to the party rather than to an individual president. Aside from the fact that the *National Intelligencer* was presumably speaking for the president, who was indebted to the party it supported, there is no historical record of Harrison using the paper for his own purposes. Given his avowed philosophy on the proper role of the presidency in the field of public policy making, though, it is unlikely that Harrison would have made much use of this avenue of communication had he lived.

John Tyler (1841–45): Democrat in Whig's Clothing

John Tyler turned out to be a much different story, for both the Whigs and for students of presidential communication. Tyler, who had served as a Democratic senator from Virginia until he resigned because of his mounting policy disagreements with Andrew Jackson, seems to have been added without much thought to the Whig ticket in an attempt to appeal to southern states (Harrison's home was in Indiana). The Whigs soon came to regret this strategy because Tyler quickly demonstrated that both his conception of the presidency and some of his policy positions differed markedly from those of Harrison and most Whigs.

In his first public message after being sworn in, Tyler did not say, as Harrison had, that Congress knew better than he what the people wanted. He attempted to lay out the principles that would "govern [him] in the general course of [his] administration," thereby endorsing the decidedly non-Whiggish notion that a president might have principles independent of Congress and his party.[20] Tyler also hinted broadly that he was opposed to the cornerstone of Whig policy, the restoration of the Bank of the United States, which he years earlier had helped kill under Andrew Jackson.[21]

At first the *National Intelligencer* continued to be regarded as the Tyler administration's official organ, which meant that its pages were filled not only with supportive statements about the administration but also numerous official government advertisements and announcements.[22] The paper argued in favor of Tyler's compromise proposal to create a bank in the District of Columbia that would be able to establish branches in states that gave their permission, and carried three editorials by Secretary of State Daniel Webster in favor of the plan.[23]

Just a few months after his inauguration, however, Tyler set off a firestorm of protest when he vetoed the Whigs' bill to reestablish the Bank of the United States. The veto was such big news that the *New York Herald* chartered a train to carry Tyler's veto message to New York, where more than a hundred thousand copies of a special morning edition with the message in it were sold.[24] A month later, on September 9, the president vetoed another compromise version of the legislation. Two days after that, all of Tyler's cabinet officers (all of them Whigs and holdovers from Harrison's brief administration) resigned except for Daniel Webster.[25] On September 13, between fifty and seventy Whig congressmen met in the capital to adopt a manifesto expelling Tyler from the party. According to historian Norma Lois Peterson, the main reason for their anger was Tyler's assertion of presidential independence. There was even an abortive move, led by ex-president and now congressman John Quincy Adams, to impeach Tyler for his impertinent use of the veto. Tyler sent a message to Congress defending his actions, but the House refused to officially receive it, just as the Senate had refused to officially receive Andrew Jackson's reply to its censure of him over the bank deposits withdrawal controversy.[26]

Tyler's actions strained and eventually ruptured his relationship with the *National Intelligencer*. The paper, forced to choose between the Whig Party and a president who was turning out to be an apostate, became gradually more critical of Tyler. Finally, Tyler could take no more. He wrote Daniel Webster sometime in early September, 1841: "I can no longer tolerate the *Intelligencer* as the official paper. Besides assaulting me perpetually, directly and indirectly, it refuses all defensive articles, as appears by the *Madisonian* of Saturday. There is a point beyond which one's patience cannot endure."[27] Later that month, Tyler wrote to close associate Henry Wise: "The *Madisonian* is the official organ and is now enjoying the Executive patronage."[28]

Thomas Allen founded the *Madisonian* in 1837 to serve as a voice for disaffected Democrats during the administration of Martin Van Buren.

In the first issue, Allen jibed that "If the Globe has an *exclusive* patent right to be the organ of the *executive,* perhaps he will allow us to be the organ of the [Democrat] Republicans in the *legislative* department." By 1840 Allen was on good terms with both Harrison and Tyler, so his paper offered Tyler an appealing alternative to the *Intelligencer,* particularly because it had strenuously defended the president from the attacks of that paper as well as the Democratic Party's *Globe* throughout the summer of 1841.[29]

Tyler was not content with merely trading warhorses, however; he wanted to change jockeys as well. After a "free conversation" with Allen, the president negotiated the sale of the paper to thirty-one-year-old Baltimore novelist and journalist J. Beauchamp Jones, who was known to Tyler and his friends.[30] In November, 1841, Tyler's new editor boldly proclaimed his paper was the "Official Organ of the Government." Jones wrote that, as "the only Administration Journal in the District of Columbia," his paper was dedicated to "publishing officially the proceedings of the Government, and cherishing and defending honestly and earnestly the principles upon which the public acts of President Tyler have thus far been founded."[31]

Although many of Tyler's and Jones's papers have been lost, there are still records of several instances in which Tyler gave very specific instructions to his editor on what to write. During the winter of 1843–44, as the next presidential campaign was getting started, Jones focused his editorial attacks on Martin Van Buren, who at that time was widely expected to run again. Concerned that Jones's attacks might be interpreted by Democrats as favoritism by Tyler toward Henry Clay, the likely Whig nominee, Tyler told Jones he had said enough about Van Buren and should find some "general subject" to discuss to avoid further antagonizing the Democrats. Tyler wrote again a few days later, this time urging Jones to maintain "an exact balance" in his treatment of the candidates so as to avoid having the *Madisonian* identified with any party.[32] Having thus finetuned the campaign coverage of his administration's paper, Tyler then instructed some three hundred local newspapers that held government printing contracts to follow the *Madisonian*'s approach when writing about the campaign.[33]

On two other occasions, Tyler had Jones clarify the origins of his Exchequer Plan, which would have created a central depository for federal funds and made them more readily transferable throughout the country.

Tyler authorized Jones to deny "by authority" that Nicolas Biddle, the notorious president of the Bank of the United States, had been consulted. To emphasize that Daniel Webster had not been involved in the development of the plan, Tyler also had Jones state in another article—in italics—that the president alone had developed the plan.[34]

The openness with which the *Madisonian* was acknowledged to be Tyler's mouthpiece is remarkable. A year after first trumpeting his special relationship to the president, Jones reiterated the fact even more forcefully. After again describing his paper as the "organ of the Administration," he reminded the world that the "views and purposes of the Administration, will, as heretofore, be made known through the columns of this paper.[35] Rival papers recognized that the *Madisonian* spoke for the president. The *Globe* sneered about the "factitious importance" the *Madisonian* enjoyed "as the journal which the Executive has constituted the exponent of its 'views and purposes.'"[36]

Tyler's use of the *Madisonian* to convey his administration's views to the public was even discussed on the House floor. During the debate over awarding government printing contracts, Tyler's friend Henry A. Wise, who had helped Tyler establish the *Madisonian* as the administration's new paper, complained that the Democrats and Whigs were conspiring to deny the paper government printing work. Their successful efforts, Wise said, were an unfair attempt to "strike at the *Madisonian*, and thus deprive the Executive of what had always been enjoyed under every previous Administration—the advantage of having a public press at the seat of Government to speak in his behalf, while other presses expressed the views of the opposition."[37] As Wise's candid complaint shows, the presidential newspaper had by that point in the nineteenth century become an accepted, well-known means of going public.

Foreshadowing a technique that Abraham Lincoln would later use extensively, Tyler on at least two occasions used public letters to express his opinions on policy matters. On one occasion he wrote to a Saint Patrick's Anniversary Celebration Committee expressing his "liveliest interest" in Irish independence efforts.[38] Another time, Tyler used a letter to the editor of the Cincinnati *Republican* to urge his Whig critics in Congress to put aside the "spirit of faction." The letter was widely reprinted in other newspapers, including the *Madisonian* and the *Intelligencer.* The *Intelligencer* expressed "surprise and concern" at both the contents of the letter and at "its apparently authorized publicity" by Tyler.[39] It criticized

Tyler and defended the conduct of the Whigs in Congress, while the *Madisonian* did the opposite.

The *Madisonian* even figured in negotiations between Tyler and James Polk, who was campaigning to succeed him, during the last days of Tyler's presidency. In June, 1844, discussions began about the *Madisonian* either supporting both Polk's candidacy and Tyler's presidency, with one of Polk's men serving as a coeditor of the paper, or being absorbed into a new Polk organ. Although these schemes faltered, the negotiations continued. Finally, in August, the *Madisonian* carried Tyler's announcement that he was withdrawing from the race, and the next day the paper announced that Tyler was endorsing Polk. Polk biographer Paul H. Bergeron states that the deal was finally made when Polk and his aides "cajoled the *Washington Globe* into putting an end to its criticisms and attacks upon Tyler."[40]

James Polk (1845–49) and the Importance of Going Public

The actions of Tyler's successor, James Polk, demonstrate the importance a president could attach to having an official paper in Washington to "speak in his behalf" in the mid-nineteenth century. Although his nomination and election were unexpected, James Polk came to the presidency as a highly experienced politician. He had served seven terms in the House of Representatives and been governor of Tennessee, a state where the arts of political scheming and attack journalism had been raised to a high level. He also came into the presidency with an activist conception of the office, believing that "The people, by the Constitution, have commanded the President, as much as they have commanded the legislative branch of the Government, to execute their will."[41]

As president-elect, Polk not surprisingly had very definite ideas about what he wanted from his administration newspaper.[42] According to presidential press historian James Pollard, "Polk understood clearly what was widely comprehended, namely, that an effective, even aggressive, president had to 'manage' the news to build support for his administration and to gain leverage with the Congress.[43] Late in 1844, Polk outlined his thinking: "As to the *press* which may be regarded as the Government organ, one thing is settled in my mind. It must have no connection with, nor be under the influence or control of any clique or portion of the party which is making war upon any other portion of the party—with a view to the succession and not with a view to the success of my administration."[44] To Andrew Jackson, he explained: "I must be the head of my own administration, and will not be controlled by any newspaper or particular individual whom it serves.[45]

Jackson, Francis Blair, and many other Democrats at first assumed that the *Globe* automatically would become the Polk administration's official voice. That was not what Polk wanted, however, because he thought Blair had become an independent, divisive influence who would blow apart the party's delicate coalition if he were returned as the editor of the new administration's paper.[46] Although Jackson continued to entreat Polk to retain the *Globe* as his administration's paper, the new president was not deterred. In the end, Polk brokered a complicated and mysteriously funded deal in which two experienced newspapermen, Thomas Ritchie, editor of the *Richmond Enquirer,* and John P. Heiss, publisher of the *Nashville Union,* bought out both the *Globe* and the *Madisonian.* The former papers of Jackson, Van Buren, and Tyler were replaced with a new paper that was to be Polk's mouthpiece: the *Washington Union.*[47] The transaction was funded by the surreptitious transfer of $50,000 in U.S. Treasury funds to a small-town bank in Pennsylvania.[48]

Having fought so hard to get his own presidential newspaper, Polk made good use of it over the next four years. The first issue, appearing on May 1, 1845, trumpeted a prospectus that had been edited and approved by Polk. Promising to carry out Polk's pledges, the paper said it would defend strict constructionism, oppose a national bank, fight for a revised national tariff system, push for Texas' absorption into the Union, and discourage abolitionists, who, it said, were attempting to interfere with the "essential compromises in the Constitution which secured its adoption."[49]

Polk kept a detailed diary during his White House years that documents an extremely close working relationship between the president and his editor. Ritchie was often at the White House for long periods of time, and Polk frequently consulted him on the "best ways to present policies and ideas to the public and to Congress." The paper usually received copies of executive department announcements in advance, and during the Mexican War news dispatches from the front were released through the *Union.* The paper, of course, overflowed with paid government advertisements.[50]

Polk was intimately involved in the *Union*'s daily operations as he used it to convey the news and opinions of his administration. Numerous examples of the president's involvement abound, ranging all the way up to occasions on which he authored articles that were then promptly printed in the paper. In September, 1845, stung by an article claiming that he had not been the real author of a much-admired campaign letter on his national tariff views, Polk summoned Ritchie to the White House and read him his "authorized contradiction." It was immediately published in the *Union*.

In April, 1846, Polk, dissatisfied with an editorial Ritchie had written about a recent Senate resolution on the Oregon question, again summoned the editor to the White House, where he rebuked him in the presence of Secretary of State James Buchanan for not having indicated a preference for the House-passed resolution. Buchanan had prepared a corrective editorial, but, after reading it, Polk rejected it and presented both men with an "explanatory article" he had just written.[51] A "supplementary editorial" appeared the next day, apologizing for the previous day's editorial and presenting the "clarified" Polk position on the resolutions.[52] The editorial foul-up prompted Sen. William Allen of Ohio, chairman of the Foreign Relations Committee, to visit Polk to complain about Ritchie. Allen argued that the Democratic Party would disintegrate if Ritchie remained as editor and urged that Francis Blair be brought back to replace him. Polk understandably defended Ritchie and rejected the idea.

Polk used the *Union* extensively to whip up public and congressional sentiment for his major foreign policy initiatives. Shortly after receiving word that U.S. forces led by Zachary Taylor had skirmished with Mexican forces in disputed territory along the Rio Grande, Polk had the *Union* swing into action. The paper resolved any doubts about the administration's position on the question of war with Mexico to settle Texas' boundaries by trumpeting: "We mean to conduct war against Mexico with all the vigor in our power. . . . [W]e shall even TAKE HER CAPITAL, if there be no other means of bringing her to a sense of justice." After all, said the paper, "American blood has been shed on American soil!"[53]

Within a week of the first mention of the dispute with Mexico in the *Union*, other Democratic papers began taking up the cause at the state level. As had been the case with Andrew Jackson and the *Globe*, the state papers frequently recycled the words and imagery of Polk's presidential newspaper. The papers that followed the *Union's* lead numbered in the hundreds.[54]

Early in 1847, unhappy that Congress was balking at his war legislation, Polk had Ritchie run regular attacks on the war's opponents in the *Union*. The attacks so offended some Whig senators that they introduced resolutions citing Ritchie for having libeled the Senate, and banning *Union* reporters from the press gallery for having misreported a recent Senate floor debate on the war. After two days of partisan debate, the second resolution was withdrawn and the first was defeated by a close vote.[55]

Later, when he decided to dispatch an emissary to explore a negotiated peace with Mexico, Polk decided to keep the mission a secret so that the Whig press, led by the *National Intelligencer*, would not be able to sabotage the mission. Polk took Ritchie into his confidence, however, because, in Polk's words, "it was necessary that he should know it in order to shape the course of his paper in reference to it."[56]

In late 1846, when the controversy between Britain and the United States over the Oregon Territory was heating up, Polk resolved to propose in his upcoming annual message to Congress that it abrogate the treaty under which the two countries jointly occupied the region. To pave the way for the announcement, the *Union* began arguing in its columns that there should be no compromise with Britain and that the United States should insist on acquiring all of the territory.

Polk also used the *Union* to attack renegade government officials. In 1846, a letter from Maj. Gen. Zachary Taylor criticizing the administration's plans for war with Mexico was published in the New York *Express* and *Herald*. Incensed, Polk instructed the secretary of war to prepare a "proper article vindicating the government" and have it published in the *Union*.[57]

On another occasion, Polk chose to publish official reports in the *Union* rather than transmit them to Congress. The reports, from federal officers in California, concerned the anarchical state of affairs there caused by the Gold Rush of 1849. Polk wrote in his diary that, after reading the reports, his first inclination was to transmit them directly to Congress with a message urging that a civil government be set up in California. Upon polling his cabinet members, however, Polk found that, while two agreed with his idea, four thought the reports should instead be published in the *Union* and then transmitted to Congress when requested. The reason the four gave for their position provides an intriguing example of how the Whig conception of a restricted presidential role in policy making could affect the actions of a Democratic president: "They said that I had already in my annual message said all that could be said to induce Congress to act, and that exception might be taken by the Whig members, and perhaps some Democrats, if I repeated my views."[58]

Polk's political opponents were well aware that the *Union* spoke for the president. Indeed, the *National Intelligencer* once contrasted *Union* editorials with an ambassador's speech to show that the Polk administration's public position on the Oregon controversy was different from its diplomatic position.[59] The Whig leader in the Senate, John J. Crittenden, referred to the *Union* as "the 'oracle.'"[60]

To be sure, both Polk and Ritchie from time to time proclaimed their independence from each other. For example, Polk told a visitor in December, 1845, that he had "little opportunity to read newspapers, and could at no time do more than glance hastily over them."[61] In light of the massive evidence to the contrary, including entries in the president's own diary, however, Polk's insinuation of noninvolvement with the press rings hollow. As James Buchanan said, the reality was that, when Polk's organ "fell out of tune," as it often did, the president "set to adjusting its pipes." Historians have suggested these protestations of independence seem to have been disingenuous attempts by Ritchie to claim the mantle of journalistic integrity and by Polk to maintain the option of disavowing statements in the *Union* if necessary.[62]

The only president to surpass Polk's usage of a presidential newspaper was Andrew Jackson. His paper, the *Globe*, was the ultimate presidential newspaper for several reasons: it was the head of a massive chain of party newspapers throughout the country, the independent press had not yet begun to arise, and Jackson used his editor not merely as a mouthpiece but as one of his most confidential and influential advisers. Nevertheless, Polk's accomplishments in the area of presidential communication were impressive and have prompted some historians to declare that Thomas Ritchie was the "equivalent of a modern-day presidential press secretary," with Polk himself a sort of executive editor.[63]

Polk treated his written messages to Congress as messages to the American public as well, a fact documented in the diary he kept during his presidency. While writing his fourth annual message to Congress, Polk wrestled with his conflicting desire to have the message be a "full examination" of national issues while still being accessible to the general public. He described the difficulty in his diary: "To make it as full as I desire, the danger is that it will be so long that it will not be read by the mass of people, and by none but the politicians."[64]

As documented in this book, Polk, Jackson, Lincoln, and Grover Cleveland all treated their presidential messages as having two audiences: Congress and the American public. Other nineteenth-century presidents undoubtedly did the same.[65] This dualistic attitude calls into question the inferences that have been drawn from the fact that these messages were nominally addressed to Congress and not the people.[66] Rather than signifying presidential recognition of an overarching constitutional order, addressing these messages to Congress seems to have been little more than a formality.

Zachary Taylor (1849–50): A Whig Goes Public

Polk's successor, Zachary Taylor, carried on the practice of having an activist official administration newspaper. The Whig Party, deeply divided over slavery, chose Taylor, a hero of the Mexican War, as their best hope for winning the election even though he had no political experience. He and running mate Millard Fillmore barely won over an even more divided Democratic Party.

Taylor revived the *Republic,* a paper that had sprung up in 1847 to support his candidacy but which failed during the presidential campaign, rather than use the Whigs' flagship paper, the *National Intelligencer,* because the *Intelligencer* had long supported Henry Clay and Daniel Webster, from whom Taylor wished to distance himself.[67]

The *Republic* served the president well, "continually going to the defense of Taylor, explaining and interpreting his position," although this meant daily war with the Democrats' *Washington Union,* which pressed fierce attacks on Taylor and his paper.[68] In response to an attack by the *Union* that it was a mere "pensioned organ" of the president, the *Republic* defined itself instead as "The Presidential Organ," but then asserted that it owed "no favors and no allegiance as a public journal in any quarter but to the Whig *people of the United States.*"[69]

Taylor used the paper on many occasions to announce his views, and at one point even changed editors because he was dissatisfied with the paper's tone. In 1850, William H. Seward, regarded as Taylor's trusted ally, gave an impassioned speech in the Senate condemning slavery on moral and constitutional grounds. The speech contradicted Taylor's position and enraged the president, who immediately ordered his editor to denounce the speech in the *Republic* "authoritatively and decidedly."[70]

Four days later, a *Republic* editorial condemned Seward's invocation of natural law in his argument against slavery as a "law breaking, Constitution defying, disunion doctrine" that contradicted "Whig teaching as understood and practised everywhere." Because the statements appeared in a paper that was "widely considered Taylor's own echo," they had a "profound impression" on the editorial tone of newspapers throughout the country. Even Seward himself believed the statements accurately reflected the president's attitude toward his speech.[71]

Taylor also used the *Republic* in his battle with Sen. Henry Clay over the issue of slavery in new western states. When Clay made a proposal that would have required the president to compromise his own announced position, the paper published a short statement that Taylor remained firmly committed to his own proposal and had no intention of compromising. Clay, provoked by Taylor's stand, promptly took the offensive. He attacked the president's recalcitrance in a Senate speech and wrote an article for the Democratic *Globe* showing point by point how his plan was superior to Taylor's.[72] In response, Taylor authorized publication of a long editorial in the *Republic* attacking Clay and responding to his policy arguments.[73]

In 1849, Taylor went on a tour of Pennsylvania and New York, making speeches on two of the chief policy issues of the day—tariffs and slavery—advocating higher duties on steel, and proclaiming his opposition to the extension of slavery into any new states. His pronouncements and even his speaking style were much discussed in the papers of the time, and his statements about slavery antagonized southerners and figured prominently in the calculations of congressional leaders on both sides of the issue.[74]

Taylor's speechmaking and active use of a newspaper to defend and advance his administration's causes are unusual in light of his avowed Whiggishness. Most Whigs, as we have seen, believed as a matter of constitutional doctrine that Congress was the only legitimate maker of public policy, and that the chief executive had no business interfering with the process. A president who shared this view of the presidency would have considered public communications on policy matters to be inappropriate for his office. On several occasions, Taylor professed that important matters should be left to Congress without presidential interference, and his friends maintained that he was not trying to influence Congress.[75]

Paradoxically, many Whigs also criticized Taylor for not being a more active president on behalf of the party's cause. These conflicting pressures prompted the *National Intelligencer* to come to Taylor's defense. Those Whigs who wanted Taylor to do more, said the paper, were in effect blaming the president for not behaving like another Andrew Jackson, who was the epitome of executive excess from their perspective.

Taylor, said the *Intelligencer,* had taken office against "the Executive influence, Executive patronage, Executive dictation, and the Executive veto." Under Jackson, these elements had "resolved the Government into the one-man power and almost annihilated the Legislature." Moreover, Congress under Jackson and the Democrats had "ceased to be what it was intended to be under the Constitution, the independent and only legitimate organ for the expression of the public will." Taylor's critics apparently had forgotten that correcting this "great evil" had been the major reason for electing him president.[76]

As this Whig editorial shows, the Taylor presidency is a manifestation of the conflict between the active and reserved conceptions of the office that festered throughout the nineteenth century. Taylor, who after all was a military leader and not a career partisan, might well have found value in both conceptions of the office and acted according to one or the other depending on the particular situation confronting him. This philosophical or strategic ambivalence would explain his ambivalent involvement as president in the national public policy-making process.

Millard Fillmore (1850–53): The Dutiful Whig

When Taylor died after just sixteen months in office, Millard Fillmore became president. An experienced politician who well knew the value of the party press, he wrote in 1840 to Thurlow Weed, the Whig's political boss in New York state, about the effect the *Extra Globe*, the Democrat's campaign newspaper, was having: "Unearthly efforts are now making by the administration party to turn the current again in their favor. . . . The *Extra Globe* is a perfect Bohon Upas [poisonous tree] in the field of truth and virtue. Its noxious leaves are falling in every town and hamlet. . . . We are making arrangements to give a little more efficiency to the *Madisonian*. It is the only paper that we have here that exposes the corruptions of the administration. The *Intelligencer* is . . . good in its sphere but worth nothing to meet the vile slanders and base fabrications of the *Globe*."[77]

During Fillmore's vice presidency, he and Weed engaged in a vicious battle over control of the presidential patronage appointments in New York. Fillmore was also under constant attack by Taylor's cabinet; the attacks were carried out through the chain of papers controlled by Weed. Because the head of the chain was the influential Albany *Evening Journal*, Fillmore began planning to start a rival paper in that city. This maneuver, he thought, "would restrict and tame Weed and his dependencies—harmonize and strengthen the party—protect our friends from proscription and slander, and weaken, if it does not destroy, this arbitrary and over-shadowing central influence."[78]

After trying and failing to purchase the *Evening Journal* from Weed, the vice president and his allies created the *New York State Register*. Fillmore himself contributed $250 toward the paper's $10,000 start-up cost. After he became president, Fillmore tried to crush Weed, discharging his allies from the patronage positions they had obtained under Taylor and encouraging the post office to interfere with the circulation of Weed's paper through the mail.[79]

When he took office after Taylor's death, Fillmore discharged both Taylor's cabinet and his newspaper, the *Republic*. The new administration paper was the old Whig standard bearer, the *National Intelligencer*. The *Republic*, for its part, continued to "defend and praise Fillmore with the same loyalty that it had shown to Zachary Taylor."[80]

Unlike his predecessor, Fillmore did not give public speeches or use his administration newspaper as a public communications tool. While the *National Intelligencer* was designated as the administration's "official" paper, carrying government announcements and paid advertisements, Fillmore otherwise virtually closed off his administration to all newspapers, including the *Intelligencer*. Tebbel and Watts assert that the change was due to Fillmore's belief that a hands-off policy was the only way to "gain the confidence of both sides" in the battle over the slavery question, for which he desperately sought a viable compromise.[81]

Another explanation is that Fillmore was the prototypical Whig, and his public silence reflected the reserved Whig attitude toward the presidency's role in the public policy-making process. Prior to becoming president, Fillmore, like many other Whigs, had used newspapers extensively in political campaigns. However, his abandonment of that communications tool after occupying the White House may be evidence of the power of the Whig proscription against presidential involvement in the public policy process.

Franklin Pierce (1853–57): The Beginning of the End

Franklin Pierce succeeded Fillmore after winning the election of 1852. By then, big, independent newspapers like Horace Greeley's *New York Tribune,* the *Chicago Tribune,* and the *New York Herald* had huge national circulations and were covering national politics intensively.[82] A president could no longer hope to control public communications through his own newspaper, as had previously been possible when there were few papers with a Washington presence. Both the Whig and Democratic Parties were splintering over the slavery issue, and Congress, flexing its muscles, had taken full control over granting the lucrative government printing contracts that presidents had always used to subsidize the publishers of their administration "organs."[83]

Against this backdrop, it is not surprising that the story of the Pierce administration's communication with the public is an uneven one. On one hand, Pierce's paper, the *Washington Union,* is said to have reflected and explained the president's views on a daily basis in its editorials, which places his presidency in the Mobilizer category. On the other hand, Pierce was not always able to control the editorial course of the paper, resulting in numerous embarrassments to his administration.[84] Since throughout Pierce's presidency much of the real political power lay with other party leaders in Congress, it is easy to see how the paths of the president and those running what was really the Democratic Party's paper might have diverged.[85] Such difficulties contributed to the demise of the presidential newspaper under the last president before the Civil War, James Buchanan.

James Buchanan (1857–61) and the Death of an Institution

James Buchanan's presidency marks the end of one era and the beginning of another in the story of presidential communications. Buchanan came to realize that the real influence over public opinion lay in the hands of the giant independent newspapers and their formidable, highly opinionated editors, and began the kind of concerted effort to influence the media that has been the focus of many presidents since.

At the beginning of his administration, Buchanan maintained the *Washington Union* as his administration's paper. Like his predecessor, he had trouble controlling the editorial course of the paper because most of the power in the Democratic Party, including control of government printing contracts, was in the hands of congressmen and not the president.[86]

An even bigger impediment to the efficacy of Buchanan's paper, though, was that the country was awash in the newsprint of newspaper giants that were commercially and often politically independent. In 1856, annual newspaper circulation was 156 million in the North and 50 million in the South.[87] A poorly edited and underfunded Washington newspaper thus would have been of little help to a president. Buchanan recognized this new reality and set about trying to cope with it by carefully cultivating a friendship with James Gordon Bennett, publisher and editor of the immensely influential *New York Herald.* On October 20, 1856, the president wrote Bennett to say how happy he was for their recently renewed friendship, and to ask Bennett to use his paper to help restore friendly relations between the North and South.[88] To Mrs. Bennett, he fawned that the *Herald* was "a powerful instrument and it would be vain for me to deny that I desire its music should be encouraging and not hostile."[89]

Buchanan tried to treat the *Herald* well. He sent Bennett an advance copy of his first annual message to Congress, and frequently gave *Herald* reporters scoops on upcoming changes in his administration.[90] Over time, as his presidency began sinking under the weight of congressional attacks and sectionalism, Buchanan's appeals to the New York newspaperman intensified. Finally, in late 1860, Buchanan desperately entreated Bennett, as head of "the most powerful organ in the country for the formation of public opinion," to throw his paper's support behind the recently passed Kansas-Nebraska Act, which had voided the Missouri Compromise by permitting slavery in the new territories.[91]

Within a few days of this appeal to a paper that represented the new era in presidential public communication, the old era ended with another presidential letter. Buchanan's own paper had shrunken from a daily to a weekly paper and changed its name to the *Constitution.*[92] Moreover, it had exasperated Buchanan by its failure to consistently follow the administration line, leading the president to require notices to be printed in the paper advising readers that its editorials did not necessarily represent his views.[93] Buchanan's attempts at going public, hindered as they were by an uncooperative administration paper that was serving other masters as well, nevertheless place his presidency in the Mobilizer category.

Matters came to a head for Buchanan on Christmas Day, 1860, when the president saw an editorial in the *Constitution* disagreeing with his position that secession by southern states was unwarranted and arguably unconstitutional. Enraged, he wrote the paper's editor: "I have read with deep mortification your editorial this morning. . . . You have a perfect right to be in favor of secession, and for this I have no just reason to complain. The difficulty is that the *Constitution* is considered my organ, and its articles subject me to the charge of insincerity and double dealing." Buchanan then issued an order withdrawing all executive branch advertising from the paper. Within a month, the *Constitution* was dead.[94]

Postmortem for the Presidential Newspaper

James Buchanan's *Union/Constitution* was to be the last of the presidential newspapers, a passing brought on by several factors. With sectionalism plaguing both parties beginning in the 1840s, presidents had found it increasingly difficult to control the editorial output of papers whose sponsorship they essentially shared with their parties. Moreover, there were so many newspapers with large circulations in the vastly expanded nation that the presidential newspaper had become a very feeble means of public communication.[95]

The real key to the demise of the presidential newspaper, however, is that Congress gradually took control of this political tool. Presidential newspapers were expensive to maintain, but, since the time of Jefferson, presidents had solved the problem by steering lucrative government printing contracts to the publishers of their administration newspapers. Executive branch printing business could be awarded directly by presidents to the publishers of their choice, whereas House and Senate printing work went to whichever printer was selected by the chambers for that purpose.

Each new session of Congress meant the selection of a new printer, and this biennial affair became highly politicized as the president and Congress jockeyed and bargained for their favorites. A strong president with a working majority in Congress, such as Andrew Jackson, was usually able to get congressional printing contracts awarded to the publisher of his presidential newspaper. The contracts were usually rigged to provide excessive profits of 50 percent or more, leaving plenty of money to subsidize the presidential newspaper. On the other hand, as discussed above, politically hobbled presidents such as John Tyler saw their publishers denied congressional printing work.

In the 1850s, Congress began turning the screws on the presidency even tighter. In 1852, the Whig majority in Congress established the Office of Superintendent of Public Printing. This officer was appointed by the president and Senate for each Congress, and was supposed to be a "practical printer" who would monitor the work of contract printers to prevent cost overruns and other abuses.

Dissatisfied with this solution, Congress in 1860 eliminated this source of political largesse by creating the U.S. Government Printing Office.[96] This final move came after the Covode Committee laid bare in sensational detail the financial and political intricacies of the government printing business during House hearings. Cornelius Wendell, owner of the *Washington Union,* testified candidly about how presidential newspapers were funded:

> The editor of the organ is generally supposed to command the patronage of the President. There is a good deal of this work at the disposal of the President—say an aggregate of one hundred thousand dollars per year, more or less.
> Q. At the disposal of the President?
> A. Yes sir. That patronage the organ has commanded for years, it being impossible to keep a paper up here without government support.
> Q. Is this one hundred thousand dollars worth of patronage you speak of at the disposal of the President personally?
> A. The law provides that it shall be under the control of the heads of the departments; but . . . as a matter of course they will obey his wishes. It has been a matter of custom for the President to dispose of it. Mr. Buchanan has done it, and his predecessor, Mr. Pierce, did it. . . .
> Q. Was there ever any understanding with you while you had that printing that a portion of the profits should be used towards sustaining the organ?
> A. Yes, sir; it was given for the purpose of sustaining the organ.[97]

With the advent of the Government Printing Office, there was no longer any way left for presidents to subsidize a personal administration newspaper. Moreover, according to William Seaton, owner of the *National Intelligencer,* that newspaper lost two-thirds of its circulation when the South seceded and the Civil War began.[98] Any Washington-based paper would have faced similar circulation losses with the advent of war, making survival without subsidies even harder. Like an old soldier, the presidential newspaper just faded away with the inauguration of Abraham Lincoln. The presidential newspaper had become a casualty in the war for power between Congress and the presidency.

CHAPTER 4

The Old Norm against Going Public

Constitutional Principle or Partisan Fancy?

THREE NOTABLE PRESIDENCIES followed the demise of the presidential newspaper in 1860. Taken as a group, the presidencies of Abraham Lincoln, Andrew Johnson, and Ulysses Grant are notable because they contain one example of each of the three approaches toward public communications that have characterized all subsequent presidencies. The contrasts in the approaches of Johnson and his successor Grant illuminate the conflicting constitutional conceptions of the office of the presidency that underlay their different styles. On the other hand, Abraham Lincoln's careful approach toward going public represents a thoughtful synthesis of the presidential office with the realities of coping with the modern media.

The presidencies of Lincoln and Johnson also happen to be the ones that Jeffrey Tulis relies on as the best evidence of the existence of a norm against going public in the nineteenth century. Consequently, this chapter contains a critical reexamination of the evidence.

Abraham Lincoln (1861–65): Going Public Carefully

For Tulis, Lincoln's presidency is at once both a challenge to and a confirmation of his theory. It is a challenge because Lincoln made quite a few speeches: almost nineteen speeches per year in the four years and one month that he was president.[1] On the other hand, Lincoln's presidency is regarded as proof of the "doctrine of the nineteenth-century constitutional order" because Lincoln is said to have "offered his rhetoric in forms consistent with the doctrine." Thus, on the trip east for his inauguration, Lincoln repeatedly refused to say anything specific about the issues of the day, which, of course, included the impending civil war between the North and the South. Tulis cites this reticence as evidence of the doctrine having restrained Lincoln's rhetoric. He finds further evidence in statements Lincoln made on his way to Washington in which he supposedly "reflected upon the doctrine."[2]

Tulis lists five reasons Lincoln cited in declining to speak out on specific issues prior to his inauguration.[3] The first four reasons essentially amount to variations on the same theme: Lincoln saying that it was too early for him to begin making such pronouncements. Thus, the first reason is that Lincoln did not yet know enough about the situation to speak wisely and authoritatively. Second, Lincoln expressed the hope that problems might "work themselves out" without his involvement. Third, Lincoln wanted to wait until he was sure he was right because he would not easily be able to change positions. Fourth, Lincoln argued that his words were being so closely followed that it would be unwise for him to say anything because trivial statements would be unacceptable and he therefore could not "be expected to be prepared to make a mature one just now." None of these four reasons contain even the faintest allusion to any constitutionally based norm against going public. On their face at least, they provide no support for the supposed existence of the norm.

It is true that such blandishments might be polite substitutes for a president telling a crowd that he is not going to speak to it because there is a norm against playing to the passions of the easily swayed masses. On the other hand, it is equally possible that the reasons Lincoln gave were his full, truthful reasons. After all, Lincoln was a highly strategic public communicator, and the reasons he offered all have an element of strategy in them.

It also may be true that the four kinds of reasons Lincoln gave were not entirely truthful, and that they were a cover for some other reason.

Yet if that is so, then why must we further assume that the true, hidden reason was the existence of a norm against going public? Why could the real reason not be something else, such as, for example, the custom that presidents-elect follow even today of saying little about their policy plans until their inauguration? In fact, in the speech quoted below, Lincoln explains his refusal to comment as required by exactly that custom. And if Lincoln were covering up for a norm against demagoguery, might he not have used explanations somewhat closer to the truth, such as saying: "You know it's not a president's place to comment on such things"?

Finally, if this was such a universally felt norm, then why is Lincoln always being asked to violate it? After all, if he was declining to speak on issues, then someone—perhaps even a whole crowd—must have first asked him to speak on those issues. The simple fact that Lincoln was being asked for such comments is actually evidence against the existence of any such universally felt norm.

According to Tulis, the fifth reason Lincoln gave for refusing to speak is that he needed to wait to make his pronouncements on Constitutionally "proper" or "authoritative" occasions. As evidence for this fifth reason, Tulis quotes part of a speech by Lincoln: "I have kept silence for the reason that I supposed it was peculiarly proper that I should do so until the time came when, according to the customs of the country, I should speak officially [Voice, partially interrogative, partially sarcastic, 'Custom of the country?'], I heard some gentleman say, 'According to the custom of the country'; I alluded to the custom of the President elect at the time of taking his oath of office. That is what I meant by the custom of the country. . . . And now, my friends, have I said enough? [Cries of 'no, no,' 'Go on,' etc.] Now my friends there appears to be a difference of opinion between you and me, and I feel called upon to insist upon deciding the question myself. [Enthusiastic cheers.]"[4]

While this speech can be read to support Tulis's argument that it was an example of Lincoln being constrained by a constitutionally based norm, a more direct reading suggests exactly the opposite. First, note that when Lincoln refers to the "custom of the country," he is met with a quizzical and sarcastic challenge that in effect asks, "What custom?" If the norm were so pervasive, then why would anyone have challenged Lincoln's assertion? If there was a norm against going public, and that is what Lincoln was referring to, then the meaning of Lincoln's allusion should have been obvious to everyone. Even though perhaps just one person challenged

Lincoln's reference to a "custom," no one else in the crowd apparently voiced any support for such a custom after its existence was challenged. In fact, a short time later several others in the crowd urged Lincoln to say more.

Second, and perhaps most tellingly, when Lincoln responds to the challenge, he defines the "custom" not in terms of some norm against going public, but merely as the custom of the president to speak first on matters of public import at his inauguration and not before. If Lincoln was being restrained by a much more all-encompassing norm, would he not have said so? Finally, note that when Lincoln asked whether he had "said enough" several listeners implore him to continue. If the norm was so well known and pervasive, why should there have been such cries? Such a response appears to reveal the counterexpectation and desire of the audience for Lincoln to speak more and, most likely, to say something about the specific issues of the day.[5]

Another reasonable assessment of this exchange between Lincoln and a boisterous crowd is that the exchange signifies nothing more than the sharpness of Lincoln's stump-speaking skills. It can well be argued that the exchanges and the circumstances under which they were made are too ambiguous to count as evidence for or against the existence of any norm, especially since we have no way of knowing how accurately the speech was reported. The point here is not so much to convince the reader of what Lincoln's words might really have meant. Rather, it is to convince the reader that the speech is hardly conclusive evidence of a universally felt norm against going public, as Tulis implies.

Moreover, Lincoln's personal correspondence indicates that his refusal to speak on specific issues of the day at the beginning of his presidency had nothing to do with the supposed influence of any norm. That reticence was due to the strategic calculation (by an ex-criminal defense lawyer, no less) that his opponents would inevitably use anything he said against him. Lincoln certainly knew he had many opponents; he had won the election with just 40 percent of the popular vote, and almost all of that had come from northern states.

In response to the editor of a Democratic Party paper who had written him in November, 1860, suggesting that a public declaration by the president-elect might "favorably affect the business of the country," Lincoln wrote (in a letter marked "private and confidential"): "The Republican newspapers now and for some time past are and have been republishing copious extracts from my many published speeches, which would at once reach the whole public if your class of papers would also publish them. I am not at liberty to shift my ground—that is out of the question. If I thought a repetition would do any good, I would make it. But in my judgment it would do positive harm. The secessionists *per se*, believing they had alarmed me, would clamor all the louder."[6]

A few days later, in a letter to the editor of the *New York Times* he defended his silence by citing how the opposition papers had taken a recent conciliatory speech which had been given by Sen. Lyman Trumbull in an attempt to "quiet public anxiety," and had instead used it to "further inflame the North and South." Lincoln wrote: "This is just as I expected, and just what would happen with any declaration I could make. These political fiends are not half sick enough yet. Party malice, and not public good, possesses them entirely. 'They seek a sign, and no sign shall be given them.' At least such is my present feeling and purpose."[7]

These two letters reveal Lincoln's real purpose in staying quiet after his election—and it had nothing to do with any norm. The only consideration behind Lincoln's "present feeling and *purpose*," as he put it, was to avoid saying something that would inevitably be used by his opponents for their own purposes against him.

When writing to newspaper editors, whom one would expect to be aware of any supposed norm regarding presidential communications to the public, it makes sense that Lincoln would have referred to a norm if one had indeed influenced his actions. That he did not is strong evidence that such a norm did not exist or, if it did, had little influence on him. Conversely, the fact that these editors were interested in Lincoln making statements to the public may well be additional supporting evidence against such a norm. It is true that some editors might have been motivated to try to get around such a norm for the sake of a good story. Yet one may just as plausibly speculate that editors would have respected it and not sought Lincoln's comments. That one of the editors who asked Lincoln to comment on policy matters was a Democrat is also consistent with the fact that the Democratic Party's philosophy saw nothing wrong with public presidential involvement in policy matters.

Tulis makes no mention of another Lincoln speech that explains the president-elect's reluctance to say much about policy matters, again without any reference to a norm against going public. On February 13, 1861, just a few weeks before his inauguration, Lincoln told the Ohio legislature: "Allusion has been made to the interest felt in relation to the policy of the new administration. In this I have received from some a degree of credit for having kept silence, and from others some deprecation. I still think that I was right. In the varying and repeatedly shifting scenes of the present, and without a precedent which could enable me to judge by the past, it has seemed fitting that before speaking upon the difficulties of the country, I should have gained a view of the whole field."[8]

This speech is significant for two reasons. First, note that Lincoln does not refer to any norm against going public even though he is addressing an audience of political elites who surely would have been aware of, and respected, the invocation of any universally felt political norm. He instead explains his silence as a matter of prudence. Second, note that Lincoln reports he had received both support and criticism for his silence on policy matters. This divided reaction surely proves the absence of any universally felt norm.

In another short speech not mentioned by Tulis, Lincoln, called upon to say something to the citizens of Frederick, Maryland, on October 4, 1862, began by saying: "Fellow Citizens: I see myself surrounded by soldiers, and a little further off I note the citizens of this good city of Frederick, anxious to hear something from me. I can only say, as I did five minutes ago, it is not proper for me to make speeches in my present position."[9] We do not know why Lincoln thought it would be inappropriate for him to make a speech. One inference might be that this was a reference to a norm against going public. However, the problem with this inference is that the crowd, according to Lincoln, was "anxious to hear something" from him. As noted previously, the eagerness of a crowd to hear Lincoln speak hardly indicates the existence of a universally felt norm against presidents speaking on substantive policy matters. Another explanation for Lincoln's statement may therefore be that it is yet another instance of Lincoln declining to speak for pragmatic rather than normative reasons.

Lincoln certainly was no stranger to the political world of public communications. "From the very beginning of his public career," writes James E. Pollard, Lincoln was "keenly aware of the importance of public opinion. He deliberately cultivated the press, especially that of his own neighborhood and party."[10]

In addition to reading several newspapers regularly, Lincoln in the 1830s began writing editorials and news reports for a Whig Party newspaper in Springfield, Illinois, the *Sangamon Journal*. According to Pollard, the articles "were not signed but in some cases the authorship was known and in others it was more or less evident." The paper also carried the full text of important Lincoln speeches in the state legislature and elsewhere. In the late 1830s and early 1840s, Lincoln engaged in a series of newspaper exchanges with political foes. One such exchange almost forced Lincoln into a duel with the Illinois state auditor, James Shields, who had been ridiculed in several articles attributed to Lincoln. (In reality, Lincoln had written only one of the articles; Mary Todd, his wife, and a friend had written the others).[11]

In the late 1840s, Lincoln wrote a series of articles and editorials for the *Illinois State Journal* about abolition and slavery. In 1855, he sent the editor of another Illinois paper a political article. When the editor declined to publish it, explaining that he printed only his own editorials, Lincoln replied that the editor had "a lofty but proper conception of pure journalism," thus subtly reminding him that they were living in the real world, where the line between politics and journalism was often quite blurred.[12]

In 1858, Lincoln made his famous "house divided" speech at the Republican convention that nominated him to run for the U.S. Senate against Stephen Douglas. The text of the speech was to be carried in the *Illinois State Journal,* and Lincoln carefully read the page proof, marking parts that should be italicized for emphasis.[13] When he was about to give a campaign speech in that race, Lincoln was stopped by a reporter, who told him that he could not begin until the paper's shorthand reporter arrived. Lincoln waited.[14] Clearly, the newspaper had become a tool for Lincoln to communicate with the public.

When a Springfield, Illinois, German-language newspaper that was thought important to securing the German vote for Republicans failed in 1858, Lincoln bought it from publisher Theodore Canisius and then entered into an extraordinary arrangement with him. Their carefully drafted contract provided that Canisius be given immediate possession of the paper's printing press and that he resume publishing it as a "Republican newspaper, . . . said paper, in political sentiment, not to depart from the Philadelphia and Illinois Republican platforms." If Canisius attempted to move the newspaper from Springfield or printed anything "opposed to, or designed to injure the Republican party," Lincoln could immediately repossess it. If, on the other hand, Canisius lived up to his part of the bargain "until after the Presidential election of 1860," the paper's assets would become his property, with the proviso that it would not be used against the Republican Party or removed from Springfield without Lincoln's consent. Both men honored the contract, and on December 6, 1860, Lincoln reconveyed the paper to Canisius and subsequently appointed him to serve as consul in Samoa.[15]

This account of Lincoln contracting for the political support of a newspaper is a dramatic illustration of the symbiotic relationship that existed between the press and the master politicians of the nineteenth century. Even more significantly for the purposes of this study, it illustrates Lincoln's determination to use newspapers to communicate with the public on the political issues of the day.

When he became president, Lincoln, unlike his predecessors a quarter of a century earlier, had no Washington-based newspaper through which to communicate with the public. He subsequently acknowledged that not having his own presidential newspaper affected his approach toward public communications. In 1864 Lincoln was enduring withering attacks over his conduct of the war from all sides, including the widely read and highly influential *New York Tribune,* whose activist editor was Horace Greeley. At a cabinet meeting, Lincoln was urged to write a letter to the public defending himself against Greeley's criticisms. Lincoln rejected the idea, explaining: "Mr. Greeley owns a daily newspaper, a very widely circulated and influential one. I have no newspaper. The press of the country would print my letter, and so would the *New York Tribune.* In a little while the public would forget all about it, and then Mr. Greeley would begin to prove from my own letter that he was right, and I, of course, would be helpless to reply."[16]

Although his options were limited, Lincoln still made strategic use of newspapers to communicate with the public. In early 1862 there was much agitation in the press and Congress for emancipation of the slaves. Greeley, who was in the forefront of the movement, wrote an editorial addressed to Lincoln entitled "The Prayer of Twenty Millions," which appeared in the *Tribune* on August 19. Lincoln responded in a letter to the editor dated August 22, which, in a classic display of "going public" nineteenth-century style, he gave to a prominent capital newspaper, the *National Intelligencer,* for publication.[17] The letter appeared a few days later and was subsequently reprinted in newspapers across the country.

Contrary to the claim that nineteenth-century presidents who made public statements avoided addressing specific matters of public policy, Lincoln's letter tackled the issue of slave emancipation head on:

I have just read yours of the 19th, addressed to myself through the New York Tribune. . . .

I would save the Union. I would save it by the shortest way under the Constitution. . . . My paramount object in this struggle is to save the Union, and is not either to save or to destroy slavery. If I could save the Union without freeing any slave, I would do it; and if I could save it by freeing some and leaving others alone, I would also do that. What I do about slavery and the colored race, I do because I believe it helps to save the Union; and what I forbear, I forbear because I do not believe it would help to save the Union. I shall do less whenever I shall believe what I am doing hurts the cause, and I shall do more whenever I shall believe doing more will help the cause.[18]

Less than a month later, on September 19, Lincoln issued the Emancipation Proclamation, which was in fact limited to slaves in the rebel states.

Lincoln also granted several interviews that served to convey messages to the public. At the outbreak of the war, for example, a correspondent for the New York *Herald* wrote: "I am authorized by the President to say that he is determined to prosecute the war begun against the government of the United States, with all the energy necessary to bring it to a successful termination. He will ask for a large additional force, rely upon Providence and the loyalty of the people to the government they have established."[19]

An interview with two Wisconsin officials resulted in a conversation about the upcoming election in 1864 that one of the officials published in a Wisconsin paper. It was reprinted in *Harper's Weekly,* the London *Spectator,* and numerous other papers in the United States and England.

Although Lincoln could not control the newspapers, he sought to influence them in less direct ways. One way was the bestowal of political "gifts." He appointed newspapermen to a number of positions in his administration (ranging from postmaster to ambassador), did favors for them (such as pardoning southerners and court-martialed soldiers on whose behalf friendly editors had interceded with Lincoln), and threatened to withdraw government printing business from unsupportive papers. Another way was to simply keep "on the good side" of key newspaper people by maintaining close contact with them. For example, Lincoln engaged in regular correspondence with the most influential editors of the time, including Greeley, James Gordon Bennett of the *New York Herald,* and Henry J. Raymond of the *New York Times.*[20]

Lincoln sent long annual and special messages to Congress in which he discussed wartime policy issues in frank detail. However, these messages always had two audiences: Congress and the American people. This was because their text was immediately published in newspapers across the country. Moreover, since the messages were public and would be subjected to extensive public discussion, there is an element of "going public" even in messages not formally addressed to the people.[21] Lincoln undoubtedly would have considered and crafted his messages to Congress with the idea that he was communicating directly with the American public as well.

In a similar vein, Lincoln wrote several letters to citizens' groups or other public bodies that served to communicate his positions on policy matters to the nation when they were promptly published in the newspapers.[22] Lincoln wrote one such letter to the new Confederate Virginia assembly, in reply to a letter requesting that he explain his intended policy toward the newly seceded states. Among other things, Lincoln wrote that he would repel "force by force," defend, and retake if necessary any federal property seized by the rebel states, and probably cut off federal mail service. He also wrote a long letter to a citizens' group in Albany, New York, defending the constitutionality of his actions during the war; one to the Ohio Democratic convention of 1863 defending the constitutionality of his suspension of the writ of habeas corpus privilege; and another to a Missouri citizens' committee that was unhappy with Union military rule in that state.[23]

On at least one occasion, the letter Lincoln sent was actually a speech, read on his behalf by Sen. James Conkling, a trusted supporter, to a group of self-styled "unconditional Union men" in Illinois who were unhappy with his Emancipation Proclamation. This speech-letter defended the constitutionality of the proclamation, argued that no political compromise with the Confederacy was possible at that time given the South's military successes, and, in response to the group's complaint that its members were not happy fighting "to free negroes," suggested, "Fight you, then, exclusively to save the Union."[24]

Lincoln biographer Carl Sandburg describes this letter as "really a paper aimed at the masses of people in America and Europe," and a "carefully wrought appeal in simple words aimed to reach millions of readers." The letter spawned intense newspaper comment in the United States and abroad, and numerous American politicians wrote to congratulate

Lincoln on his fine piece of rhetoric. One of them, Sen. Henry Wilson, wrote: "God Almighty bless you for your noble, patriotic and Christian letter. It will be on the lips and in the hearts of hundreds of thousands this day."[25]

Even letters that Lincoln sent to individuals were turned into a form of public communication. In the fall of 1863, a Boston publisher distributed *The Letters of President Lincoln on Questions of National Policy.* The twenty-two-page pamphlet contained the Albany and Springfield letters discussed above as well as letters to Maj. Gen. George B. McClellan, Horace Greeley, a governor, and others.[26]

Of the public speeches Lincoln gave, many were short and fairly general in tone. Others, however, were more substantive, as the following examples illustrate. In a long speech to a "Committee of Colored Men," Lincoln outlined to a group of freedmen his idea to establish a Central America colony where African Americans could be sent to live. In another, he sought to convince a delegation of Indian chiefs that they should abandon their traditional hunting ways and turn to cultivating the earth like the more successful "white race." On September 13, 1862, he engaged in a spirited dialogue with a citizens' group from Chicago that had brought a petition urging him to issue a proclamation emancipating the slaves. He used other speeches to deny he was planning to replace Maj. Gen. Winfield Scott as commanding general of the army, to deny that there was any disagreement between his administration and Maj. Gen. George B. McClellan, to declare that he would carry on the Civil War for years if necessary until its "worthy object" was attained, and to assure the nation he had no plans to seize control of the government if he was not reelected.[27]

In another speech, Lincoln also attacked those who called the North's war efforts an attempt to impose "tyranny" on the South. Then, after saying "it is not very becoming for one in my position to make speeches at great length," he went on to address "some anxiety in the public mind" by reassuring his listeners that, "having determined to use the Negro as a soldier," he was committed to "give him all the protection given to any other soldier." Lincoln promised that this protection would include the retaliatory killing of Confederate prisoners of war if captured black Union soldiers were found to have been massacred.[28]

Finally, on April 11, 1865, just a few days before his assassination, Lincoln gave a speech in Washington in which he discussed his plans for reintegrating Confederate states into the Union. He explained in detail his handling of the situation in Louisiana, using it as an example of the general principles he would follow with the other vanquished southern states.[29]

In sum, Lincoln went public in several ways, albeit always very carefully. His approach might be summed up in the cautious, lawyerly attitude that "what you don't say can't hurt you." As Pollard puts it, "in the White House Lincoln's policy toward the press was often one of expediency. Where it served administrative purposes and he could do so he made use of it. Where it might hamper or complicate pending matters he sought to avoid it." This cautious attitude can be found in both Lincoln's writings and his speeches. In an opinion he wrote on the draft during the war, Lincoln affirmed that "It is at all times proper that misunderstanding between the public and the public servant should be avoided; and this is far more important now than in times of peace and tranquillity."[30]

Lincoln remained cautious even on the day that news of Lee's surrender reached Washington. Called to the portico of the White House to address a large crowd that had gathered outside, the president said he knew that he would be expected "to say something" either then or the following day. He said he preferred to wait because "Just now, I am not ready to say something that one in my position ought to say. *Everything I say, you know, goes into print.* If I make a mistake it doesn't merely affect me, or you, but the country. I, therefore, ought at least try not to make mistakes."[31]

Two days later, when someone noticed with surprise that he had written down the remarks he was going to make after a White House dinner, Lincoln said: "I know what you are thinking about. You think it mighty queer that an old stump-speaker like myself should not be able to address a crowd like this outside without a written speech. But you must remember I am, in a certain way, talking to the country, and I have to be mighty careful."[32]

The picture that emerges from this account of Abraham Lincoln's presidency reveals no evidence that he was affected by a norm against going public. Instead, one finds occasions when Lincoln clearly did communicate directly with the public, not only through speeches but also through newspapers. His avowed reticence in many of his public speeches and the relatively small number of times he used the newspapers for public communications seem clearly to have been manifestations of a cautious, strategic presidency rather than a normatively restrained one. This approach, which might be termed "going public carefully," is one that was utilized with great success by Dwight Eisenhower in the twentieth century.[33]

Andrew Johnson (1865–69): Going Public Carelessly

For proponents of the "rise of the rhetorical presidency," Andrew Johnson is the exception that proves the rule. In a view advanced most explicitly by Jeffrey Tulis, Johnson committed the sin of going public by embarking on a speaking tour of the country while he was president, and was then severely punished for his infraction.[34] The punishment took the forms of public censure, impeachment by the House of Representatives and a U.S. Senate vote that fell one short of conviction. Thus, the tribulations visited on Johnson are said to be proof of the power of the norm. There are, however, more plausible explanations for Johnson's troubles.

Some historical background helps in understanding what happened to Johnson. The most important fact is that Andrew Jackson Johnson (his full name) was a Democrat. Lincoln chose him to be his running mate in 1864 as part of his grand plan to replace the Republican Party with a new national organization called the National Union Party. Lincoln began this effort in 1861, when he and his allies decided that the Republican Party's northern-based antislavery program constituted too narrow a base of support in the national electoral arena. Their idea was to create a party that, by making its main platform the preservation of the Union rather than the elimination of slavery, could draw supporters from the South as well as the North and appeal to Democrats as well as Republicans. Lincoln had worked throughout his first administration to build up the appeal of the National Union Party through patronage, cabinet appointments, carefully measured moves in the war against the South, and "his use of the presidential pulpit to define the purpose of the war as a restoration of the Union rather than abolition or social revolution in the South."[35]

By 1864, Lincoln was ready to cut the cord. At the Republican national convention, he engineered the formal renaming of the party as the National Union Party and dumped Vice President Hannibal Hamlin in favor of Johnson as his running mate. Hamlin's replacement with Johnson was intended by Lincoln to be a clear signal to voters that "the Union party was both bipartisan and bisectional."[36]

From this perspective, Andrew Johnson must have looked like the perfect choice. Not only was he a Democrat, he was also from Tennessee—one of the southern border states Lincoln was hoping to appeal to through the new National Union Party. To top matters off, Johnson had served Lincoln as military governor of the Union-occupied parts of Tennessee for three years after that state, which Johnson had represented as a U.S. senator, had seceded.[37]

Johnson had a thirty-year career as a Tennessee politician, progressing from alderman to mayor of Greenville, to the state legislature, to Congress for five terms, the governorship for two terms, and finally the U.S. Senate.[38] A sense of how Johnson succeeded so well comes through in this description of his roots: "Politically, Johnson's plebeianism served him wonderfully well in the fundamentalist atmosphere of the East Tennessee upcountry. Long hours of cultivating his voice in the solitude of his [tailor] shop had made him a superb speaker. . . . The simple mountaineers were deeply impressed by his philippics, and they would shiver in appreciation as his words rang through the valley in the gathering twilight."[39]

Another historian describes Johnson as a "tireless campaigner, able to endure long hours of traveling over wretched roads to speak or debate at town after town, day after day."[40] This is what Tennesseans of the time expected, according to an 1855 sketch of politics in the state: "As face answereth to face in water, so must the popular favorite answer to the genius and character of the people. Only a bold, frank, decisive man could rise to power in such a community. He must shrink from no danger; he must fear no responsibility; he must wear no mask; he must wait for no cue; he must be able to appeal to the strong feelings and the manly common-sense of the people."[41]

Unfortunately for Johnson, his peculiar position as a Democrat on the National Union-Republican ticket left him with few natural allies when he succeeded to the presidency after Lincoln's assassination. Johnson quickly compounded his problems by antagonizing the Radical Republicans, who controlled Congress, had resisted Lincoln's renomination, and wanted to control the presidency—and with it the reconstruction of the South. He refused to reorganize the cabinet he had inherited from Lincoln or to accept the Radicals as his unofficial advisers. After at first giving the Radicals the impression that he would cooperate with Congress in significantly toughening the terms by which southern states could be readmitted, he then attempted to present Congress with a fait accompli by completing reconstruction on his own terms during the seven months that Congress was out of session.

Congress eventually rejected Johnson's reconstruction efforts, including the state governments he had recognized, and imposed its own plan in 1867. Not surprisingly, relations between Congress and the president had seriously degenerated. By then, Johnson had lost the support of many leading semi-nonpartisan newspapers, including the *New York Times,* the *Chicago Tribune,* and the *New York Tribune.* Regarded by many Democrats as a traitor, and by Republicans as a tricked-up Democrat who was never meant to be president, Johnson would not have found much automatic support among the many still avowedly partisan papers across the country, either.[42]

Against this backdrop, Johnson's decision to go on a speaking tour to drum up support would have been a natural one for him. After all, that is what he had done for years as a politician in Tennessee. According to James Pollard: "It was perfectly in character for Johnson, at the drop of a hat, to 'go to the people.' Such was the nature of his constituency, combined with the simple values which he represented, that not only was the direct appeal successful time after time, but Johnson's own experience, in the process, could develop and sustain in him an almost religious sense of 'the people.'"[43] Moreover, Johnson was a believer in the activist, publicly engaged conception of the presidency. He and all other Americans who held this view of the presidency would have regarded the trip as a perfectly appropriate presidential endeavor.

Unfortunately for the president, his three-week trip through nine states was, on balance, a public relations failure. Johnson's plan was to make a series of speeches defending his policies as he journeyed to Chicago to give the keynote speech at the unveiling of a memorial to Stephen A. Douglas. Concerned that Johnson might say the wrong thing in the heat of an extemporaneous moment, several of his friends advised him to either make no speeches at all or at least stick to a carefully prepared script. The basis for this advice was strategic, not constitutional. As Sen. James R. Doolittle of Washington put it: "You are followed by the reporters of a hundred presses who do nothing but misrepresent. I would say nothing which has not been most carefully prepared, beyond a simple acknowledgment for their cordial reception." At first, the trip went well, with Johnson receiving warm welcomes from the large crowds that turned out along his route.

Grant's chief of staff wrote his wife that Johnson was making "innumerable speeches every day, and the people cheer him lustily."[44]

According to historian George Fort Milton's 1930 account of Johnson's tour, the news of the president's popular successes alarmed Radical Republican leaders back in Washington: "The President was carrying his case to the common people and it seemed as if the people were hearkening to his words. It was a disastrous development. The Radicals could not permit the President's trip to be successful. If this 'ovation' continued, Andy would carry the North that fall!" Milton asserts that the Radical Republicans set out to sabotage Johnson's tour. Their method was to take advantage of Johnson's well-known propensity as an old stump speaker to respond to hecklers. Drawing Johnson out in this way, they hoped he would make intemperate remarks that could then be used against him in the Republican press. The tactic worked beautifully in Ohio and Missouri, with Johnson making numerous wild statements in response to hecklers, including comparing himself and the Radical Republicans to Christ, Judas, and the other apostles. At one point, Johnson even challenged a heckler to come out of the crowd and confront him personally.[45]

Johnson's enemies had gotten what they wanted and made good use of it. Just as Lincoln might have predicted, Johnson's numerous opponents in the press used his own often carelessly chosen words against him as they painted a highly derogatory picture of his conduct on the trip. According to Pollard: "The trip loosed an avalanche of abuse from the opposition newspapers. Johnson was attacked as a 'renegade,' a 'traitor,' 'the great apostate,' a 'faithless demagogue,' the 'great accidental,' the 'great pardoner,' and as 'the man made President by John Wilkes Booth.' . . . He was pictured as a drunken demagogue and the impression was given that the trip was just a drunken orgy. Throughout the long hot ordeal Johnson was plagued by a lying press."[46]

Newspaper accounts of Johnson's speeches varied greatly, depending on the papers' partisan leanings. The Cleveland newspapers, for example, took conflicting views of Johnson's visit to their city, where he had encountered hecklers. The Democratic *Plain Dealer* wrote:

> The President of the United States was greeted in this city last night by an enormous crowd. The vast majority of citizens who listened to his speech behaved as gentlemen should have, but a small portion of the crowd . . . disgraced themselves and the glorious city they live in by

interrupting the President in his speech, and by assailing him with vile epithets which they glean from the columns of the Cleveland *Leader.* The President of the United States should have passed these interruptions with silent contempt, but Andrew Johnson . . . cowers before no man, nor shrinks from any conflict that may be urged upon him.

The Republican *Leader* saw the speech much differently:

When the President forgets his official dignity and prostitutes his official position; when he abandons the chair of State and "takes the stump;" when he insults his hosts by stigmatizing them as traitors, and inciting a mob to hang their cherished leaders, he throws away all claim to respect or consideration as President. . . . We regard the manner of Monday night's throng as one of extreme toleration under grievous insult, and we thank the people that they were so moderate and forbearing.[47]

Johnson's experience thus appears to have shown the wisdom of Abraham Lincoln's twin strategies of avoiding public statements because they might be used against him by opponents, and of avoiding unscripted speaking situations that might lead to saying the wrong thing, either inadvertently or through provocation.[48] There is no need to postulate a universal norm to explain the trouble Johnson's tour got him into: simple partisanship feeding on poor rhetorical strategy suffices.

Tulis views the tenth article of impeachment against Johnson as evidence of a general attitude in Congress that the president had transgressed a constitutional norm by making his speaking tour. Article 10 charged that Johnson made and delivered "with a loud voice certain intemperate, inflammatory, and scandalous harangues, and did therein utter loud threats and bitter menaces as well against Congress as the law of the United States. . . . Which said utterances, . . . highly censurable in any, are peculiarly indecent and unbecoming in the Chief Magistrate of the United States." However, Tulis concedes, "many congressmen participating in the proceedings were skeptical that 'bad rhetoric' constituted an impeachable offense," and most historians regard the charge as frivolous.[49]

More importantly, however, the interpretation of Article 10 as evidence of a norm against going public glosses over another, more likely explanation. The charge reflects not an overriding constitutional precept, but a highly partisan conception of the presidency. As was discussed in chapter 2, there were two partisan-based conceptions of the policy-making role of the president in our constitutional system. One, the Democratist conception held by most Democrats, was that the president was a legitimate participant in the policy-making process. Indeed, as Andrew Jackson showed, the president could be conceptualized as the only truly nationally elected representative of the people whose job was to see that the people's will was carried out, mobilizing them as necessary to pressure Congress to follow the lead of the people and their tribune, the president.

The other view, the Classicist conception held by Whigs and then Republicans in the nineteenth century, was very different. In the Whig-Republican American constitutional system, Congress, as the true representative of the people in their sovereign capacity, was the only appropriate institution to deliberate upon and make national policy. In this view, mass public opinion was something to be almost feared and certainly filtered, so that the true "common good" could be distilled through the legislative process. There was no room for presidents in this process, and certainly no room for them to be making public statements to the people about legislative matters.

Thus, to many Republicans, Johnson's tour, in which he explicitly sought to rouse public opinion in favor of his positions and against those of the Republican majority in Congress, would have been doubly outrageous. In their eyes, not only was the president acting against the majority will, but his appeals to the public would have been perceived as a clear violation of the prevailing Republican Classicist conception of the proper role of the presidency in the constitutional order and, therefore, legitimate grounds for impeachment. On the other hand, as noted earlier, this reserved conception of the presidency was only one of the two conceptions that existed in the nineteenth century. The second, and in retrospect more modern, Democratist view of the presidency held that presidential involvement in the public policy process was perfectly appropriate.

Andrew Johnson was, of course, a populist Democrat who shared the Democratic Party's Democratist conception of representative democracy and the president's role in it.[50] It is therefore highly significant that not one Democrat voted to impeach him. Because the impeachment did not have bipartisan support, the act of impeachment and the specific articles of impeachment that were approved cannot be considered evidence of any *universally felt,* constitutionally based norm. Rather, the decision to impeach Johnson was a purely partisan one.[51]

The history of Article 10 also reveals that the Republicans could not solidly agree on the charges. The original impeachment resolution reported to the full House by the House Reconstruction Committee contained only nine articles, all essentially indicting Johnson for his attempt to remove Secretary of War Edwin Stanton without congressional approval, in violation of the Tenure Act. Article 10 was written by Rep. Benjamin F. Butler, a leader of the Radical Republican contingent in Congress that was attempting to remove Johnson. According to Wilfred Binkley, the Radical Republicans thought of the president as nothing more than "Congress's chief minister," and planned to impeach him for essentially political reasons to secure "the permanent subordination of the Executive to Congress" through the equivalent of a parliamentary vote of no-confidence. Some sense of this attitude comes through in Butler's response to Johnson's assertion that removal of executive branch officials was an executive prerogative under the Constitution and therefore not an impeachable offense as the Radical Republicans asserted. Butler sanctimoniously replied that this argument raised the "momentous question . . . whether the Presidential office (if it bears the prerogatives and power claimed for it) ought, in fact, to exist, as a part of the constitutional government of a free people."[52]

Butler, who seems to have been regarded as somewhat of an extremist on the role of the president even within the Radical Republican ranks, proposed Article 10 to the Reconstruction Committee when it was drafting the articles of impeachment against Johnson, but the committee *rejected* the article. Undeterred, Butler brought Article 10 up again when the full House, then comprised of 189 members, was considering the impeachment articles. The first time he did so, March 2, 1868, the House voted 74 to 48 *against* adding it to the impeachment charges.

The next day, however, Butler persuaded the House managers to bring Article 10 up for vote again. The article immediately "met the opposition of representatives who argued that it charged no indictable crime," to which Butler responded that the idea that presidents could only be impeached for indictable crimes "was dead and buried—I knew it stunk." Reversing itself for reasons that are not clear, the House then approved the addition of Article 10 by a vote of 87 to 43. Significantly, however, 11 Republicans voted against the article, and 7 others who were present apparently abstained from the vote. Thus, there were at least 43 representatives—over a fifth of the House, including 18 Republicans—who ultimately did not support the "scandalous language" charges of Article 10.[53] Other prominent Republicans shared this attitude. Joseph Medill, editor of the *Chicago Tribune*, complained: "If Johnson can't be impeached and ousted from office for violating the Tenure-of-Office law, he will never be put out for anything he *said*. . . . We are in danger also of causing a reaction in the popular mind against Congress and the Republican Party by dragging in this extraneous and unnecessary matter."[54]

Article 10 fared even worse in the Senate impeachment trial: it never came up for a vote. After votes on what the Republicans thought were the three strongest articles fell one short—35 to 19—of the two-thirds majority required for impeachment, the Senate gave up and adjourned. At least 10 Republican senators were on record as opposing Article 10 if it had come up for a vote. Interestingly, all 7 of the Republican senators who voted against Johnson's impeachment left the mainstream Republican Party after the trial (1 returned later). Two who had represented Democratic border states retired at the end of their terms, and 2 others moved to the Democratic Party, where they had long and successful careers.[55] This suggests that at least some of the moderate Republicans in Congress who did not toe the party line on impeachment votes may have been closer to Democrats on the ideological spectrum, and so may well have not shared the radical Republicans' reserved conception of the presidency.

In sum, Article 10 failed to attract the support of any Democrat in either the House or Senate, and also was not supported by a significant number of Republicans in both chambers. To argue that Article 10 is evidence of a *consensus* view of the impropriety of Johnson's public speaking, therefore, goes much too far.[56] Given Butler's and the Radical Republicans' Whiggish/Classicist view of the presidency and the absence of any Democratic support for Article 10, the assertions made in it are most accurately viewed as reflecting one possible, partisan-based view of the president's place in our constitutional system. In fact, Johnson's Democratic defenders in the impeachment proceedings argued that the president's speeches criticizing Congress were entirely appropriate exercises of his right to free speech.[57]

Public communication played a prominent role in the impeachment trial itself. The trial was conducted as much in the newspapers of the time as on the Senate floor. Demonstrating his populist streak once again, Johnson insisted to his lawyers that he wanted his defense made not only

to the Senate, but to "the people" as well. To that end, he continued giving interviews to Washington correspondents while the trial was going
on, prompting his lawyers to insist that he stop the practice to avoid being misquoted and divulging their defense strategy. Even Benjamin Butler, who was to make the initial presentation to the Senate on behalf of
the House impeachment managers, was concerned about the public aspect of the trial. Butler mailed and telegraphed advance copies of his
speech to newspapers around the country, complete with notations of
imagined applause and cheers. Republican newspapers everywhere, including the *Chicago Tribune* and Horace Greeley's *New York Tribune,* im-
plored readers to contact their senators to urge Johnson's impeachment.[58]

Put into its proper historical context, the story of Andrew Johnson's
failed presidency is not, as Tulis argues, the most dramatic illustration of
the power of a universally felt nineteenth-century norm against going
public. It represents instead the dramatic collision of two competing partisan-based conceptions of the American presidency in the nineteenth
century. In a great battle between the proponents of the two views, those
supporting a populist-oriented, activist concept of the presidency barely
avoided defeat. However, as the following examination of the presidency
of Ulysses S. Grant shows, their victory was a fleeting one.

Ulysses S. Grant (1869–77): The Rise of the Silent Figurehead

During his eight years in office, President Grant issued no significant public
statements and had virtually no direct contact with newspapers. Two
explanations have been offered for Grant's isolation. The first, by James
Pollard, is that, as a career military officer, Grant "had no particular prior
experience with the press and did not understand its functions or its methods any too well. As with most military men the uses of the press were
foreign to him."[59] This explanation is not entirely convincing, however,
since it relies on a generalization disproved by generals such as Andrew
Jackson, Zachary Taylor, Dwight Eisenhower, and Colin Powell.

The second explanation is more plausible because it concerns Grant's
conception of the presidency as it relates to the people and to Congress.
According to Wilfred Binkley, Grant "except on rare occasions . . . was, as
President, disposed to accept without question the work of Congress as
the authoritative expression of the will of the American people. Not having divested himself of the military mentality, he would now dutifully

defer to the civil authority vested in Congress." Grant manifested this attitude early and often. During the attempt to impeach Johnson, Grant made a bargain with the Radical Republicans. In exchange for Grant's promise to lobby senators to vote for impeachment, which he did vigorously, Republican leaders promised to support Grant's nomination for the presidency. Their promise was in turn contingent on Grant's commitment to appoint to his cabinet men who had been hand-picked by the Radical caucus, thus ensuring, in Binkley's words, that "the Executive would be mortgaged to Congress for some years in the future at least."[60]

When the Republicans nominated him for president, Grant declared in his acceptance speech that he viewed the president as a "purely administrative officer." Moreover, one of his first acts as president was to agree to an amendment to the Tenure Act that essentially maintained Congress' veto power over the removal of executive branch officials by the president. Grant's action was widely perceived as a capitulation to Congress.[61]

Most Republicans, including powerful Sen. John Sherman, shared Grant's conception of the presidency. According to Sherman: "The executive department of a republic like ours should be subordinate to the legislative department. The President should obey and enforce the laws, leaving to the people the duty of correcting any errors committed by their representatives in Congress."[62] According to Binkley, Grant's ascendance to the presidency meant that "for the first time in the history of the Republican party its most influential members had found . . . a man who approached their ideal of a President."[63]

With his philosophy that the will of the people was expressed through an institutionally preeminent Congress, Grant would have had little reason to want to influence public opinion even if he had possessed the necessary newspaper skills and tools. For him, the president's role was to follow Congress, not to try to lead it by appealing to the people. Any effort to communicate with the people on matters of public policy would not only have risked the wrath of the party that had nominated him but would also have been regarded by him as inappropriate. This reserved notion of the presidency dominated politics until William McKinley's election in 1896.

CHAPTER 5

Presidents and Public Communication in the Late Nineteenth Century

The Reign and Fall of the Whigs

THE LAST QUARTER of the nineteenth century was a time when the powers of Congress were at their zenith and those of the presidency at their nadir. Woodrow Wilson, writing in 1885, said that the legislative branch had "virtually taken into its own hands all the substantial powers of government," and that the presidency was merely the "clerical part" of government.[1] There had been only one Democratic president since the Civil War, the discredited Andrew Johnson, and the Republican Classicist conception of the presidency inherited from the Whigs—in which the chief executive's duties were limited to approving cabinet decisions, passing out patronage positions, and enforcing laws passed by Congress—dominated political thinking in the country.[2]

To modern ears, the way that some Republicans—especially congressional Republicans—described their conception of the presidency then sounds quite foreign. In 1885, less than a year into his first term, Grover Cleveland became embroiled with the Senate in a dispute over executive privilege. In defense of his refusal to turn over to the Senate Judiciary

Committee certain papers related to his decision to not reappoint a U.S. district attorney in Alabama, Cleveland sent the Senate a special message.

The sending of the message was taken as a great affront by the Republican chair of the Judiciary Committee, Sen. George F. Edmunds of Vermont. The senator said that the message Cleveland delivered on March 1, 1886, marked the first time in history that a president had "undertaken to interfere with the deliberations" of Congress—except for State of the Union messages "which the Constitution commands him to make from time to time." Edmunds went on to say that Cleveland's special message reminded him of "the communication of King Charles I to the Parliament, telling them what, in conducting their affairs, they ought to do and not do."[3]

In light of such strident expressions from a leader of the party that dominated presidential politics in the last quarter of the nineteenth century, it is not too surprising that the story of this period is, with one stunning exception, a story of presidents indeed acting in accordance with the view that presidents should avoid direct public communication on policy matters. However, this view represented only one of the two prevailing views of the presidency in the nineteenth century. Plenty of other presidents earlier in the century had actively communicated their policy positions and arguments to the public, sometimes through speeches or written messages, but mostly through the device of the presidential newspaper.

America had six presidents during this period: Rutherford Hayes, James Garfield, Chester Arthur, Grover Cleveland (twice), Benjamin Harrison, and William McKinley. Five of the six—including Cleveland the Democrat—generally conformed to the reserved conception of their office, although two, Hayes and Harrison, delivered many generally nonpartisan speeches. This time of presidential disengagement from the public policymaking process then ended dramatically with the presidency of William McKinley, who inaugurated the "modern" era of going public by making scores of policy speeches across the nation.

Rutherford B. Hayes (1877–81): A National Cheerleader

Republican Rutherford Hayes was a former member of the Whig Party. In his presidency, he generally adhered to the Whig theory of executive authority, which held that the president's role was to passively carry out the policies developed by Congress. Hayes did, however, use his veto power in a few instances to thwart congressional attempts to weaken the presidency even further.[4] This overall restrained presidential attitude fit with Hayes's reserved personality. According to one biographer, Hayes did not enjoy life in Washington as a congressman because the future president "did not believe in unnecessary and intrusive eloquence, nor did he seek to make himself conspicuous through 'noisy exhibition.'" Moreover, according to another historian, Hayes in both his "public utterances and in his correspondence . . . was extremely cautious lest they be distorted or otherwise misused by a careless or hostile press."[5]

Hayes owed his presidential nomination to his party's need, after the scandal-ridden Grant years, for a nominee who had an unblemished public and private record and was not tied to corrupt party politics. In the eyes of many Republicans, however, Hayes probably wound up carrying the independence a bit too far. Taking office with the motto, "He serves his party best who serves his country best," Hayes pursued an avowedly nonpartisan course as president.[6]

This attitude manifested itself in Hayes's approach to the press during his presidency. In 1880, the last full year of his presidency, Hayes listed in his diary twenty points in which his administration had "been successful to a marked degree." One of the points concerned the press. Hayes wrote: "The Administration has never had a newspaper organ in Washington or elsewhere. As Mr. Evarts said: 'The Administration has not been well edited.' This is good as a joke, but with the newspapers so enterprising and able as they now are, *no organ* is wisdom. It gives all a fair chance, and gives the Administration a fair chance with all." Carrying this approach to an extreme, Hayes never intentionally gave any newspaper interviews.[7]

Hayes was also hobbled politically by a number of factors. His avowed nonpartisanship, by his own admission, attracted "few supporters in Congress and among the newspapers." The Democratic press never forgave Hayes for the dealings in the House of Representatives that made him president by one Electoral College vote even though he had lost the popular vote to Samuel J. Tilden by 51 percent to 48 percent. Partisan Republican newspapers opposed him over his civil service reform efforts, and independent or Republican reform papers, which included the *New York Times,* often were unhappy with Hayes for not doing more on civil service reform.[8]

One aspect in which Hayes was not reserved was travel. Indeed, he "spent much of his four-year term traveling throughout the United States . . . . Beset by critics in both the political arena and the press, he strove to put his cause and himself directly before the American people."[9] Hayes made official tours across New England, the South, and the West (all the way to California and Washington State) as well as numerous shorter excursions for various ceremonial functions.

The more than one hundred speeches Hayes gave on these tours were brief and generally nonpartisan in nature, although they did touch on some matters of national concern.[10] Hayes himself described his stock speech in this diary entry:

> One week from today, Thursday, we expect to start for Ohio and thence on our tour to the Pacific Coast. When I meet assemblages of citizens, of necessity, I must talk to them. Brief as these conversations must be I ought to be in some measure prepared for them. As I now see it congratulations on the condition and prospects of our Country will almost always be appropriate. In order to make them of some interest let me gather facts as to restored Union, sound financial condition, increase of exports of Agricultural & Manufacturing products—balance of trade and the like. In order to make the talks practically useful, not merely vain boasting, let me trace the favorable conditions to the adoption of sound principles, and warn the people of some of the evils existing which threaten our future, such as clipped silver dollars—unredeemed government paper—a redundant currency, popular illiteracy, Sectional and race prejudices, &c&c.[11]

In addition to routinely mentioning the silver and race questions, Hayes on this tour occasionally referred briefly to other policy issues in his speeches. For example, in Portland, Oregon, at a newly established government school for Native Americans, Hayes said: "Some people seem to think that God has decreed that Indians should die off like wild animals. With this we have nothing to do. If they are to become extinct we ought to leave that to Providence, and we, as good patriotic, Christian people, should do our best to improve their physical, mental, and moral condition. We should prepare them to become part of the great American family. If it turns out that their destiny is to be different, we shall have at least done our duty. This country was once theirs. They owned it as much as you own your farms. We have displaced them, and are now completing that work. I am glad that Oregon has taken a step in the right direction."[12]

Significantly, Hayes's diary contains his own explanation for the overall nonpartisan tone of his speeches, and that explanation does not refer to any broad, constitutionally based norm against going public. Wrote Hayes: "When strangers meet in Mixed assemblages their talk is about the weather, their health, the Crops, the condition and prospects of business and the current news foreign and domestic. It is only after they are more intimately acquainted that in mixed companies they talk of religion and politics. For my general talks on miscellaneous occasions this usage must govern. All of my audiences must of necessity contain men of different creeds and parties."[13]

Clearly, if any norm was influencing Hayes, it was by his own account one of sheer politeness mixed with nonpartisanship. This polite, public nonpartisanship was a natural reflection of Hayes's reserved, Classicist conception of the presidency. As Benjamin Harrison was to do twelve years later, Hayes seems to have been following the model of the president as patriot leader established by George Washington. By avoiding much discussion of potentially controversial issues, of course, he in effect ceded to others, most notably Congress, the right to influence public opinion on important national issues. Given his Classicist conception of the presidency, Hayes would have wanted it that way.

James A. Garfield (1881): Reserved Whig

Another Republican, James Garfield, succeeded Hayes. Garfield fit right in with the tenor of the times. He was suspicious of presidential power, saw the office primarily in administrative terms, and "thought that the president could make recommendations to Congress but should never inflict his views on the legislature."[14]

The main battle Garfield fought in his short tenure as president was over reserving the power of political appointments to himself instead of Congress. He once gave an extensive interview to a reporter for the *Philadelphia Press* after his inauguration. In the interview, he explained and defended his decision to fill the New York customs collector position with Judge W. H. Robertson, who was an enemy of the ruling New York Republican boss, Sen. Roscoe Conkling.[15] A few months later, Garfield was dead, shot by a disappointed office seeker who just happened to be a

Conkling sympathizer—as was vice president and former New York customs collector Chester Arthur.

Chester A. Arthur (1881–85): Quietest Whig of Them All

If there ever was a president who fit the model of the reserved nineteenth-century presidency, it was Chester Arthur. He "had no active or regular dealings with the press, he gave few interviews, and he had few intimates among the newspapermen." He consistently refused to discuss political issues or make political speeches or visits, and "possessed an aristocratic disdain for the masses." An old-time Whig, Arthur was inclined to defer to Congressional initiative.[16]

Arthur also labored under several limitations. He was severely ill during most of his presidency, a fact he worked hard to conceal from the public, and died just twenty months after leaving office. He had to contend with a Democratic majority in both houses of Congress in the last two years of his administration, and had so antagonized the Republicans that he has been described as "a President without a party."[17] Not surprisingly, he made few legislative proposals and, consistent with his conception of the office, exhibited little presidential leadership.

Grover Cleveland (1885–89; 1893–97): Democratic Whig

Even Grover Cleveland, the only Democratic president in the late nineteenth century, essentially adhered to the reserved view of the president as an administrator with no role in the legislative process except to exercise the veto if he determined that Congress had passed unwise legislation "under the inspiration of popular excitement or political cowardice." According to Richard E. Welch's history of Cleveland's presidency, Cleveland attempted to influence the shape of pending legislation only twice in his eight years as president.[18]

Moreover, like Benjamin Harrison, who served as president between Cleveland's two terms, Grover Cleveland considered demagoguery a virtual sin. This attitude was probably influenced by the fact that Cleveland was not a talented speaker. Talkative with friends, he was reserved in public and "believed it well matched the dignity of the presidential office."[19]

On the other hand, Cleveland vetoed more legislation than all of his predecessors combined. During his first term alone, he sent 304 veto messages to Congress. These messages expressed his positions on a wide range of legislation and, coupled with his annual messages and special messages to Congress, conveyed his positions quite clearly—sometimes even haughtily—to Congress. Cleveland was reclaiming the right of the president to participate in the legislative process, prompting Woodrow Wilson to refer to him as "the extraordinary man who is now president." Tellingly, Welch reports that "Republican cartoons often portrayed Cleveland in the toga of a Roman emperor," and there was a "general belief that Cleveland was exerting the authority of the presidential office and intervening in legislative policy in an unprecedented manner."[20]

Because Cleveland utilized veto, annual, and special messages so extensively, his actions fit the Deliberator Model of the presidency. The story, however, is not quite so simple, for like other presidents such as Jackson and Taylor before him, Grover Cleveland had more than one audience in mind in his messages that were addressed nominally to Congress. Take, for example, Cleveland's special message to the Senate on March 1, 1886, defending his absolute right to make executive branch appointments without interference from the Senate. Richard Welch observes that the message "was addressed to the Senate, but it was directed as well to the American public." Moreover, the strategy worked because the message "inspired considerable support from the public and the press."[21]

Thus, we see once again, this time in the case of one of the few pre-twentieth-century presidents who actually seem to be have behaved consistently with the deliberative model of the presidency, that even presidential communications to Congress were often styled to sway the public as well. The fact that a presidential message was addressed to Congress does not necessarily mean it was not an attempt to also appeal directly to the American public for presidential support.

Cleveland occasionally used other techniques to communicate with the American public. One of these was the press interview. After winning the 1884 election despite lurid newspaper stories about his fathering a child outside of marriage and living the "low life" during his early professional years in Buffalo, New York, Cleveland went to New York City in February, 1885, to confer with party leaders shortly before his inauguration. While there, he gave daily interviews to the press.[22]

As president, Cleveland would occasionally give interviews to reporters on public policy matters.[23] In early 1886, with fairly disastrous results, Cleveland used an interview to contradict a New Year's prediction by the *New York Herald* that he would take a tough line with Congress on his policy positions on the tariff and silver issues. In a January 4 interview with several newspaper correspondents, Cleveland said the *Herald* had been mistaken. The presidency, he said, was just one of the coordinate branches of government, and members of the legislative branch had "responsibilities of their own, grave and well-defined." Saying he meant to be a strictly constitutional president, Cleveland proclaimed: "I believe that this is an executive office, and I deem it important that the country should be reminded of it. I have certain executive duties to perform; when that is done my responsibility ends." Accordingly, when asked if he thought Congress would follow his recommendations on the tariff and silver issues, Cleveland said he had no way of knowing because the matters were out of his control. Furthermore, he said, he had "no desire to influence Congress in any way beyond the methods he had employed in directing their attention to the topics."[24]

According to Cleveland biographer Allan Nevins, the effect of this interview at the time was to seriously weaken Cleveland's presidency by invigorating his opponents and dispiriting his supporters. Nevertheless, it is obvious from Cleveland's words that, in his first term at least, he was following the then-dominant conception of a constitutionally reserved presidency. As he moved through his second term, Cleveland apparently moved away from the limited view of his office, but for other reasons discussed below still avoided direct engagement with the press.[25]

Two years into his second term, Cleveland used a newspaper interview to defend the plan he had developed to keep the country on the gold standard by floating several huge bond issues. Convinced that the president was planning to sell bonds privately to J.P. Morgan and other big bankers, Joseph Pulitzer, publisher of the *New York World,* launched a frenzied newspaper campaign to force the government to sell the bonds via a public offering. After the bonds were sold publicly (as Cleveland apparently had been planning all along), the president gave an interview to a Boston newspaper in which he explained the details of the bond issue and expressed his conviction that the sale would cause more small holdings of gold to flow into the U.S. Treasury, his ultimate goal.[26]

Another technique Cleveland employed was to make use of what is today known as the press release. As David S. Barry, a long-time Washington reporter who covered the White House during Cleveland's administrations, described the technique, Cleveland "seldom if ever talked to a newspaper correspondent. When he had something to communicate to the public he wrote it out and gave it to his private secretary to hand to the representative of the press associations." Cleveland also timed his releases in a way that would make a modern president proud. According to Barry, Cleveland "invariably selected Sunday evening for having his messages promulgated, evidently believing that on Monday morning the newspapers had ample space to devote to his utterances."[27]

Cleveland's messages must not have been very frequent or substantial, however, because Barry said the administration operated under a "policy of secrecy." Writing in 1897, he said that the policy had become "rapidly popular during the past ten years" in Washington, until "under the Cleveland administration it became so firmly fixed that information on public questions" had to be obtained by reporters "much after the fashion in which highwaymen rob a stage-coach."[28]

There are only a few documented instances of presidential statements released by Cleveland to the press. The only one pertaining to a significant policy matter is an appeal to voters in 1896 to oppose congressional proposals for the free coinage of silver. Cleveland also issued a few press releases to clarify his policy positions between his two terms of office.[29]

When Cleveland was reelected, he turned to old friend and newspaperman George F. Parker to handle the increasing media inquiries. According to Parker, "Mr. Cleveland simply would not consent to see representatives of the newspapers or press associations, day by day, and to tell them what he had done or had in mind." Instead, Parker began meeting with Cleveland daily and formed a sort of "news-syndicate, so that each day, where there was anything to publish, it would be given out to my papers with authority."[30] Parker, described by one historian as the "self-appointed press secretary" of Cleveland's 1892 campaign, put together a published compilation of Cleveland's speeches and statements from 1882 through 1891 and encouraged him to cooperate with the press and thereby turn it into a tool for his reelection.[31]

Cleveland never really took this advice, however. It not only conflicted with his early conception of the presidency, he just did not much like dealing directly with reporters and had a low opinion of newspapers in general. Parker later wrote that Cleveland had a "strong aversion" to newspapermen. Cleveland's own language is less polite. At various times during his presidencies he referred to reporters as "animals," "the pestilence," "scavengers," and the "dirty gang."[32] One year into his first term, he told a magazine editor that there had never been a time "when newspaper lying was so general and so mean as at present. . . . The falsehoods daily spread before the people in our newspapers . . . are insults to the American love of decency and fair play of which we boast."[33] Given these opinions, Cleveland's reserved approach to public communications is understandable. Even when he might have yearned to get his side of a story out, Cleveland would have been inhibited at first by his sense of presidential propriety and then by the difficulties he saw in overcoming the base tactics of the press.

Benjamin Harrison (1889–93): Another National Cheerleader

The next president had no such reservations about cooperating with reporters. Thanks to the Electoral College, Benjamin Harrison became president in 1888 despite being outpolled in the popular vote by almost four hundred thousand votes. Harrison ran an unusual "at home" campaign for the presidency. Numerous citizens' delegations journeyed to his home in Indianapolis, where he would greet them with a speech. Harrison gave ninety-four such speeches, which were taken down by stenographers, edited by his campaign managers, and then distributed to the press, attracting "daily national comment." As president-elect, he remained in Indianapolis until one week before the inauguration, poring through bags of mail and greeting still more delegations. During this period, he attended a number of public functions, and "most of the time he was asked to speak after it was known that he was in the crowd."[34]

Harrison, a Republican, was also, according to the most recent account of his presidency, "a Whig at heart."[35] As Harrison himself put it: "There is not much that a President can do to shape [national] policy. He is charged under the Constitution with the duty of making suggestions to Congress, but, after all, legislation originates with the Congress of the United States, and the policy of our laws is directed by it. The President may veto, but he cannot frame a bill."[36]

An excellent public speaker, Harrison was inundated with invitations to speak all over the country. He made grand tours of the United States, including one of 2,851 miles in 1890 across the Midwest to campaign for congressional candidates, and another of 9,232 miles in 1891 all the way to the West Coast. He traveled for weeks in a plush railroad car from which he would give short speeches to assembled crowds at train stops. The almost three hundred speeches he made during his single term were recorded by a stenographer and distributed to the news media. Indeed, he said of his month-long tour of the United States in 1891 that "this whole journey has been a succession of speeches" due to the "great and predominant and all-pervading American habit of demanding a speech on every occasion," and noted that he had given 138 speeches on the tour.[37]

The most recent history of Harrison's presidency points out that "almost none of his speeches were bona-fide political ones," but instead treated general themes such as "interest in the flag, loyalty to the nation, the value of education, and the prosperity enjoyed by all American citizens." In but a handful of speeches, and then only briefly, did Harrison address any policy specifics.[38]

Harrison began many of his speeches by saying that time permitted only a short address, that the condition of his voice would not permit him to say much, or, rather implausibly, that he had not had time to prepare anything formal because of his duties in Washington.[39] There are a number of possible explanations why Harrison made such statements so often. They may have been his attempt to ingratiate himself with his audience, a recognition of the difficulties of public speaking before amplification, or even a way of explaining his Whiggish reserve in a politically tasteful way.[40]

Nevertheless, from this "hesitant" language in Harrison's speeches, Tulis argues that the president "comes close to expressions of guilt at violating a norm he knew he should respect."[41] Tulis supports his argument with excerpts from three of Harrison's "road" speeches. In the first two excerpts, though, Harrison plainly says why he avoids policy specifics: to avoid offending those who may have other, *partisan-based* views.

In the first excerpt quoted by Tulis, Harrison says he wants to be "careful not to trespass upon any forbidden topic, *that I may not in the smallest degree offend those who have forgotten party politics in extending this greeting to us.*" Similarly, after slipping briefly into a discussion of the need for a strong dollar and good overseas markets, Harrison hastens to add: "But, my countrymen, I had not intended to speak so long. I hope I have not intruded upon any ground of division."[42] The next sentence in Harrison's speech, omitted by Tulis, makes Harrison's meaning clear: "I am talking, not as a partisan, but as an American citizen, desiring by every method to enhance the prosperity of all our people."[43] In both of these speeches, Harrison is actually referring only to a desire to behave in a nonpartisan manner in public.

In its edited form, the third excerpt quoted by Tulis does indeed seem to indicate the existence in Harrison's mind of a constitutionally based norm against public policy discussions by presidents. This is the entire excerpt presented by Tulis: "You ask for a speech. It is not very easy to know what one can talk about on such an occasion as this. Those topics that are most familiar to me, because I am brought in daily contact with them, namely, public affairs, are in some measure prohibited to me."[44] The quotation ends too soon, however, for what was omitted explains quite clearly why Harrison thinks that topics of public affairs are in "some measure prohibited" to him. Here is Harrison's entire sentence: "Those topics that are most familiar to me, because I am brought in daily contact with them, namely, public affairs, are in some measure prohibited to me, *and I must speak therefore only of those things upon which we agree; for I have no doubt, if we were closely interrogated, some differences would develop in the views of those assembled here.*"[45]

According to his own, unabridged statements, Harrison avoided discussion of "public affairs" not because of any constitutionally based norm against public policy statements by presidents, but rather out of respect for those who might hold different views on the subjects and a desire to project a nonpartisan image as president.[46] While there is little doubt that Harrison, due to his Classicist conception of the presidency, avoided making policy pronouncements in his speeches, it is worth noting that his speeches make no specific mention of such a norm.

Harrison spelled out his understanding of appropriate presidential rhetoric in another speech at the beginning of his nine-thousand-mile tour in 1891. He observed that, although the president is elected only by a majority of the people, "he should always act and speak with a reserve and a respect for the opinion of others that shall not alienate from him the good-will of his fellow-citizens, without regard to political belief."[47] Toward the end of that tour, Harrison explained his speech-making rule in plainer terms: "I do not like to say anything anywhere that makes a line of division; for I know that these assemblages are without regard to politics, and that men of all parties have extended to us a cordial greeting."[48]

Given his goal of trying to keep the good will of all Americans, "without regard to political belief," Benjamin Harrison would naturally have steered clear of controversial issues in his speeches. This strategy would have been based on the Classicist-inspired notion that the president should manifest a proper, patriotic air of impartiality as the "servant of all the people." Harrison is another example of a president following an ideal of public reserve and nonpartisanship, consistent with the model of a patriot-leader established by George Washington.

William McKinley (1897–1901): The Forgotten Man of Going Public

While Benjamin Harrison hesitated to tread into political controversies, William McKinley strode boldly into them. As he is portrayed by Jeffrey Tulis, however, William McKinley was the paradigmatic reserved nineteenth-century president: McKinley's speeches, writes Tulis, "emerged as general discussions of the requisites of prosperity and make no mention of pending bills or treaties. There is no speech that even alludes to the Spanish-American War, the sinking of the *Maine,* the problem of 'Jim Crow' laws, or United States policy toward the Philippines, all major issues faced by McKinley. Indeed, much of McKinley's rhetoric was characteristic of the century as a whole: expressions of greeting, inculcations of patriotic sentiment, attempts at building 'harmony' among the regions of the country, and very general, principled statements of policy, usually expressed in terms of the policy's consistency with that president's understanding of republicanism."[49]

This is a highly inaccurate portrayal. In fact, even the circumstances of McKinley's death contradict it. The president was assassinated on September 6, 1901, just one day after giving a speech at the Pan-American Exposition in Buffalo before fifty thousand people in which he argued strenuously on behalf of several reciprocal-tariff treaties that had been negotiated by his administration but were being held up in the Senate. Copies of the speech, one in a series McKinley made in 1901 to urge ratification of the treaties, had been provided in advance to newspaper reporters.[50]

McKinley also made numerous speeches about U.S. policy toward the Philippines, which had become a U.S. possession in 1899 as a result of the treaty with Spain settling the Spanish-American War. The war and subsequent acquisition of the Philippines ignited a stormy national debate. Teddy Roosevelt, Henry Cabot Lodge, and Harvard president Charles W. Eliot were among those who equated territorial expansion with national pride and destiny. Benjamin Harrison, Andrew Carnegie, and Mark Twain led those who argued that colonialism was contrary to

American ideals, would destroy the distinctive national character, and would ultimately lead to despotism.[51]

McKinley entered the controversy in full rhetorical force, making scores of speeches in which he vigorously defended keeping the Philippines. He began the defense with a speech to the Dinner of the Home Market Club in Boston on February 16, 1899. After stating that the Spanish-American War had "added great glory to American arms and a new chapter to American history," McKinley went on to argue at length that

> The Philippines, like Cuba and Porto Rico [sic], were intrusted to our hands by the war, and to that great trust, under the providence of God and in the name of human progress and civilization, we are committed. (Great applause.) It is a trust we have not sought; it is a trust from which we will not flinch. . . .
>
> We could not discharge the responsibilities upon us until these islands became ours either by conquest or treaty. There was but one alternative, and that was either Spain or the United States in the Philippines. (Prolonged applause.) The other suggestions—first, that they should be tossed into the arena of contention for the strife of nations; or, second, be left to the anarchy and chaos of no protectorate at all—were too shameful to be considered. The treaty gave them to the United States. Could we have required less and done our duty? (Cries of "No!") . . .
>
> Did we need (the) consent (of the people of the Philippines) to perform a great act for humanity? . . . We did not ask these things; we were obeying a higher moral obligation, which rested on us and which did not require anybody's consent. (Great applause and cheering.)[52]

McKinley gave another major speech on August 28, 1899, where, among other things, he said there was "no flaw in the title" of the United States to the Philippines, and that the territory had become "ours as much as the Louisiana Purchase, or Texas, or Alaska."[53] In October, 1899, he then embarked on a two-week swing through the Midwest to welcome back returning soldiers and assure everyone that he had no intention of abandoning the Philippines.

McKinley made some eighty speeches in his two-week tour, and, as can be seen in Appendix C, most of them contained references, both direct and indirect, to the Spanish-American War, the Philippines question, or both. Many of his statements on the Philippines were colorful and adamant, echoing the sentiments he expressed in the speech quoted above. McKinley fully expected that the Philippines issue would, in his words, be the "'paramount and dominating" issue in the 1900 presidential campaign.[54]

McKinley made other tours. He toured the Midwest and South in late 1898 and the Far West in 1901. The two-week Midwest tour began in October, after the United States had defeated Spain, and was obviously made to celebrate that success while aiding Republican congressional candidates in the upcoming November election.[55] McKinley made fifty-six speeches of varying length, almost all of which referred to the great patriotism and sacrifices of those who had participated in the war and of the need to, as he put it in one speech, "do our duty" and not "dim the splendor" of our military achievements. Reporters were given advance copies of McKinley's prepared speeches and stenographic copies of his informal ones.[56]

In his week-long swing through the South in December, 1898, McKinley made ten speeches in which he applauded how soldiers from the North and South had fought side by side in the Spanish-American War, and argued strenuously that, having done our "supreme duty" in defeating Spain and capturing the Philippines, "is there any less duty to remain there and give to the inhabitants protection and also guidance to a better government?" His Far West tour in the spring of 1901 lasted six weeks, and McKinley used it "to talk to the country about two subjects which had previously been overshadowed by the postwar issues: the control of trusts and the extension of commercial reciprocity."[57]

McKinley's speaking tours differed markedly from the tours made by Hayes and Harrison. They rarely alluded to matters of controversy or partisan disagreement when they spoke. Instead, their words were generally celebratory in tone, with a focus on current bright prospects for the nation and nonpartisan, patriotic themes such as loyalty to the nation and the value of education and hard work.

McKinley's tours, in contrast, were made precisely so that the president might put before the American people his positions on major policy questions of the time. When the president invoked patriotic themes, they were not invoked as ends in themselves but rather as justifications for McKinley's policy positions. As the quotes in Appendix C from some of his speeches on the Spanish-American War and the Philippines show, there was nothing timid or obscure about McKinley's policy statements. They were clearly designed to whip up public support for his positions and thus put pressure on Congress.

McKinley also used a speech in early 1900 to counteract the national controversy generated by a speech by a Republican senator, Albert J. Beveridge of Indiana, on the floor of the Senate. In that speech, Beveridge, who had recently visited the Philippines, spoke in racially disparaging terms about the ability of the inhabitants to govern themselves, and argued that the United States should hold onto the Philippines "forever." His words, which were splashed across the front pages of the country's newspapers, reignited the smoldering debate over U.S. "imperialism"— especially since Beveridge was known to have been meeting with McKinley to discuss the territories. On March 3, 1900, McKinley gave a speech at a banquet in New York, in which he thundered, "There can be no imperialism. . . . The liberators will never become the oppressors. A self-governed people will never permit despotism in any government which they foster and defend." McKinley biographer Margaret Leech writes that the speech had a profound calming effect on the nation: "His words were an inspiration to the army of his adherents. The significance of the speech was enhanced because it was delivered at a time of great uneasiness about the colonial policy. The Philippines were not, for the moment, in question."[58]

While the dispute between the United States and Spain over Cuba was simmering in 1897 and early 1898, and even after the shocking sinking of the battleship *Maine* in Havana harbor on February 15, 1898, McKinley said nothing publicly. While that may seem curious to us now, it turns out that McKinley said nothing *privately* either: "Fearing to add impetus to the problem by discussing it, he followed his customary silence. All who talked with him noted that as usual he listened rather than talked. In all of his personal correspondence no position is outlined; the word 'Spain' is never mentioned." It turns out that this silence was part of a deliberate strategy. McKinley hoped to resolve the crisis through private diplomatic means, so "He said nothing in public, . . . and made no appreciable effort to placate any opinion arrayed against him. By maintaining this statesmanlike pose above the battle he hoped to rally all as yet undecided sentiment to his side and to hold his own ranks firm, while at the same time denying information to the press and public that might be distorted."[59]

In retrospect, even McKinley appears to have regarded this silent approach as a failure. However, there is no evidence that his silence was due to anything more than a simple strategic calculation to limit his public discussion of this particular issue.[60] On the subject of keeping the country on the gold standard, for example, McKinley in 1898 assured members of the National Association of Manufacturers of his intent to follow through on that part of the Republican Party's 1896 campaign platform.[61]

McKinley demonstrated his "modern" attitude toward presidential communications in other ways. His staff gave him a file of press clippings daily, and he had a press secretary who met with reporters daily. Reporters were given a table and chairs on the second floor of the White House, which came to be called "Newspaper Row," from which they could monitor visitors and attempt to interview them. Although McKinley gave only two known interviews to reporters, he was friendly with them and occasionally engaged in "off the record" conversations.[62] His administration also employed press releases on numerous occasions to announce presidential policy positions.[63]

In fact, McKinley was so successful in publicly asserting his place in the national policy-making sphere that commentators began writing about executive supremacy and excessive presidential power. Joseph Pulitzer asked in an article in 1899, "Has Congress Abdicated?" and Henry Litchfield West, in a 1901 article about the "Growing Powers of the President," wrote that "'in the legislative branch, it is the executive which influences, if it does not control, the action of Congress.'"[64]

Somehow, William McKinley's intensive speechmaking on the most critical public policy issues of his time has escaped the notice of presidential scholars.[65] This is unfortunate, because McKinley's is a crucial presidency in the history of going public. He was the first Republican president in decades to depart from the conception of the president as someone who avoided statements on public policy issues out of deference to Congress. He was, however, just one of numerous nineteenth-century presidents who went public; many others did not. What remains to be considered is why the view that presidents should go public ultimately prevailed.

CHAPTER 6

The Evolution of Going Public

THE EMPIRICAL DATA presented in the preceding chapters show that going public was a far more common activity by nineteenth-century presidents than has previously been thought. Prior scholarship has held that only Andrew Johnson tried to go public in the nineteenth century.[1] As Table 2 shows, however, fully half of the twenty-two nineteenth-century presidents were actually quite active in communicating their public policy positions to the American people. On the other hand, an equal number of presidents did not go public.

What accounts for this division? Mainly, as was discussed in chapter 2, it is due to the existence in the nineteenth century of two competing partisan concepts of the role of the presidency in the policy-making process. The reserved, Classicist conception of the presidency, which held that the president had no substantive role in the policy-making process and thus no need to communicate with the public on policy issues, was a basic tenet of the Whig Party, which inherited it from Federalist political philosophy. Many Whigs, including most notably Abraham Lincoln, moved to the Republican Party in the 1850s when the Whig Party disintegrated.[2] Not surprisingly, therefore, the Whiggish/Classicist conception of the presidency became a tenet of the Republican Party, influencing several presidents—including Democrat Grover Cleveland—in the last third of the nineteenth century. On the other hand, Democrats did not generally share this view, opting instead for the Democratist view that the president should be at least an active and coequal participant in the public policy and communication processes as the one official in the national government who was elected to represent all the people.

This partisan division manifested itself in the different approaches toward going public taken by presidents of different parties. Of the eleven presidents who went public in the nineteenth century, eight were Democrats, either formally (Jefferson, Jackson, Van Buren, Polk, Pierce, and Buchanan) or informally (Tyler and Johnson). Of the three presidents on the other side of the partisan ledger, one (Taylor) was a Whig; one (McKinley) was a Republican; and one, Lincoln, was a sort of hybrid Republican, having run for election in 1860 on the Republican ticket and then for reelection in 1864 on the National Union Party ticket as part of his plan to create a new, more broadly based party to replace the Republican Party.

Of the eleven who did not go public, only three were Democrats (Madison, Monroe, and Cleveland) while the other eight were either Whigs (William Harrison and Fillmore), Republicans (Grant, Hayes, Garfield, Arthur, and Benjamin Harrison), or a Whig precursor (John Quincy Adams).[3] The high percentages of Democrats who went public, and of Whigs and Republicans who did not, strongly indicate that partisan affiliation rather than a universally felt constitutional norm determined whether presidents in the nineteenth century went public.[4]

Table 2 also shows how public communications activity by presidents ebbed and flowed in the nineteenth century. There were three distinct phases. In the first phase, actually running from Washington's election in 1789 to the end of John Adams's term in 1829, only one out of six presidents went public. While George Washington himself did not go public, he did permit the two most influential members of his administration, Alexander Hamilton and Thomas Jefferson, to do so through their own sponsored newspapers. There are at least two reasons why going public was not practiced by presidents during this period. First, most of them held highly reserved conceptions of their office. Second, until the mass public became more relevant to the public policy and electoral processes in the 1820s with the expansion of suffrage, population growth, and more direct voting for the president, there was far less need to go public even if a president wanted to influence policy making.

TABLE 2

Pre-Twentieth-Century Presidents and Their Approaches toward Going Public

President	Party	Went Public	Did Not
Phase 1: 1789–1829			
Washington	Federalist		x
J. Adams	Federalist		x
Jefferson	Democratic-Republican	x	
Madison	Democratic-Republican		x
Monroe	Democratic-Republican		x
J. Q. Adams	Coalition		x
Phase 2: 1829–69			
Jackson	Democratic	x	
Van Buren	Democratic	x	
W. Harrison	Whig		x
Tyler	Whig/Democratic	x	
Polk	Democratic	x	
Taylor	Whig	x	
Fillmore	Whig		x
Pierce	Democratic	x	
Buchanan	Democratic	x	
Lincoln	Union/Republican	x	
Johnson	Union/Democratic	x	
Phase 3: 1869–1900			
Grant	Republican		x
Hayes	Republican		x
Garfield	Republican		x
Arthur	Republican		x
Cleveland	Democratic		x
B. Harrison	Republican		x
Cleveland[*]	Democratic		
McKinley	Republican	x	
Total (1800–1900):		11	11

*Grover Cleveland served two nonconsecutive terms, one before Benjamin Harrison and one after, but is counted only once because he followed basically the same approach toward going public in both of his presidencies.

In the second phase, from 1829 to the end of Andrew Johnson's term in 1869, the pattern reversed and only two out of eleven presidents did *not* go public. This was a period when the size of the electorate mushroomed as suffrage requirements were eased and the nation grew in size and population, and when most states switched to a more direct method of electing the president by selecting presidential electors according to the popular vote.[5] Times had changed, and master politicians like Andrew Jackson and Martin Van Buren saw that national politics could also be changed by appealing not to the elites but to the burgeoning legions of "commoners." Going public suddenly made more sense as a way of influencing Congress, and presidents began making much more use of the technique.

Seven out of the eleven presidents during this period were either actually or functionally (Tyler and Johnson) products of the Democratic Party, which had a populist creed and activist conception of the presidency. All seven of those presidents went public, usually through chains of regional and local newspapers that took their cues from the president's official newspaper in Washington. Two other pragmatic politicians, Zachary Taylor and Abraham Lincoln, went public during this period even though the Whig-Republican creed did not countenance the practice.

In the third phase, 1869 to 1900, the pattern reversed again, and only one out of seven presidents went public. Although there are several probable factors behind this switch to the nonactivist model of the presidency, the most obvious is party affiliation. Of the six Republican presidents during this period, five avoided much involvement in the public policy process in general and none went public. Their actions would have been consistent with the prevailing Republican Classicist conception of the presidency, which held that Congress and not the president controlled the making of national public policy.

These last two periods correspond almost exactly with the dominant phases of national campaign strategy identified by historian Michael E. McGerr in *The Decline of Popular Politics*. From the 1820s until the end of the 1860s, says McGerr, political parties and their candidates relied on spectacle in their campaigns, employing vivid, demonstrative devices such as marches, partisan newspapers, and symbolic pageantry to appeal to voter's emotions.[6] This is precisely the time period identified in this study as a time when most American presidents went public.

McGerr then identifies a second period from 1870 to 1896 when, thanks to the efforts of what he terms elitist reformers, there was a shift away from the spectacular to the educational campaign, in which parties and candidates took an unemotional, intellectual approach to politics.[7] This is precisely the time period identified in this study when no president went public.

Why did the Whig-inspired reserved conception of the presidency dominate presidential thinking during this last period? One reason might be that this conception was a tenet of the Republican Party and, being good Republicans, the men selected as the party's presidential candidates would have acted accordingly.[8] Owing their nomination to the party leaders and their election to the party machine, and with Congress dominating the budgetary and policy processes, Republican presidents of the time would have been unlikely to deviate from the party line on this crucial point.

This was also a sensitive time for a country just starting to recover from a wrenching civil war. Presidents might well have chosen to steer clear of public involvement in controversial issues and instead cast themselves as grand symbols of national reunification and healing. Avoiding controversial public issues would also have had the virtue of minimizing the risk of antagonizing any parts of the electorate and appealing to undecided voters in a time of political stalemate. Throughout the last quarter of the nineteenth century, presidential elections were decided by razor-thin margins, and one party rarely controlled both houses of Congress.[9] Presidents who knew they would have to deal with members of both parties legislatively might also have sought to avoid taking many overtly partisan positions to preserve their bargaining power, a technique employed in varying degrees by Bill Clinton and George W. Bush in similar circumstances.

Another explanation may be that this was simply a period in American history where political reality seems to have converged with a political and scholarly prescription. Congress had emerged supreme from its struggle with the executive in Andrew Johnson's presidency, and had, in Woodrow Wilson's famous description, become "unquestionably, the predominant and controlling force, the centre and source of all motive and of all regulative power, . . . until it has virtually taken into its own hands all the substantial powers of government."[10]

This was as it should be in the eyes of many influential Americans. According to one senator of the time, the "most eminent senators . . . would have received as a personal affront" any message from the president seeking their support on a legislative matter. "If they visited the White House, it was to give, not to receive advice," wrote Sen. George Hoar of Massachusetts. Woodrow Wilson confirmed these sentiments in his 1885 treatise on American government, in which he wrote that "no one, I take it for granted" would disagree that Congress was the "proper ultimate authority in all matters of government and that administration [i.e., the President] is merely the clerical part of government."[11]

How this reserved conception of the presidency managed to achieve such widespread approbation, influencing even Democrat Grover Cleveland, so soon after such strong presidencies as those of Andrew Jackson and Abraham Lincoln is unclear. One factor may have been the long shadow cast over the activist conception by the antics of another assertive but discredited president, Andrew Johnson. Another factor may have been the country's infatuation with the patriot-leader image of George Washington. The power of this image is illustrated by the immediate elevation of Washington's Farewell Address, a paean to patriotic nonpartisanship, to the status of a "sacred statement of American political principles." Until the 1970s, the address was read in Congress every year on February 22, Washington's birthday.[12] The day carried so much symbolism that when the planned House impeachment vote of Andrew Johnson had to be adjourned from Saturday, February 22, to the following Monday, the House leaders "set back the clock of the House in order that Monday should appear on the House journal as Saturday, February 22."[13] In the 1890s, top political figures, including President McKinley and Sen. Henry Cabot Lodge, followed the "custom of giving orations on February 22 concerning 'The Character of Washington.'"[14]

This was also a time when science and technology were producing a rational, mechanistic worldview. Congress' involved legislative process thus could have come to be regarded as a sort of machine that had been set up by the Founders to produce the best possible legislation if simply left to do its work without outside influence from anyone, including the president. That there was some such intellectual underpinning to the primacy accorded Congress during this period is suggested by Wilson's description of the Founders' "Newtonian" view of the government as a "machine."[15]

This phase of the "quiet presidency" ended dramatically in 1896 with the election of William McKinley. McKinley quickly abandoned the reserved Republican conception of the presidency and began going public in scores of speeches on fundamental policy issues of his day. Significantly, Michael McGerr finds that, beginning in 1896, a twentieth-century political style arose: advertised politics, which relied on careful packaging of the presidential candidate and his personality to sell him and his party to the voters.[16] Having gone through such a campaign to get elected, McKinley may well have seen the advantage of similarly promoting himself and his policies once he was in office.

The research reported here also answers two other important questions about the behavior of nineteenth-century presidents. The first is, when presidents went public before the twentieth century, how did they do it? The second is, for those presidents who did not go public, which of the three possible models—the Deliberator, the Celebrator, or the Reserved/Silent Figurehead—did they follow? Table 3 displays these two additional sets of data for the pre-twentieth-century presidents. The "Went Public" column shows in italics the major means of communication used by every president who went public. The "Did Not" column shows, again in italics, the conceptual model of the presidency followed by each president who did not go public.

Table 3 also explains why historians have overlooked the fact that half of the pre-twentieth-century presidents communicated directly with the American people on policy matters. The reason for the oversight is that many presidents used a now extinct institution, the presidential newspaper, as their primary means of going public. The means may have been different, but the intent to influence public opinion and thus the public policy process by communicating the president's positions to the people was the same then as it is now.[17]

That so many presidents maintained these newspapers indicates the presidency was automatically accorded its own, separate place in the "public sphere" or "public arena" of political and social dialogue as it developed in this country.[18] Going public is hardly a twentieth-century phenomenon, as has heretofore been assumed. Rather than having been at first constitutionally consigned to the fringes of the democratic policy-making process, those presidents who wanted to be involved, it turns out, have been deeply engaged in that process from almost the beginning of our nation, presenting their cases directly to the American people and not through Congress. There clearly was no universally felt "common law" constitutional norm against such direct presidential involvement in the public policy-making process.[19]

TABLE 3

Pre-Twentieth-Century Presidents: Techniques of Those Who Went Public,
Philosophies of Those Who Did Not

President	Party	Went Public	Did Not[*]
Phase 1: 1789–1829			
Washington	Federalist		Reserved
J. Adams	Fedederalist		Deliberator
Jefferson	Democratic-Republican	newspaper	
Madison	Democratic-Republican		Deliberator
Monroe	Democratic-Republican		Celebrator/ Deliberator
J. Q. Adams	(Coalition)		Reserved
Phase 2: 1829–69			
Jackson	Democratic	newspaper	
Van Buren	Democratic	newspaper	
W. Harrison	Whig		Reserved
Tyler	Whig/Democratic	newspaper	
Polk	Democratic	newspaper	
Taylor	Whig	newspaper/speeches	
Fillmore	Whig		Reserved
Pierce	Democratic	newspaper	
Buchanan	Democratic	newspaper	
Lincoln	Union/Republican	newspaper/speeches	
Johnson	Union/Democratic	speeches	
Phase 3: 1869–1900			
Grant	Republican		Reserved
Hayes	Republican		Celebrator
Garfield	Republican		Reserved
Arthur	Republican		Reserved
Cleveland	Democratic		Deliberator
B. Harrison[**]	Republican		Celebrator
Cleveland	Democratic		
McKinley	Republican	speeches/newspapers	
Total (1800–1900):		11	11

* See Appendix A for an explanation of the rules followed in classifying presidents according to the four possible categories.

** Grover Cleveland served two nonconsecutive terms, one before Benjamin Harrison and one after, but he is only counted once in this table because he basically followed the same approach toward going public in both of his presidencies.

Given a place in the public policy process by a constitutional frame-work that provided for their popular election and the right to veto any legislation, many presidents even in the nineteenth century sought ways to appeal to and influence public opinion as a means of enhancing their power in the policy-making process. To be sure, there have been many later presidents whose efforts at going public dwarfed the efforts of nine-teenth-century presidents—except perhaps for Andrew Jackson, who worked daily with his editor shaping the day's media strategy. The goal of this study has not been to compare the frequency or intensity or quality of going public by presidents in the nineteenth and twentieth centuries, but rather to show that many nineteenth-century presidents *did* go pub-lic.[20] The fully developed practice today represents a constitutionally le-gitimate, logical evolution of the office that has been aided by the explo-sion of mass communication theory and technology in this century.

What has been mistakenly identified as a norm against going public was in reality one of two competing conceptions of the institution of the American presidency, only one of which survived to any significant ex-tent in beyond the nineteenth century. The surviving conception is that of a president actively engaged in the legislative process and communi-cating with the American people on public policy matters. The extinct, or at least currently dormant, conception is one of a publicly reserved president who is not actively involved in the legislative process and re-frains from public communications on policy matters because policy making is the province of Congress. Thus, one of these conceptions pre-scribed public rhetoric by presidents, while the other proscribed it.

The reserved, Classicist conception of the presidency exerted a power-ful constraining influence on numerous presidents prior to the twentieth century. Perhaps the most dramatic example is John Quincy Adams, who wrote disdainfully in 1827 that he would not use "purchased news-papers" and "stipendiary editors" to get reelected.[21] In the meantime, An-drew Jackson and his campaign manager, Martin Van Buren, were set-ting up a partisan newspaper chain across the country to appeal to and mobilize the vastly expanded national electorate. Adams lost the 1828 election in a landslide, and Jackson's presidential newspaper, the *Wash-ington Globe*, became the classic example of going public nineteenth-century style.

Even presidents who did not go public did not all behave in the same fundamental way. The model of a Deliberator president—one who is involved in public policy but only by working and communicating directly with Congress—has been cited by Tulis, Kernell, Ceaser, and others as a constitutional ideal that was manifested in nineteenth-century presidential behavior. However, the actions of only three nineteenth-century presidents—James Madison, James Monroe, and Grover Cleveland—fit the model of a Deliberator president. (Another Deliberator Model president, John Adams, served in the eighteenth century.)

Of the eight nineteenth-century presidents who did not go public and were not involved in the policy process, there is a division between those who followed the Celebrator Model, making public speeches largely devoid of policy content, and those who followed the Reserved/Silent Figurehead Model and communicated with the public hardly at all. Two of these presidents, Rutherford Hayes and Benjamin Harrison, fit into the Celebrator Model, along with James Monroe whose presidency encompassed both the Celebrator and Deliberator Models. The six nineteenth-century presidents who fit the Reserved/Silent Figurehead Model are: John Quincy Adams, William Harrison, Millard Fillmore, Ulysses Grant, James Garfield, and Chester Arthur.

Of course, the concept of a constitutionally reserved presidency influenced the actions of other political figures besides presidents. The best example of the potency of this influence is the attempt by adherents of the restrained presidency to impeach Andrew Johnson for both resisting Congress and then trying to drum up public support for his actions.

The concept of a publicly reserved presidency even in some sense influenced the actions of presidents who favored instead the activist conception of their office. The practice of using presidential newspapers can itself be viewed as a bow by activist presidents to the illusion of a restrained presidency. By using newspapers to present their positions indirectly rather than through speechmaking, activist nineteenth-century presidents were able to present their positions and arguments to the American people in a way that still insulated them from any claim by proponents of the restrained presidency of improper presidential meddling in the public policy process.[22]

There are some other factors that may have played a part in influencing presidents to go public via their own newspapers rather than through speechmaking. Two very pragmatic factors are the sheer difficulty of making oneself heard before the advent of speech amplification, and the rigors of long-distance travel for much of the nineteenth century.[23]

There are two favorable strategic factors as well. First, in theory at least, it should have been easier to deliver a message with more precision through one's own newspaper rather than through speechmaking, because a speech would have to be filtered through other papers' reporters and editors. However, as has been seen in the problems some presidents had with their editors, this advantage did not always prove true in real life. Second, presidents could always disavow messages delivered through nominally independent newspaper editors if the message still came out wrong or had an unfavorable effect.

Another intriguing factor that might have dissuaded some presidents from making speeches about public policy was the belief among the educated elite in the nineteenth century that important ideas were more properly presented in writing rather than through speechmaking. This belief began being taught at Harvard in the 1820s and spread quickly to most other American colleges. The notion of the written word as the preferred form for higher-level communications was a fundamental precept in the teaching of rhetoric throughout the century.[24]

The shift toward presidential policy speechmaking and other public communications put in motion by William McKinley at the end of the nineteenth century became common presidential behavior in the twentieth century. While Teddy Roosevelt and his bully pulpit have received much of the credit for this shift, the equally important theoretical contribution to this change made by Woodrow Wilson in his prepresidential years as a political scientist has not received its due appreciation.

Wilson wrote two influential works on the American political system, the first in 1885 and the second in 1908. In his 1908 book, *Constitutional Government,* Wilson dramatically changed his position on the president's involvement in the public policy-making process. Wilson had previously written in his 1885 book, *Congressional Government:* "No one, I take it for granted, is disposed to disallow the principle that the representatives of the people are the proper ultimate authority in all matters of government, and that administration is merely the clerical part of government. Legislation is the originating force. It determines what shall be done; and the President, if he cannot or will not stay legislation by the use of his extraordinary power as a branch of the legislature, is plainly bound in duty to render unquestioning obedience to Congress."

In his later book, Wilson argued instead that our system of government had so evolved over its first century that the presidency had become "the vital place of action in the system," with presidents the only ones truly capable of interpreting, influencing, and marshaling public opinion on matters of national policy.[25] Wilson now asserted that either presidential approach was legitimate under the Constitution. "Governments are what politicians make them," he said. Consequently, it is "easier to write of the President than of the presidency" because "the presidency has been one thing at one time, another at another, varying with the man who occupied the office and with the circumstances that surrounded him."[26]

At various times in the nation's history, Wilson said, some presidents had held what he called the "strict literary theory of the Constitution, the Whig theory, the Newtonian theory," and had acted as if it would be wrong to try to "lead the houses of Congress by persuasion." Such presidents had "scrupulously refrained" from trying to influence either the "subjects or character of legislation."[27]

On the other hand, he asserted, there had been other presidents with very different attitudes. These presidents had felt the need for some "spokesman of the nation as a whole," and had "tried to supply Congress with the leadership of suggestion, backed by argument and by iteration and by every legitimate appeal to public opinion." Such presidents, Wilson argued, could dominate their party, Congress, and the nation by "being spokesm[e]n for the real sentiment and purpose of the country," and thus "giving direction" to public opinion.[28] Here, Wilson's words echoed those of another great president and theoretician, Thomas Jefferson. In early 1801, just as he was taking office, Jefferson articulated this vision of the presidency in a letter to a friend: "In a government like ours, it is the duty of the Chief Magistrate, in order to enable himself to do all the good which his station requires, . . . to unite in himself the confidence of the whole people. This alone, in any case where the energy of the nation is required, can produce a union of the powers of the whole, and point them in a single direction, as if all were constituted by one body and one mind."[29]

Although the "practice and influence" of presidents had varied greatly over time, Wilson wrote, "there can be no mistaking the fact that we have grown more and more inclined from generation to generation to look to the President as the unifying force in our complex system, the leader both of his party and of the nation." There was nothing wrong with this development, and certainly nothing unconstitutional. The men who framed the Constitution had indeed been "Whig theorists," who had sought to create a Newtonian machine of government in which there was no single "dominating force" but instead a number of counterbalanced forces. "The trouble with the theory," said Wilson, is that "government is not a machine, but a living thing." And this government had evolved just as any organism would, "accountable to Darwin, not to Newton." Shaped by the "sheer pressure of life," our system of government had changed with the times, sometimes drawing from the president the leadership and coordination that were essential to successful government, and at other times drawing its energy from Congress. In all cases, however, "leadership and control" had to reside somewhere in the system. After all, said Wilson, "we have all been disciples of Montesquieu, but we have also been practical politicians."[30]

Wilson argued that presidential assumption of an active role in public policy and public opinion making was "not inconsistent with the actual provisions of the Constitution; it is only inconsistent with a very mechanical theory of its meaning and intention." For Wilson, the restrained "Whig theory" of the presidency was no more than some "law of taste" which in the minds of some had wrongly "become a constitutional principle." The Constitution itself, he asserted, "contains no theories." Consequently, "those presidents who have not made themselves leaders have lived no more truly on that account in the spirit of the Constitution than those whose force had told in the determination of law and policy."[31]

When he became president, Wilson practiced what he had preached in *Constitutional Government.* During World War I, for example, Wilson created a "Division of News" to put out his administration's views on the war. The division issued more than six thousand press releases. It had seventy-five thousand "Four-Minute Men" who traveled the country and delivered more than 755,000 speeches to a total of over 300 million people. Boy Scouts were enlisted to deliver annotated copies of the president's addresses to American households, and six hundred thousand teachers received biweekly pamphlets on the war. Wilson could no longer draw on the resources of a presidential newspaper, but he came up with some effective substitutes.[32]

Wilson's scholarly theorizing, coupled with his own activist presidency, must have had a significant influence. By 1947, *Constitutional Government* was in its eighth printing, indicating the book's ideas had achieved a wide circulation.[33] Two or three generations of students of American government would have been doubly impressed with the notion of an activist presidency, having not only read Wilson's eloquent prose but also lived through the presidencies of such publicity giants as Wilson and the two Roosevelts.

Wilson explained brilliantly why either conception of the presidency was constitutionally valid. In doing so, he also demonstrated that no universally felt "norm" had controlled all presidents. However, his explanations for why the activist conception of the presidency should prevail are not very illuminating. The system had to have a leader, he said, and the practical demands of governing—what he called the "sheer pressure of life"—were moving the American presidency inexorably toward the activist-leader approach. And why did so many presidents previously follow the restrained conception of their office? Again, Wilson offers little by way of explanation except to say that either view was a "matter of taste."

A more specific answer to both of these questions has its roots in the essential ambiguity of the presidency at its constitutional founding, and in the institutional attributes of the office. Although it is commonplace to talk about "what the Founders did" or "what the Founders intended," in fact, as was shown in chapter 2, there was almost no agreement among the Founders (let alone the Antifederalists or Americans in general) on virtually any aspect of the office of the president.

Many of the Founders and other influential politicians saw the presidency as a generally reserved and deferential institution, with Congress far more powerful and important. Meanwhile, many others, beginning with Thomas Jefferson, viewed the presidency as an active participant in all aspects of the government, serving as a coequal or even in some senses a superior to Congress in the American political system.[34] As we have seen, the two conflicting conceptions of the presidency became central components of the party orthodoxies of the Democratic and Whig/Republican Parties throughout the nineteenth century. This partisan difference meant that, as different presidents took office, they would behave differently depending on which conception of their office they held.

As for the question of why the activist concept of the presidency came to prevail, the answer from a political science perspective lies in the institutional logic of the office. Arguably, the single most important occurrence in the history of the development of the American presidency was the democratic movement in the early 1820s that prompted the states to enfranchise most white males and then make the popular vote, rather than the votes of legislators, the method for allocating state electoral votes. The results of this movement, in combination with rapid population growth, became evident in the 1828 presidential election, when 1,155,340 males voted—eight hundred thousand more than in the previous election.[35]

The new reality of mass politics, coupled with the massive growth in newspaper circulation that began in the 1820s, injected into the American system a powerful inducement to presidents to communicate with the public.[36] More politicians were adopting the "rhetoric of mere reflection, as if their voices really came from the electorate," and the claim was increasingly being made that "the president was the sole authentic spokesman for and representative of national majorities."[37]

This conceptualization grew naturally out of the Democratist political philosophy, which originated in Antifederalist philosophy and then became a part of the overall orthodoxies of the Democratic-Republican and Democratic Parties, that political representation should be as direct and as unmediated as possible. Given such a goal, the presidency would be the best institution in the national government for accomplishing it, because the president would have the greatest potential for immediate, unmediated institutional responsiveness to public opinion.

The judiciary, of course, would be far too insulated. Congress, too, although to a far lesser extent, would be potentially less responsive to public opinion due to its institutional constraints. These constraints would be especially pronounced in the Senate, which elects only one-third of its members every two years, has a filibuster rule that requires a supermajority to pass legislation, and, until 1914, was elected not by popular vote but by state legislatures. Even the House of Representatives has had throughout its history some significantly antidemocratic features, such as the committee and seniority systems and the power of the House leadership to control its agenda.

In contrast to the other two branches, the only barriers between the presidency and popular opinion would be those a particular president chose to maintain. This may well have not been the intent of the writers of the original Constitution. However, the presidency was given some essential attributes, such as the veto power and a national electoral base, which at least made this alternative use of the office an attractive option for others with different ideas about the meaning of the terms *republic* and *representative democracy.*[38]

Presidents who were planning to use their office to actively influence and participate in the legislative process as the "people's representative" could see that much of their power, as Neustadt wrote of twentieth-century presidents, was in reality the power to persuade. After all, just like modern presidents, nineteenth-century presidents had few means of legislative influence at their disposal aside from patronage or log rolling.[39] Party leadership is one such means, but for much of the nineteenth century that leadership lay in the hands of congressmen or regional political bosses. Moreover, the tool is not much help unless one's party has a solid working majority, which was not always the case for nineteenth-century presidents. Even a presidential veto could be overridden by a vote of Congress.

Nevertheless, these limited presidential tools of policy leadership can be enhanced by presidential communication with the public. As Neustadt described the process, members of Congress "anticipate reactions from the public" in "deciding how to deal with the desires of a President."[40] This political calculus was just as valid in the nineteenth century as it is today. After exhausting or dismissing his ability to simply command the result through partisan maneuverings, a nineteenth-century president who desired a particular course of action would consider going public to generate increased public support for the presidential initiative, thereby bolstering its chances in Congress. Representatives who perceived increased support for a president's initiative would be less likely to oppose it, anticipating electoral punishment by their constituents.

Similarly, a president who is planning to veto legislation knows that the veto can be overridden by a congressional vote. Therefore, a president bent on exercising this ultimate presidential tool might well endeavor to stimulate public opinion in his favor and thus dissuade representatives from voting against his stand. Alexis de Tocqueville, who based his classic account of the workings of American democracy on his observations during Andrew Jackson's first term, saw this connection clearly. "The veto," he wrote, is "a sort of appeal to the people. The executive power . . . can then argue its case and make its reasons heard" to the public through the veto message.[41] In 1842, James Buchanan, then a member of Congress, invoked the concept of the president as the direct representative of the people in defending President Tyler's vetoes against Whig claims that policy-based vetoes were constitutionally illegitimate. A veto,

Buchanan argued, was a "mere appeal by the President of the people's choice from the decision of Congress to the people themselves." The fallacy in the Whig's argument, Buchanan asserted, was their "assumption that Congress, in every situation and under every circumstance, truly represent the deliberate will of the people. The framers of the Constitution believed it might be otherwise; and therefore they imposed the restriction of the qualified veto of the President upon the legislative action of Congress."[42]

For a long time, as is the wont of old habits and traditions, the Classicist conceptualization of the presidency lived on in the new world of mass politics, causing many American presidents after the 1820s to continue to behave (or at least act publicly) as if the times and the political system had not changed. This is quite understandable, considering the impressive pedigree conferred on the paradigm by the Founders and classical political thought.[43]

Eventually, however, three new realizations began dawning on more of the key actors in the American political system. The first reality was that, as Andrew Jackson articulated so forcefully, the president was the only government official elected by all the people and therefore arguably *primus inter pares* or at least a coequal in the process of divining and enacting the public will.[44] The second reality was that the veto power was a potent tool in the hands of a president who wanted to exert control over the legislative process. As time went on and more and more presidents exercised the veto for policy and not constitutional reasons, the legitimacy of using the veto power as a presidential policy-making tool increased. The third reality was that, as mass communications technology improved, it was becoming easier to communicate quickly and directly with the American public.

These three factors were mutually reinforcing. As the country grew in size and population, getting elected president became an ever greater achievement of mass mobilization and communication, which in turn made it easier for the winners to claim electoral mandates and to try to implement those mandates through their only direct legislative weapon, the veto. However, presidents who were contemplating or exercising their veto power realized that it could be overridden by a two-third's vote of Congress. How might that possibility be prevented? As the literature attests, legislators can often be quite responsive to their constituents.[45] Thus, for activist presidents in any era, going public in some form would have been critical to marshaling the support that would then inhibit legislators from voting against the president's position.

Presidents who want to be influential in the public policy sphere must go public. This is the institutional logic of the new American system, which granted an element of influence over the legislative process to not just one actor—the legislature—but two: Congress and the president. Once the electorate expanded in the 1820s, presidents who wanted to maximize their power over legislation were impelled by the realities of that power to "take their case" directly to the people in ways that would have seemed unnecessary and even inappropriate to those steeped in the classic concept of a "republic."[46]

As presidents increasingly came to be viewed as at least coequals in the public policy process, the original reserved attitude toward going public fell into such deep disfavor among presidents, political scientists and historians, the media, and the American people that it is hard to even conceive of a president following such an approach today. In its place arose the paradigm of the president as an independent representative of the people, advancing his or her own public policy agenda and communicating with the public about that agenda. This institutional evolution would have been influenced considerably by environmental factors in the twentieth century such as changing social expectations, a dramatic expansion in the size of the electorate due to population growth and the enfranchisement of previously excluded groups, and major advances in communications technologies.

Thus, the story of going public is not of how one universally felt behavioral norm came to be superseded by a new norm, but rather of how only one of the two original competing constitutional conceptions of the presidency in the nineteenth century has come to dominate our current understanding and expectations of that office. With the governmental system established in this country, especially as modified with popular presidential election and expanded suffrage in the early nineteenth century, presidents with an activist conception of their office would have increasingly turned to making appeals to the public that some of their predecessors, steeped in another tradition, would have had no need for and even disdained. The need to go public would be heightened for presidents during times of divided government—particularly prevalent since the 1950s—when even America's lightweight version of party discipline would be of little use to an activist president.

We see today that continued need and legitimacy for presidents going public, motivated institutionally by the political system in which they find themselves. The present, paradigmatic practice of going public is in reality the refined, technologically enhanced version of a venerable American concept: talking—and listening—to the people.

CHAPTER 7
The Legitimacy of Going Public

THE DISCOVERY that far more nineteenth-century presidents than previously thought went public in one form or another is more than a historical curiosity. That nineteenth-century presidents did *not* go public is a crucial underlying tenet of the two main works in this field, *Going Public* by Samuel Kernell and *The Rhetorical Presidency* by Jeffrey Tulis. The removal of this factual underpinning necessarily calls into question the analyses that have been built on this incorrect empirical claim.

The basic problem with the arguments of both Kernell and Tulis is that they mistake the reserved Federalist-Whig-Republican nineteenth-century conception of the presidency for the only original constitutional conception of the office. Any variation from that conception represents a change in the constitutional order. Once this historical dichotomy is set up, supposedly newer ways of presidential behavior can then be labeled as deviations from the "original intent." From this intellectual haven, it is then an easy step to label any allegedly newer way of presidential behavior as wanting or even corrupted.

Consider, first, the "original intent" world portrayed by Samuel Kernell. Kernell makes the historical underpinnings of his analysis evident early on, as the following excerpt from his introduction shows: "Clearly, going public appears to foster political relations that are quite at odds with those traditionally cultivated through bargaining. One may begin to examine this *new* phenomenon by asking, *what is it about modern politics* that would inspire presidents to go public in the first place?"[1]

Kernell then proceeds to construct an original world of American politics that would make any Federalist or Whig proud. According to him, this original Washington world was one that was to be "insulate[d] against short-term swings in popular sentiment." It was therefore to be "a stable and a somewhat insular community in which even a new president may be viewed as an interloper." In this isolated political world, "public pressure has little place in the community." Kernell contrasts this world with the modern world, in which "modern communications and transportation have brought Washington prominently to the attention of the nation so that over-the-shoulder inspection by constituents can easily *contaminate* the transactions of politicians."[2]

Tulis's world has a similarly biased viewpoint that is also based on Federalist-Founders principles. The fear of "'direct' or 'pure' democracy" is manifest. Our entire "constitutional government . . . was established in contradistinction to government by assembly." From these Founders' perspective, it would "not do to suggest that in a democracy good legislation reflects the majority will." These attitudes are reflected in the institution of the presidency itself: "With respect to the presidency, the founders wanted to elicit the 'sense of the people,' but feared an inability to do so if the people acted in a 'collective capacity.'"[3]

The flaw in these constructed worlds is obvious. Their skewed conception of the proper constitutional order leaves no place for direct public involvement in the policy-making process. It is this other strain of original American political thought that underlay the activist conception of the American presidency. Some of the *Federalist Papers* certainly speak about the undesirability of direct democracy, but that does not mean that a contrary strain of political thought was not present among early American political thinkers. Indeed, as James S. Fishkin has observed, the "vision of direct democracy or, as second best, a small democracy kept as close to the people as possible," was at the heart of the writings of the Antifederalists.[4] As Herbert Storing has pointed out, the goal of the Antifederalists was "to keep representatives directly answerable to and dependent on their constituents. This is the reason for the concern with short terms of office, frequent rotation, and a numerous representation."[5]

This attitude was not confined to a bunch of now unknown Americans who wound up on the losing side of the battle over ratification of the Constitution. While he is not considered an Antifederalist, Thomas Jefferson certainly shared the views of many Antifederalists on democratic government. As we have seen, that populist democratic vision was behind the actions of the Antifederalists and of Jefferson, Jackson, Johnson, and several other nineteenth-century presidents, who saw direct appeals to the public on policy matters as appropriate and even necessary components of the American political system.

The vision did not just go away once the Constitution was ratified. Rather, its adherents continued to pursue it as the new government evolved. For Antifederalist believers in direct democracy, ratification of the Constitution hardly meant that their vision was wrong and should be abandoned. Instead, the vagueness and thus malleability of its language merely meant that there was room for both sides—the believers in direct democracy, whom I have called the Democratists, and the believers in "filtered democracy" or representative republicanism, whom I have called the Classicists—to go forward in political life, each acting within the governmental framework as if their vision were correct, and each battling the other side as necessary. The nineteenth century is full of examples of the struggle between these competing visions, ranging from the newspaper battles between Hamilton, Madison, and Jefferson in the 1790s to the impeachment of Andrew Johnson by Whigs and Republicans for, among other things, public speechmaking that was contrary to their reserved conception of the presidency.

Today, it is obvious that, as Fishkin says, "The direct-majoritarian vision that animated the Anti-Federalists, while it lost the initial battle over the Constitution, has largely won the war in the long march of history— the war to determine the vision of legitimate politics directing change in American democracy. . . . The modern presumption has become that anything more direct and majoritarian must be more democratic."[6] There is, however, nothing illegitimate about this development. It is simply the triumph of an idea, rooted in the radical Antifederalist populist ideal that has always been one of the main currents in American political thought.

From the standpoint of constitutional law and development, the story of the evolution of going public is a remarkable saga of two conflicting interpretations of the Constitution coexisting in American politics for much of our history. Constitutional development is usually depicted linearly, with theoretical or political ferment ultimately resulting in some sort of cataclysmic event after which the nation is then set on a new course of action. A good example of this method of portrayal is Bruce Ackerman's thesis that the United States has gone through three changes of "constitutional regimes" in its history: the Founding, Reconstruction, and the New Deal. Following each of these regime changes, he says, a new "professional narrative" on the Constitution was produced which then colored all future thinking by judges and lawyers on cases of constitutional interpretation.[7]

In contrast, the inherent contradiction between the two prevailing attitudes toward going public in the nineteenth century never really produced a defining moment of change. In fact, it only produced one moment of high-profile conflict: the impeachment of Andrew Johnson by Whigs and Radical Republicans for, among other things, daring to make "inflammatory" speeches on public policy matters. Perhaps because that was hardly the main reason for Johnson's impeachment (his attempt to undermine congressional policy on Reconstruction was), this "constitutional moment" did not resolve the issue of the constitutional propriety of presidents going public. Instead, presidents temporarily retreated from going public, only to resume the practice later in the century. Thus, the nineteenth century as a whole can be characterized as a century in which the comparative strength of two competing constitutional conceptions of the presidency ebbed and flowed, usually without much sign of conflict between the two.

In this ebb and flow of presidential conceptions, we find a rather unusual case of constitutional interpretation. Rather than taking place in the courts, the interpreting was done by presidents and other politicians and political actors as they directly applied their interpretations to the conduct of particular presidencies. This type of interpretation never resulted in the kind of dramatic, defining moment that interpretation in the judicial and even legislative forums are said to produce. Rather, there was a very long, usually low-key, political give-and-take process that ultimately resulted in the institutional logic of one conception of the presidency winning out quietly, with the other conception never really dying but just fading away.

The perception that going public is a twentieth-century development has resulted in it being wrongly labeled as a constitutionally illegitimate political tool. The real nature of going public can be seen in one of its earliest forms, the presidential newspaper. These papers were really tools for mobilizing partisan support, with the message being passed from the president's Washington-based paper to partisans throughout the nation by means of chains of party-supported papers throughout the country.

It is not correct to assert, as Kernell does, that, because "other Washington elites [already] legitimately and correctly represent the interests of their clients and constituents," going public as a strategy of presidential leadership is "incompatible with the principles of pluralist theory."[8] Nor is it fair to assert, as Tulis does, that going public is a wholly new development that is at odds with the original understanding of government expressed in the Constitution of 1789.[9] These views ignore the fact that constituents—in the best Antifederalist tradition of direct, populist democracy—have an expectation that they can communicate their wishes to their representatives via elections, protest marches, referenda, recalls, mail, and any other accepted form of political communication, *and* that their representatives will follow their wishes if they are in the majority on an issue. In other words, these views ignore the very real expectation of most Americans that their representatives represent them according to the "delegate" and not the "trustee" model of representation.[10]

By going directly to the American public over the heads of Congress, presidents try to present their arguments and appeals to the people in such a compelling way that constituents will then pressure their individual congressional representatives to go along with what the president wants. Going public thus is a classic exercise of political mobilization by a political actor, the president, who is at the very center of the American democratic process. When they go public, presidents widen the scope of conflict, precisely as E. E. Schattschneider described the workings of a representative democracy.[11] They also very explicitly follow the Antifederalist/Democratist rather than the Federalist/Classicist conception of what a democratic republic means.

Going public is not, as Kernell asserts, necessarily a departure from the president's proper place in the constitutional order. Nor is going public a tool that must be considered to interfere with the president's "classic" role of bargaining within the system. Going public—that is, mobilization—is more properly viewed as one of three equally valid political tools that are available to presidents. As Kernell, Richard Neustadt, and others make abundantly clear, bargaining is one of those tools, and perhaps even the most effective.[12] However, as many presidents have shown, direct mobilization of voters and their intensities by presidents who go public is the second arrow in an activist president's quiver. The third is the perhaps underestimated power of a president to actually command other government officials to act as he or she desires.[13] When scholars evaluate strategic presidencies, therefore, they need to examine how well a president used each of these available tools, just as they might examine how well a civil rights or labor leader had used all of the tools that were legitimately available in those situations.

This study shows that going public historically has been viewed by many presidents as complementing, rather than conflicting with, their proper role in our system of government. From this enlarged perspective, criticisms that are made of the technique seem more problematical. Who really can prove, for example, that going public can "damage and displace bargaining" by reducing "choices to black-and-white alternatives and to principles that are difficult to modify," as Kernell asserts? As any good union negotiator knows, labor leaders frequently are expected to take strong public positions to demonstrate their leadership ability and to inspire the membership.[14]

That such public posturing is so common casts doubt on the claim that it is counter-productive. Indeed, by staking out an unrealistically extreme position, leaders can leave room to later make essentially cost-free concessions to the other side while still ending up where they wanted to be all along. The road of American political history is littered with vivid political statements that were later rendered "inoperative." Examples include Woodrow Wilson's promise to keep the country out of war and George H. W. Bush's guarantee of "no new taxes."

And is Kernell's assertion that "the mobilization of public opinion becomes little more than an abrasive" that "can sow only ill will and ultimately reap failure" with those who are at the bargaining table really correct?[15] Politicians, school board members, newspaper editors, and business and labor leaders can all attest that such pressure is often present in their decision making. Since it is, are not efforts to generate such pressure simply considered part of the process? After all, as Kernell points out, efforts to generate public opinion pressure are not always successful. Moreover, when they fail they send just as powerful a signal to the other bargainers as when they succeed. When a representative can genuinely gauge what the majority's opinion is on an issue because the public has been mobilized, that situation is far preferable to having to guess what one's constituency thinks—or might later think—about an issue, which is the normal lot of politicians.[16]

Presidents going public actually fits quite well with the bargaining concept of public policy-making identified by Richard Neustadt. As Neustadt observed, presidential activities in the public relations sphere impact other policy makers by increasing or decreasing the "leeway" these other actors have in responding to presidential policy initiatives. This leeway is really the political actors' assessments of the political cost to them of either supporting or opposing the president's wishes.

By going public, a president attempts to increase the perceived political cost to other actors of opposing the president's initiative(s). A president who goes public knows that the real essence of the policy-making process is the bargaining that will go on between the president and Congress. Going public, however, is a way for the president to foreclose, or at least make less politically attractive, certain moves that legislators might otherwise make in response to a president's proposal.

By going public, a president can, if the effort is successful, affect the political calculations of legislators in two ways. First, the president may be able to mobilize constituents of legislators sufficiently that they actually contact their representatives to register their support for the president's position. Second, whether or not constituents are mobilized to contact their representatives, the president seeks to constrain legislators psychologically by implicitly raising the specter that, in the next election, they will either be punished or rewarded by the electorate for the position they (or their party) took on the president's proposal. In either case, a president's successful use of the public relations tool serves to narrow the range of possible legislative reaction, making achievement of the president's objectives more likely.

The policy-making process is analogous to the collective-bargaining process for labor contracts. One party, let us say the president, can be viewed as the management side, while the other party, say Congress, can be viewed as the union side. Just as in the world of commerce, where a business can only function with the cooperation of labor and management, our government can only operate with the cooperation of Congress and the president in the world of politics. Either institution can, in effect, declare a sort of strike at almost any time—Congress by using its appropriations and authorizations powers, and the president through the veto power.

In the fields of both business and government, the two parties would always prefer to avoid a strike. However, they also want to achieve their objectives to the maximum extent possible. They know there will be negotiations, but they also know that there is more to negotiations than the simple trading of quids for quos. They know that one's bargaining leverage can be increased if the other side somehow can be made to feel that its position is psychologically or even morally inferior. In the world of labor negotiations, both sides know that such noneconomic considerations can translate into economic gains by one side in the bargaining process. They know that if one side feels constrained from taking or sustaining a particular position and alters its bargaining stance accordingly, then the other side has thereby achieved a bargaining advantage even before the actual negotiations begin.

The fact that noneconomic, psychological considerations can produce economic gains is the foundation for going public. Activist presidents seeking to maximize their bargaining power with Congress go public because they hope to influence public perceptions in a way that forces members of Congress to alter their approach to the issues without the president giving up anything in return. Members of Congress may reciprocate, spawning a political war of words. Thus, properly understood, going public is not an obstacle to the bargaining that ultimately underlies the process by which Congress and the president "legislate together."[17] Rather, it is an integral part of the process in which each side seeks to maximize its bargaining advantage by appealing to the public for support.

Modern politicians sometimes are quite candid in their recognition of the role of public relations in the legislative process. In 1994, as he was gearing up to become the first Republican Speaker of the House in forty years, Newt Gingrich attacked the Clinton administration as a haven for drug users. When the propriety of his actions was questioned, Gingrich responded that America had a tradition of "hardball politics." He explained: "I'm a historian. Jefferson and Hamilton each subsidized papers to smear the other. Trying to lead America has always been a tough business and even [George] Washington occasionally got hit."[18]

A year later, as Bill Clinton prepared to counter the Gingrich-led Republican legislative initiatives, his main strategy was to try to increase negative public perception of those initiatives. After the president's health care reform package died in Congress in 1994, the Clinton administration "belatedly realized that it had allowed opponents to define the terms of the debate, using television, lobbying, and grass-roots politicking to capitalize on the public's fear of change."[19]

Learning from that loss, Bill Clinton a year later decided to play a "waiting game on negotiations" over the Republicans' budget proposals that included a proposed overhaul of Medicare. Rather than spending time negotiating with Congress, Clinton instead, through the Democratic National Committee, had weeks of television ads run portraying the Republicans' budget plan as an attack on Medicare. The idea was to "put increasing pressure on the Republicans to compromise, cause fractures in their ranks and also inoculate the President against blame if the budget battle [brought] days of crisis."[20] The strategy worked perfectly, and congressional Republicans, after in effect going out on strike by forcing a shutdown of many of the federal government's "nonessential" operations, returned to the bargaining table to negotiate a budget compromise more acceptable to the president.

Bill Clinton's successful 1995 battle with Congress over the federal budget is a classic illustration of how going public is really part of the legislative bargaining process. Within a few months of his inauguration in 2001, George W. Bush demonstrated his understanding of this reality. He made several "tours around the circle," usually to states with senators and representatives in danger of losing their seats in Congress, urging voters to send their legislators messages of support for the Bush agenda. He told one "roaring audience" in Atlanta, "If you find a member that you have some influence with, or know an e-mail address, or can figure out where to write a letter, and find out somebody isn't listening to you to do what's right for the country, just drop them a line."[21]

Despite what Tulis and others say, going public is also best viewed as a legitimate part of—rather than a detriment to—a national deliberative process for making public policy. There are two ways to look at the policy-making process, each grounded ultimately in the conflicting views of representative democracy that have been the focus of this book. The first way, the Classicist way, holds that the policy-making process is best centralized. This occurs when elected representatives of the people come together and deliberate in Washington, D.C. The other view holds that it is best to decentralize public policy making so that the people and not their representatives do it. It occurs "back home" among the people, and their elected representatives then have the job of going to Washington, D.C., to enact laws reflecting the people's (majoritarian) will.

The centralized deliberation model of policy making has been at the heart of many critiques of the modern presidency, including those of the developers of the concept of the rhetorical presidency. Tulis, for example, has argued that the increased emphasis on activism and going public by presidents tends to "subvert the deliberative process" and is part of the "continued decay of political discourse."[22] This critique, however, has been made from the perspective that there is only one original, constitutionally legitimate way of making national policy: centralized deliberation. The critiques have not taken into account the fact that there is another constitutionally legitimate way of making national policy—decentralized deliberation—that has an equally impressive political and philosophical pedigree.

Defending or analyzing the relative merits of these two models involves fundamental questions of political philosophy that are beyond the scope of this book. By drawing attention to the profound influence that the decentralized deliberation model has had on the American presidency, however, I hope that this book will prompt students and scholars of government to look more seriously at the reality of decentralized deliberation as a means of national policy making.

Many questions deserve attention. Here are a few. How much of the national policy-making process is, or has been, due to centralized deliberation and how much is due to decentralized deliberation? Are there different types of issues that are more or less amenable to resolution via one or the other of the deliberative models? And just how does decentralized deliberation occur? Somehow, out of all the messages and contacts that people receive about policy issues, many of them develop personal positions on the issues. How does that happen? From a rhetorical standpoint, is it possible to sort out the roles that the wide variety of "rhetorical media" (including not just conventional media such as speeches and writing but also unconventional sources such as radio, television, the Internet, and going to church and school and the mall) play in the decentralized deliberation process?[23]

Another intriguing question—this one for the historically inclined—is whether the current central national legislative process is any more deliberative than it was previously.[24] Since half of the pre-twentieth-century presidents engaged in a form of going public, seeking to marshal public opinion in their favor by convincing and mobilizing their supporters, it does not seem likely that the national policy-making process was significantly more deliberative then than it is today.[25] If government officials really were so insulated from "day to day currents of public opinion" before the twentieth century, then why did so many of the earlier presidents regularly expend so much effort trying to influence public opinion?[26] The answer may well be that nineteenth-century policy making was not all that different from our current process, in which public opinion, bargaining, and deliberation all play a role.

The findings presented in this book also have implications for how we view the presidency itself. The "rise of the rhetorical presidency" in the twentieth century, it has been asserted, has created a constitutionally conflicted office. The presidency is said to be an "ambivalent constitutional station," in which the "old way" of presidents deferring to Congress on policy matters conflicts with the "new way" expectation of direct presidential action and communications with the public on policy matters.[27]

The history of the evolution of going public set out in this book indicates that the two conceptions do not have to be viewed so problematically for the office. Because the two views emerged out of two equally valid and respected visions of the appropriate constitutional order, and thus have equally respectable pedigrees, presidents today can more properly be viewed as having at their disposal either legitimate conception of the presidency.

Thus, depending on the strategic circumstances confronting a president, he or she may choose to act according to any one of the four presidential models identified here. Modern presidents do, in fact, seem to do just that, utilizing all of these styles in different settings and for different purposes, with different emphases. Bill Clinton, for example, ranged from being a Celebrator on some issues, such as race relations, to a Mobilizer on others, such as health care. Perhaps due to the ambitiousness of his early agenda, which required him to work with a closely divided Congress, George W. Bush for a time seemed more exclusively a Mobilizer. Future presidential studies need to take this strategic decision-making into account in their examinations of the roles presidents assume in the fields of public policy making and communications.

With the knowledge that there have been historically four different models for presidents to follow, the current focus of scholars, journalists, and the public on just one of the models—the "Mobilizer/Going Public" Model—suddenly appears out of balance. Presidents do not all have to behave like Ronald Reagan or Teddy Roosevelt. In fact, there are principled, constitutionally based arguments for each of the four possible models of presidential behavior.

It is true that, as argued here, the institutional logic of the presidency does lead presidents who want to maximize their influence over the public policy-making process to go public. The logic dictates that result, however, only if a president can answer two fundamental questions affirmatively: Am I supposed to be involved in the policy-making process, and, if so, should I direct my communications on policy to the American people? A negative answer to either of these questions leads to very different presidential behavior than that called for by the Mobilizer/Going Public Model. These two questions for presidents in turn lead to the fundamental constitutional questions of what type of policy-making process we should have—by directed representation or representational deliberation—and what role the president should play in the process.

The existence of four possible models of presidential behavior means that, in judging presidencies, we must be careful to specify our criteria. For example, one poll of historians asked them to rank presidents from weak to strong according to "the strength of the role the President played in directing the government and shaping the events of the day." A second question asked the historians to rate "the approach taken by each President toward his administration [as] an active approach or a passive approach."[28] These rating standards are obviously biased toward the active model of the presidency; adherents of the reserved model are automatically labeled failures.

The existence of other models besides the Mobilizer/Going Public one shows how much more difficult the job of president can become for one who chooses to follow this model. First of all, a president who follows this model must have a public policy agenda. Development of an agenda cannot occur in a political vacuum. Agenda items must be politically viable or the president will waste valuable political capital on a losing cause, weakening his or her presidency in future policy and election battles. The necessity of choosing politically viable agenda items inevitably leads to presidential reliance on public polling techniques, which provide a way of measuring viability. Second, a president who follows the Mobilizer/Going Public Model must then have the skills and resources to effectively pursue this strategy. This need inevitably leads to the elevation of the presidential communications apparatus to a position of critical importance in the Oval Office.

Both of these endeavors—agenda creation and public communications—can use up a great deal of presidential energy and time. Consider how different matters are for a president who follows any of the other three models. In any of those models, the demands on a president are dramatically reduced. A president who wants to be involved in public policy but work with Congress and not the public is able to dispense with a great deal of attention to public communications. A president who wants to communicate with the public but stay out of policy matters is free to travel the country at ease, saying nice things but able to dispense with the controversy and institutional baggage that comes with agenda setting. Finally, a president who does not want to be involved in policy making or in public communications would, of course, have much less to do, at least in comparison to the other three behavioral models.

The other three models of presidential behavior may at first no longer seem very plausible (certainly not the Reserved/Silent Figurehead one) to many people. However, one ought not dismiss lightly the power or utility of any of the models. Take, for example, the model of the presidency that calls for a president to stay out of the public policy-making process. Despite the strong public policy involvement precedents set by presidents such as Jefferson, Jackson, Polk, and Lincoln in the first two-thirds of the nineteenth century, the precedents were forgotten in the last third of the century as president after president affirmed he had no place in the public policy process.

This attitude made its last significant appearance when Dwight Eisenhower announced he had no desire to follow the practice begun by his predecessor, Harry Truman, of proposing annual legislative programs to Congress in the State of the Union address. Eisenhower eventually was forced to do so, however, after strong criticism from congressional Republicans, and the practice has been followed ever since.[29] Much more recently, as noted above, Bill Clinton, a devout practitioner of the art of going public on some issues, utilized other models of behavior in dealing with other issues.

Even the mere realization that there are other models of presidential behavior besides the Mobilizer/Going Public Model serves to highlight the pathology of the current presidential paradigm, with its emphasis on going public, and to explain why the office is so demanding in its current configuration. Modern presidents who follow the Mobilizer/Going Public Model have a much more complicated job than their predecessors who chose other models.

In sum, going public is a more complex, less constitutionally suspect practice than it has been given credit for by many scholars. Contrary to many of those pronouncements, going public has been a legitimate potential tool for presidents since essentially the beginning of our constitutional republic. Like the use of other presidential tools such as the veto, its use has waxed and waned depending on strategic circumstances and the proclivities of individual presidents. That presidents have employed this tool off and on for most of our history means that, while we have unquestionably become more democratized, whether we are any less constitutional depends, in the final analysis, on with whom you are talking.

APPENDIX A

Explanation of Typology Classifications

IN THE TYPOLOGY DEVELOPED in this research, presidents can be placed in one of four categories: Mobilizer, Deliberator, Celebrator, and Reserved. These four categories represent the four possible modes of presidential behavior within the two dimensions of whether a president communicates with the public and is active in the national policy-making process.

Presidents were classified in the Reserved category if they made few public speeches (or none at all) and did not communicate with the public through other means such as a presidential newspaper, and did not communicate with Congress on policy matters, except for their required annual messages to Congress on the state of the union.

Presidents were classified in the Celebrator category if they made numerous public speeches but rarely, if at all, addressed matters of substantive public policy either in the speeches or through other means, and did not communicate with Congress on policy matters, except for annual messages to Congress on the state of the union.

Presidents were classified in the Deliberator category if they did not make public speeches or use on a regular basis other means of public communication such as newspapers, but were active in attempting to influence policy making by frequently sending messages to Congress on specific policy issues.

Finally, presidents were classified in the Mobilizer category if they frequently made public speeches or communicated with the public through newspapers and regularly addressed specific policy issues in their public communications.

APPENDIX B

Contents of the *Washington Globe* during the 1833–34 battle over Andrew Jackson's withdrawal of deposits from the bank of the United States

Date	Commentary	Other
Sept. 25, 1833	Editorial	
Sept. 26	"We have obtained permission to say that a difference of opinion has prevailed between the President and some members of his cabinet on that subject [withdrawal of deposits, disagreement of Cass], but that the president has caused it to be understood that these proceedings are not to be considered as a cabinet measure, but one upon which the members may conscientiously differ from the President and each other."	
Sept. 27		Re: whether Acting Secretary of the Treasury has authority to withdraw deposits
		Editorial reprints from *New York Standard* and *Richmond Enquirer*

Date	Commentary	Other
Sept. 28	Re: general corruption in business affairs of Bank	
		Editorial reprints from *Winchester Virginian* and *Baltimore Republican*
Sept. 30	Editorial	
		Editorial reprints from *Hartford Times, New York Standard,* and *Baltimore Republican*
Oct. 1		Editorial reprints from *Maine Democrat, Boston Daily Globe, New York Evening Post, Albany Argus, Warrenton (Va.) Spectator, Boston Morning Post, New York Working Man's Advocate,* and *Brooklyn Advocate*
Oct. 2	Editorial rejecting purported independence of the treasury secretary	
		Editorial from *Richmond Enquirer*
Oct. 3	Editorial re: independence of the treasury secretary. Also declares that the *Raleigh Star* is not a Jacksonian newspaper, contrary to the claim of the *National Intelligencer,* which had quoted a *Star* editorial against withdrawal of federal deposits from the Bank.	
		Editorials from five state papers
Oct. 4		Long excerpt (two columns) from *New York Evening Post,* excerpts from five other papers
Oct. 5	Editorial referring to the "(Bank) Intelligencer of this City" and its quotes from "the (Bank) Gazette of Philadelphia."	
		Editorials from six state papers
Oct. 7		Editorials from five state papers

Date	Commentary	Other
Oct. 8	Editorial defending Attorney General Taney	Letter from Amos Kendall denying he had any interest in Bank editorials from seven state papers
Oct. 9	Editorial responding to claim the treasury secretary is not an executive officer	Editorials from four state papers
Oct. 10	Editorial on same issue as Oct. 9	Editorial from one state paper
Oct. 12	Editorial	Editorials from six state papers
Oct. 15	Editorial	
Oct. 16	Editorial	Editorial from one state paper
Oct. 17	Editorial re: president's power to remove treasury secretary	Editorial from one state paper
Oct. 19	Editorial	Editorial from four state papers
Oct. 21		Editorials from ten state papers
Oct. 23	Editorial rebutting claim money markets damaged by withdrawal of deposits	
Oct. 24		Editorials from three state papers
Oct. 25	Editorial	
Oct. 28		Editorials from four state papers
Oct. 29		Editorial from one state paper

Date	Commentary	Other
Oct. 30		Editorials from two state papers
Oct. 31	Editorial and report re: financial ties of *National Intelligencer* to the U.S. Bank: loans that came due and were not foreclosed by Bank. Seven columns (over one page long)	
Nov. 2	Editorial re: management of Bank	
		One long editorial from *New Lisbon (Ohio) Patriot*
Nov. 11	Editorial contradicting *National Intelligencer* claim that deposits are to be restored to Bank	
		Editorials from two state papers
Nov. 13	Editorial re: Nov. 11 subject	
Nov. 14	Editorial rebutting *National Intelligencer* claims that money markets are distressed by deposit withdrawals	
Nov. 15	Editorial attacking Bank and defending Jackson's right to withdraw deposits	
Nov. 18	Editorial responding to letter from Duane in which he explained his opposition to the withdrawals	
		Editorials from two state papers
Nov. 20		Editorial from one state paper
Nov. 21	Editorial attacking Duane and *National Intelligencer*'s defense of him	
Nov. 23	Editorial attacking Duane	
Nov. 26	Editorial defending Jackson's actions	

Date	Commentary	Other
Nov. 27	Editorial replying to National *Intelligencer*'s attacks	Editorials from two state papers
Nov. 28	Editorial claiming Bank planning to induce panic by making money scarce	
Nov. 29	Editorial attacking *National Intelligencer* attacks	
Nov. 30		Editorials from one state paper
Dec. 2	Attack on *National Intelligencer* for being in debt to Bank	
Dec. 3	Same subject as Dec. 2	
Dec. 4	Reprint of Jackson's message to Congress re: Bank withdrawals	
Dec. 5	Reprint of treasury secretary's report on the withdrawals	
Dec. 6	Treasury secretary's report, continued	
Dec. 11		Editorials from two state papers
Dec. 13	Editorial attacking Bank Reprint of letter from Jackson to Senate refusing, on executive privilege, to give it the letter he had sent his cabinet re: withdrawal policy. Transcript of much of the Senate debate on Sept. 12 re: Jackson's rejection of the Senate's request for the Cabinet letter. Clay says the letter had been "published and extensively circulated by the papers in this city," and that the right of the Senate to have the letter "was founded on the ground that the whole world was already in possession of it. It was made because the document was sent forth to the American people upon an all-important subject and because it was the right of the Senate to have it."	

Date	Commentary	Other

Dec. 14 Editorial attacking Bank

Editorials from one state paper

Dec. 16 Transcript of part of House debate re: Bank

Dec. 17 Editorial responding to Bank's defense of itself

Editorials from two state papers

Dec. 18 Editorial from Dec. 17 continued: "We have not finished our castigation of these 'naughty boys'—the Biddle [Bank President] Directors."

Editorials from one state paper

Dec. 19 Transcript of debate in House re: Bank withdrawals
Editorial defending withdrawal and congressional attacks on it. Editorial notes that *National Intelligencer* wants the Bank's entire defense of itself published in the *Globe*. The *Globe* will not do it unless the Bank learns to not fill its defenses with "studied personal insult to the Chief Magistrate." But the *Globe* would cheerfully do so if the *National Intelligencer* will publish the *Globe*'s response.

Editorials from two state papers

Dec. 20 Editorial attacking Bank
Editorial responding to another Duane letter

Dec. 21 Editorial re: rechartering Bank.

Editorials from ten state papers

Dec. 23 Editorial defending Treasury Secretary Taney against attack by Clay. Response to letter sent by Bank of Philadelphia to Congress requesting redeposit of moneys into U.S. Bank Account of Dec. 19 debate in Senate over Bank

Dec. 24 Account of House debate
Editorial responding to Bank's defense, called the Bank Manifesto

Date	Commentary	Other
	Editorial attacking Clay for being financially supported by Bank	
	Editorial attacking Bank	
		Editorials from four state papers
Dec. 27	Editorial responding to Clay's "harangue in the Senate"	
		Editorials from four state papers
Dec. 28	Republication of Jackson's Sept. 18 address to cabinet re: Bank withdrawals	
	Publication of Clay's Dec. 26 response to and critique of Jackson's cabinet address	
	Editorial	
Dec. 30	Editorial defending withdrawal: The closing of the Bank of the United States was "decisively determined on [sic] by the People in the election of a President."	
	Editorial arguing withdrawal of deposits could not have produced any scarcity of money	
		Editorials from three state papers
Dec. 31	Accounts of House and Senate debates	
Jan. 1, 1834	Reprint of letter to Senate from Treasury Secretary Taney explaining his authority to withdraw deposits	
	Report of Clay's remarks in response, affirming no authority; debate in its third day, he says	
	Note from Blair that circulation is 12,100, up from 6,724 on Dec. 1	
	Long editorial arguing with Clay and arguing against Senate ordering redeposit of deposits into Bank	
		Editorial from one state paper
Jan. 2	Long editorial	
		Editorials from four state papers

Date	Commentary	Other
Jan. 3	Report of Senate debate re: Jackson's actions Editorial re: Senate proceedings	Editorials from eight state papers
Jan. 4	Report of Senate debate	
Jan. 6	Report of Senate debate Editorial	
Jan. 7	Report of treasury secretary re: Bank of United States accounts	Editorials from five state papers
Jan. 8	Report of Senate debate on Jan. 2 and Jan. 7	Editorial from one state paper
Jan. 9	Report of Jan. 7 Senate and House debates	Editorials from two state papers Reprint of Ohio legislature supporting withdrawal
Jan. 10	Report of Senate and House debates Editorial commenting on debates and rebutting Clay	Editorials from two state papers Long anonymous letter from a Virginian
Jan. 11	Report of Senate debate Editorial	Reprints of two letters to congressmen
Jan. 13	Report of Senate debate Two long editorials	Editorials from two state papers, one (from *Boston Morning Post*) as paper's lead editorial of paper
Jan. 14	Report of Senate debate	

Date	Commentary	Other
Jan. 15	Report of Senate debate	
	Editorial re: Ohio legislature resolution and more	
		Reprint of New Jersey legislature's support resolution
		Reprint of long letter to congressman
Jan. 16	Report of Senate debate	
	Editorial	
		Editorials from two state papers
Jan. 17	Report of Senate debate.	
	Editorial	
		Quotes of several anti-Bank drinking toasts
		Editorial from one state paper
Jan. 18	Blair describes himself as the "editor of the official paper in Washington" in responding to *Niles Weekly Register* editorial	
	Report of Senate debate	
		Editorials from four state papers
Jan. 20	Speech by Representative Cambreleng of New York defending Jackson	
	Editorial	
		Editorial from one state paper
Jan. 21	Speech by Representative Beardsley of New York defending Jackson	
	Report of Senate and House debates	
	Editorial	
Jan. 22	Speech by Senator Shepley of Maine	
	Editorial	
Jan. 23	Report of Senate speech by Rives	
	Editorial responding to Webster and attacking *National Intelligencer* for financial ties to Bank. Claim that Bank had	

Date	Commentary	Other

decided to make western states suffer: "What an injury, and outrage to the great valley of the Mississippi, that all its products depend for their price upon the breath of half a dozen Shylocks in the City of Philadelphia."

Jan. 24   Senate and House debates on Bank—Senate also debating Taney's renomination
Two editorials
        Editorial from one state paper

Jan. 27   Editorial re: U.S. Bank and the money market
Editorial responding to editorials in the *Philadelphia Whig* and *Enquirer,* claim that Bank spent $30,000 to establish the new paper
        Editorials from nine state papers
        Resolution of support passed at Philadelphia meeting of "2,000 freemen."
        Reports of other county party resolutions.

Jan. 28   Report of Senate proceedings re: Bank
Editorial
        Editorial from one state paper
        One anonymous letter

Jan. 29   Report of Senate proceedings and debate re: Bank Editorial
        Editorials from five state papers

Jan. 30   Senate and House debates re: Bank
Editorial
        Editorial from one state paper
        One anonymous letter

Jan. 31   Senate debates re: Bank
Editorial
        Editorials from two state papers

Date	Commentary	Other
Feb. 1	Senate debates Editorial	
		Editorials from fourteen state papers Several anonymous letters
Feb. 3	Senate proceedings Editorial	
		Editorials from six state papers Three signed letters Four state or local resolutions
Feb. 4	Senate and House proceedings, both reporting state resolutions Editorial	
		Editorials from four state papers One resolution One "unpublished play," a satire on the Bank
Feb. 5	Senate speech by Rives	
Feb. 6	House and Senate proceedings Jackson letter to Congress Editorial	
		Three state/local resolutions
Feb. 7	Senate and House proceedings re: refusal of Bank to give up soldiers' pension deposits Editorial re: Duane letter	
		Editorial from one state paper One letter
Feb. 8	Senator's speech Editorial	
		Editorials from seven state papers One resolution Two letters

Date	Commentary	Other
Feb. 10	Senate speech and proceedings	
	Editorial: the "President will not falter in his course. Speculators . . . beware!"	
		Editorials from two state papers
Feb. 11	Editorial rejecting idea Jackson will establish new bank	
		Editorials from two state papers
		Two resolutions
		Three letters
Feb. 12	Senate speech	
	Editorial	
Feb. 13	Editorial	
		Editorials from four state papers
		One resolution
		One letter
Feb. 14	House speech	
	Editorial	
		Editorial from one state paper
		One resolution
		One letter
Feb. 15	House speech continued	
	Editorial	
Feb. 17	Long editorial	
		Editorials from four state papers
		One resolution
		Two letters
Feb. 18	Long editorial	
	Senate and House debates (referring to state resolutions)	
		Editorials from eleven state papers
		Two letters

Date	Commentary	Other
Feb. 19	Senate speech Editorial	
Feb. 20	Senate and House proceedings Long editorial	Editorial from one state paper One letter
Feb. 21	Senate and House speeches Editorial re: speech in Senate on Feb. 11 by Senator Southard	Editorials from seven state papers Four resolutions One letter
Feb. 22	Senate and House speeches Editorial	Editorials from six state papers One resolution Two letters
Feb. 24	Senate speech Editorial	Editorial from one state paper Two letters (one from member of Congress saying all Congress has done is "talk, talk, talk," regarding the deposits)
Feb. 25	House and Senate speeches Editorial	Editorials from ten state papers One resolution One letter
Feb. 26	House proceedings Editorial	Editorials from seven state papers

Date	Commentary	Other
Feb. 27	Senate and House proceedings Editorial	
		Editorials from nine state papers
Feb. 28	Senate speeches and proceedings Editorial	
Mar. 1	Senate speech continued Editorial	
Mar. 3	Senate and House proceedings Editorial	
		Two letters
Mar. 4	Senate and House proceedings Editorial	
		One resolution One letter
Mar. 5	House speech Reprint of House Ways and Means committee report Editorial	
		Editorial from one state paper One letter
Mar. 6	Editorial	
		Editorial from one state paper One resolution Three letters
Mar. 7	Reprint of House committee report continued Editorial	
		Editorial from one state paper re: Fourth of July march by 15,000 in Philadelphia devoted largely to anti- Bank sentiment Resolution adopted by participants in Philadelphia march.

Date	Commentary	Other
Mar. 8	Reprint of House committee report continued Editorial	
		One letter
Mar. 9	House speech Editorial	
Mar. 11	Senate speech and proceedings Editorial	
Mar. 12	Senate speech continued Senate and House proceedings Editorial	
		One letter
Mar. 13	House speech House and Senate proceedings Editorial	
Mar. 14	Editorial re: threat of two senators to not allow Senate to adjourn until Bank rechartered	
Mar. 15	House speech continued from Mar. 13 Senate proceedings Editorial	
Mar. 16	Editorial	
		Two letters: exchange between Treasury Secretary Taney and a committee in Baltimore
Mar. 18	Senate proceedings Editorial	
		Editorial from one state paper, which said the 1832 election had posed the question of "Will you have Andrew Jackson for your president and no

Date	Commentary	Other
		Bank, or Henry Clay and a Bank?" Two resolutions One letter
Mar. 19	Senate proceedings Editorial	
		Editorials from three state papers re: big meetings in Albany and Boston where anti-Bank resolutions were adopted. Two resolutions
Mar. 20	Senate proceedings re: acceptance of resolutions from groups Senate and House speeches Editorial	
		Editorials from eight state papers Four resolutions
Mar. 21	Senate proceedings Editorial Special four-page supplement to the *Globe* reprinting speech of Sen. Wilkins re: withdrawal of Bank deposits	
		Editorials from six state papers Four resolutions Three letters
Mar. 22	House speech Senate proceedings Editorial	
Mar. 24	Senate and House speeches Editorial	
		Advertising notice headlined "Removal of the Deposits," informing customers that a boot and shoe store had moved

Date	Commentary	Other
Mar. 25	House and Senate proceedings, Senate speech Editorial	
Mar. 26	Senate speech Editorial	
Mar. 27	Senate proceedings Editorial	
Mar. 28	Senate speech Editorial on President Jackson's sentiments regarding the Bank and the national currency, as expressed to the various committees that met with him regarding "the distress which was alleged to have fallen upon the country."	Editorials from six state papers Four resolutions
Mar. 29	Senate speeches and proceedings Editorial re: New York governor's speech in *Globe*	New York governor's speech saying struggle with the Bank not causing problems for New York banking system Editorials from two state papers One resolution
Mar. 31	Senate proceedings and speeches Editorial re: Senate's censure vote of Jackson	Editorial from one state paper Two letters
Apr. 1	Editorial	
Apr. 2	Editorial	

Date	Commentary	Other
Apr. 3	Editorial	
		Editorials from three state papers
Apr. 5	Victory editorial	
Apr. 7	Victory editorial	

APPENDIX C

References (Direct and Indirect)
to the Philippines Territory
and the Spanish-American War
in McKinley's Speeches of Late 1899

Philippines		Spanish-American War	
Direct	**Indirect**	**Direct**	**Indirect**
	Aug. 15		
Aug. 25			
Aug. 28, no. 121 (extensive)		Aug. 28, no. 121 (extensive)	
		Aug. 28	
	Aug. 29		
		Aug. 30, no. 125	
			Sept. 5
		Oct. 3 (Dewey's victory "exalted American valor and extended American Authority." (p. 225–26))	

Direct	Indirect	Direct	Indirect
	Oct. 6, p. 226	Oct. 6, no. 129	
		Oct. 6, no. 130	
		Oct. 6, no. 131	
			Oct. 6, no. 132
			Oct. 6, no. 133
	Oct. 6, no. 134		

Oct. 7, no. 135

	Oct. 7, no. 136		
	Oct. 7, no. 137		
			Oct. 8 (black soldiers)
	Oct. 7, no. 138		

Oct. 9 ("from Plymouth Rock to the Philippines" (p. 245–46))

Oct. 9

Oct. 10, no. 144

Oct. 11, no. 147

Oct. 11, no. 149 (rebellion in Philippines "against the sovereignty of the U.S." (p. 256))

Oct. 11, no. 150

Oct. 11, no. 150 (rebellion)

	Oct. 11, no. 152	Oct. 11, no. 152	

Oct. 12, no. 154

Oct. 12, no. 155

Oct. 12, no. 155 (extensive rebuttal to critics citing criticisms of earlier U.S. expansions)

Oct. 12, no. 156

Oct. 13, no. 158

Oct. 13, no. 160

Oct. 13, no. 161 ("The flag of our country that floats over the Philippines floats in honor for liberty and humanity and for the American name." (p. 277))

Oct. 13, no. 162 (same image)

Oct. 13, no. 164

Oct. 13, no. 164 (rejects insurgents' offer of peace for independence)

	Oct. 13, no. 165	Oct. 13, no. 165	
	Oct. 14	Oct. 14	

Oct. 14, no. 167 ("The U.S. flag was planted in the Philippines because we have a right to do so." (p. 287)) (". . . in the providence of God, who works in mysterious ways, this great archipelago was put into our lap." (p. 288))

Oct. 14, no. 168 (promise to send enough troops to ensure "ultimate victory" (p. 290))

                                                            Oct. 14, no. 169

                        Oct. 14, no. 170

Oct. 14, no. 171 (insurrection will be "very promptly suppressed")

Oct. 14, no. 172 (Philippines became our territory; "our flag is there." (p. 297))

                        Oct. 14, no. 173

Oct. 16, no. 177 ("It is no longer a question of expansion with us; we have expanded. [Laughter and great applause.] If there is any question at all it is a question of contraction; and who is going to contract? [Applause]" (p. 302))

Oct. 16, no. 178 (We will "sustain the boys in blue" and "conquer the rebellion." (p. 303))

                        Oct. 16, no. 179–81

Oct. 16, no. 181 ("American sovereignty shall be established in every island in the archipelago. [General cry of 'Yes!' Applause.]" (p. 306))

Oct. 16, no. 182 "That territory, my fellow citizens, the President has no power to alienate if he was disposed to do so, which he is not. [Great applause]." (p. 307))

Oct. 16, no. 184   Oct. 16, no. 184

Oct. 16, no. 185

Oct. 16, no. 187   Oct. 16, no. 187

Oct. 16, no. 188   Oct. 16, no. 188

Oct. 16, no. 189 (Long and dramatic speech: "If we were going to cede the islands away, to whom would we cede them?" (p. 319))

                Oct. 16, no. 190

                Oct. 16, no. 191

Oct. 16, no. 192   Oct. 16, no. 192

Oct. 17, no. 194

Oct. 17, no. 195   Oct. 17, no. 195

Oct. 17, no. 196 (The "rebellion will be put down [enthusiastic applause] and the authority of the United States will be made supreme. [General cry of 'Good!' Great applause.]" (p. 330))

Direct	Indirect	Direct	Indirect

Oct. 17, no. 197

Oct. 17, no. 199 (The American flag floats over the Philippines "not as the symbol of enslavement, but of emancipation." (p.333))

               Oct. 17, no. 201   Oct. 17, no. 201

Oct. 17, no. 202 ("We want the sovereignty and authority of the United States recognized in that territory as fully as it is recognized in every other territory belonging to the American government. [Applause.] The American people regret that those whom they emancipated . . . should have turned upon the soldiers of the United States, foully assaulted them, and resisted our sovereignty." (p. 336))

Oct. 18, no. 203

Oct. 18, no. 204   Oct. 18, no. 204

               Oct. 18, no. 205

Oct. 18, no. 206   Oct. 18, no. 206

Oct. 18, no. 207

Oct. 31, no. 212

Note: Speech numbers follow the date on days when more than one speech was given.
Source: Compiled from William McKinley, *Speeches and Addresses of William McKinley.*

Direct	Indirect	Direct	Indirect

NOTES

Introduction

1. "Going public" has been defined as "a strategy whereby a president promotes himself and his policies in Washington by appealing to the American public for support." Samuel Kernell, *Going Public*, 2.

2. Jeffrey K. Tulis, *The Rhetorical Presidency*, 46; James W. Ceaser, Glen E. Thurow, Jeffrey K. Tulis, and Joseph M. Bessette, "The Rise of the Rhetorical Presidency," *Presidential Studies Quarterly* 11, no. 2 (spring, 1981): 158–71, 162.

3. Ceaser et al., "Rise of the Rhetorical Presidency," 159; Tulis, *Rhetorical Presidency*, 4–6, 46–47, 59.

4. On the concept of the "plebiscitary presidency," see Theodore J. Lowi, *The Personal President*.

5. See Tulis, *Rhetorical Presidency*, chaps. 6–7. For a more recent articulation of the problem and a proposed solution, see Tulis, "Revising the Rhetorical Presidency," in *Beyond the Rhetorical Presidency*, ed. Martin J. Medhurst, 3–14.

6. See James S. Fishkin, *Democracy and Deliberation*, and Bruce Ackerman, *We the People*, vol. 1, *Foundations*.

7. Samuel Kernell, *Going Public*, 254.

8. Tulis, *Rhetorical Presidency*, 62, 64. Regarding Andrew Jackson, there is only the cryptic statement, without elaboration or supporting citations, that the President's reputation as a popular leader was based on his "informal but effective support of the administrative information organ—a newspaper dedicated to publishing the president's policy positions" (Tulis, *Rhetorical Presidency*, 74). Kernell, after defining "going public" as a strategy "whereby a president promotes himself and his policies in Washington by appealing to the American public for support," does not even mention Andrew Jackson in his survey of the history of the practice (Kernell, *Going Public*, 2; for survey, see chap. 3). Ceaser et al., in "Rise of the Rhetorical Presidency," only consider presidential communications to Congress, speeches, and proclamations as possible types of popular presidential rhetoric. In his subsequent article,

"The Rhetorical Presidency Revisited," in Marc Landy, ed., *Modern Presidents and the Presidency*, 15–34. James W. Ceaser lists only three categories of direct presidential communication: inaugural addresses; "constitutionally recognized communications" such as veto and State of the Union messages; and "presidentially initiated communications," which cover any other messages or speeches from presidents.

9. Ceaser et al. note that, while presidents produce more written documents than ever and all of their speeches are transcribed, "this matters little as few in the public ever bother to peruse, let alone read, the President's words. Significant messages are delivered today in speeches" ("Rise of the Rhetorical Presidency," 164).

10. Theodore Windt, "Presidential Rhetoric: Definition of a Discipline of Study," in *Essays in Presidential Rhetoric*, ed. Windt and Ingold, xvi. See also, Martin J. Medhurst, "Introduction, A Tale of Two Constructs: The Rhetorical Presidency Versus Presidential Rhetoric," in Medhurst, ed., *Beyond the Rhetorical Presidency*, xix.

11. Philip Abbott, "Do Presidents Talk Too Much? The Rhetorical Presidency and Its Alternative," *Presidential Studies Quarterly* 18 (1988): 353; Richard E. Neustadt, *Presidential Power and the Modern Presidents*, 11, and chap. 5.

12. See, e.g., Roderick P. Hart, *The Sound of Leadership*, 2; Amos P. Kiewe, *The Modern Presidency and Crisis Rhetoric*, xvi; John Anthony Maltese, *Spin Control*, 4; Craig Smith and Kathy Smith, *The White House Speaks*, preface.

13. For example, Tulis's essay "The Two Constitutional Presidencies" is included in *The Presidency and the Political System*, ed. Michael Nelson, a popular reader on the presidency. Another basic work by Norman Thomas, Joseph Pika, and Richard Watson, has a section on the "Rhetorical Presidency" that relies heavily on Kernell and Tulis for the assertion that "the president's relationship with the American people has . . . undergone significant changes" in the area of public communications (*The Politics of the Presidency*, 134). Yet another compilation, this one edited by James Pfiffner and Roger Davidson, contains an essay by Mark Rozell on the "Press and the Presidency" which repeats the mantra, asserting that "the framers worried about the potentially harmful consequences of public appeals by presidents," and that only in the twentieth century did a "view of presidential leadership different from that of the founding era beg[i]n to emerge." (*Understanding the Presidency*, 110) A companion essay by Fred I. Greenstein, entitled "Toward a Modern Presidency," speaks of the "transformation in the 1930s of the traditional presidency into the modern variant that is the concern of this volume" (ibid., 38). See also the assertion by Sidney M. Milkis and Michael Nelson, drawn from Tulis, that the impeachment of Andrew Johnson was due to his speechmaking to "rouse public opinion in support of his policies" which was in the nineteenth century "regarded as a violation of constitutional norms" (*The American Presidency: Origins and Development, 1776–1990*, 163).

14. Stephen Skowronek, *The Politics Presidents Make.*

15. Herbert Stein, *Presidential Economics*; Barbara Hinckley, *The Symbolic Presidency*; Skowronek, *Politics Presidents Make*, 18.

16. The most prominent of these works are: Frederic Hudson, *Journalism in the United States from 1690 to 1872*; George Henry Payne, *History of Journalism in the United States*; Willard G. Bleyer, *Main Currents in the History of American Journalism*; Frank Luther Mott, *American Journalism*; and Edwin and Michael Emery, *The Press and America*.

17. Gerald J. Baldasty's *The Press and Politics in the Age of Jackson* is excellent but only the length of a pamphlet. Culver H. Smith's *The Press, Politics, and Patronage* and Richard L. Rubin's *Press, Party, and Presidency* focus mainly on the party and patronage links that bound most newspapers to government officials for much of the nineteenth century, rather than on the specific use of these partisan newspapers by presidents to communicate with the public. As their titles suggest, James E. Pollard's *Presidents and the Press* and John Tebbel's and Sarah Miles Watts's *The Press and the Presidency* deal with the relationships between presidents and the press over the past two centuries. Both books are narrative in form, covering the presidents in chronological order, and thus are excellent research sources. However, both are also largely nonanalytical historical surveys of the relationships between individual presidents and the press.

18. See Thomas, Pika, and Watson, *Politics of the Presidency*; Marcus Cunliffe, *The Presidency*; and Milkis and Nelson, *American Presidency*.

19. I wish to acknowledge here the unfortunate reality that, as noble or inclusive as some of the dialogue and concepts discussed in this book sound, they were in fact usually limited in coverage to white males. Everything said in this book comes with that implicit qualifier.

20. For an excellent discussion of the basic differences between the two philosophies, see Julie M. Walsh, *The Intellectual Origins of Mass Parties and Schools in the Jacksonian Period*, 12–15.

21. Cf., Linda K. Kerber, *Federalists in Dissent*, 197 (For Federalists, the distinction between a democracy and a republic was that in a democracy, "'the people meet and exercise the government in person,'" while in a republic, "'they assemble and administer it by their representatives and agents.'" This was a distinction Hamilton had employed in his speech on the ideal form of government at the Constitutional Convention.) For the comparable attitude expressed a century earlier by the English Whig party leader the Earl of Shaftesbury, see Edmund S. Morgan, *Inventing the People*, 103. Madison made the same points in *Federalist Papers* nos. 10 and 39 (see Will Morrisey, "The Moral Foundations of the American Republic: An Introduction," in *The Moral Foundations of the American Republic*, ed. Robert H. Horwitz, 2).

22. Harry Jaffa, "The Nature and Origin of the American Party System," in *Political Parties, U.S.A.*, ed. Robert Goldwin, 80–81. See also James W. Ceaser, *Presidential Selection*, 85.

23. See generally, Gordon Wood, *Creation of the American Republic, 1776–1787*,

175 (quoting Edmund Burke's famous expression of the two concepts) and chaps. 9 and 12; Joseph M. Bessette, *The Mild Voice of Reason*, 40–46; John Gerring, *Party Ideologies in America, 1828–1996*, 178.

24. The concept is really one of simple "direct democracy" in decision-making and maximum participation of the common people in government. See Tulis, *Rhetorical Presidency*, 36; Bessette, *Mild Voice of Reason*, 2; Gordon Wood, *The Radicalism of the American Revolution*, 243. Jackson Turner Main states similarly that, in 1787, "democracy" meant, fundamentally, "a government controlled by the people as a whole" (*The Antifederalists*, 170).

25. Joyce Appleby, *Capitalism and a New Social Order*, 58. Gordon Wood observes that, in general, during the long and gradual transformation of "republicanism" into "something we call liberalism," the participants in that transformation, such as Jefferson, "could express simultaneously, and without any sense of inconsistency," principles from both schools of classic thought (*Creation of the American Republic*, xi). Moreover, the transformation occurred in "subtle and complicated ways that kept many republican sentiments alive" (ibid., xii). Lance Banning describes the change similarly: "The revolutionary transformation of ideas was both profound and subtle. It went forward slowly, sometimes almost imperceptibly, for more than twenty years, and few were able to adjust to all its implications at once. There was no sudden break with eighteenth-century tradition. Instead, there was a gradual transition attained by different individuals with different speeds—or not at all" (*The Jeffersonian Persuasion*, 99). Cf., Stanley Elkins and Eric McKitrick, *The Age of Federalism*, 13. Sometimes, the transition was aided by the rewriting of the intellectual history of the Constitution, as Madison began to do in 1800 (Robert H. Wiebe, *The Opening of American Society*, 111–12).

Chapter 1. Just Whose Constitution Is It, Anyway?

1. Elkins and McKitrick, *Age of Federalism*, 22.
2. Charles Thach, *The Creation of the American Presidency*, 140. See also Glenn A. Phelps, "George Washington and the Founding of the Presidency," *Presidential Studies Quarterly* 17 (1987): 345–63. This vagueness is "perhaps the greatest concession the Convention made" to Alexander Hamilton, according to James MacGregor Burns, *Presidential Government*, 25.
3. Ralph Ketcham, *Presidents Above Party*, 8, 9. See, e.g., Thach, *Creation of the American Presidency*, 117–18.
4. Clinton Rossiter, *Alexander Hamilton and the Constitution*, 71; Jack N. Rakove, *Original Meanings*, 245, 256, 280. For a detailed discussion of this point, see ibid., chap. 8.
5. Jacob Ernest Cooke, *Alexander Hamilton*, 110; Milkis and Nelson, *American Presidency*, 69; Rossiter, *Alexander Hamilton*, 75 (1st quote); Rakove, *Original Meanings*, 283 (2d quote). See also James Thomas Flexner, *George Washington and the New Nation*, 406.

6. Milkis and Nelson, *American Presidency*, 72–73; Banning, *Jeffersonian Persuasion*, 118. See also Marcus Cunliffe, *George Washington, Man and Monument*, 155–56.

7. See "Responding to Britain's Sorrow, Queen Will Address the Nation," *New York Times*, Sept. 5, 1997. According to this article, "a Queen making a major speech other than the ceremonial Christmas greeting or the reading before the opening session of each Parliament of the Government's legislative goals is a departure from tradition." Queen Elizabeth's short address to the nation on Diana's death was only the third speech by her in nontraditional circumstances in the 1990s.

8. Thach, *Creation of the American Presidency*, 146; Milkis and Nelson, *American Presidency*, 76.

9. Cunliffe, *George Washington*, 161; Milkis and Nelson, *American Presidency*, 79, 83.

10. Milkis and Nelson, *American Presidency*, 79. See also Rossiter, *Alexander Hamilton*, 85, 292; Cooke, *Alexander Hamilton*, 128, Milkis and Nelson, *American Presidency*, 81; Morton J. Frisch, "Executive Power and Representative Government–1787," *Presidential Studies Quarterly* 17 (1987), 287–88.

11. Flexner, *George Washington and the New Nation*, 279, 280. See also Marie B. Hecht, *Odd Destiny*, 183.

12. Flexner, *George Washington and the New Nation*, 280; Thach, *Creation of the American Presidency*, 105; *Federalist Paper no. 44*, in *The Federalist Papers*, ed. Clinton Rossiter, 285. Curiously, in 1801 Hamilton wrote that, in the Washington administration, Jefferson had supported a "large construction" of the Constitution (see H. C. Syrett, ed, *The Papers of Alexander Hamilton*, 25:319).

13. See generally, Rossiter, *Alexander Hamilton*, 200–201.

14. Forrest McDonald, *The Presidency of Thomas Jefferson*, 130; Robert Allen Rutland, *The Presidency of James Madison*, 205. James Monroe shared these attitudes. See Noble E. Cunningham Jr., *The Presidency of James Monroe*, 46.

15. Letter to J. K. Paulding, Apr., 1831, quoted in Rossiter, *Alexander Hamilton*, 111–12.

16. Main, *Antifederalists*, 249; Henry quoted in Wilfred E. Binkley, *American Political Parties*, 59; Ackerman, *We the People*, 2:160; Forrest McDonald, *Novus Ordo Seclorum*, 185–87; Gordon S. Wood, "Interests and Disinterestedness in the Making of the Constitution," in *Beyond Confederation*, ed. Richard Beeman et al., 107. Wilfred Binkley points out that thirty-five of the thirty-nine signers of the Constitution "lived adjacent to salt water," an indication that "the regions where the opposition lived were greatly under-represented" (*American Political Parties*, 61).

17. Main, *Antifederalists*, 116, 117, 187, and chaps. 6–11.

18. See David J. Siemers, "It is Natural to Care for the Crazy Machine: The Antifederalists' Post-Ratification Acquiescence," *Studies in American Political Development* 12, (summer, 1998): 383–410. Not that all Antifederalists accepted their loss quietly, however. See Saul Cornell, *The Other Founders, 1788–*

1828, 110–20, for an account of the Antifederalist riot that broke out in Carlisle, Pennsylvania, when Federalists tried to celebrate the ratification of the Constitution by the state ratification convention.

19. Banning, *Jeffersonian Persuasion*, 106; see also Wiebe, *Opening of American Society*, 27. As one scholar puts it, "The Constitution itself did not have to be displaced since it did not prevent pursuit" of the goals of the Anti-Federalists and their immediate successors, the Democratic-(Jeffersonian)-Republicans (Walsh, *Intellectual Origins*, 46). The ambiguity of the language used in the Constitution was a common criticism of the document by Antifederalists (Cornell, *Other Founders*, 59). Moreover, "The will of the nation having been declared, Anti-Federalists immediately accepted the Constitution and assumed a positive and aggressive attitude as to the interpretation of the document" (Jesse Macy, *Political Parties in the United States 1846–1861*, 47). Cf., Joseph J. Ellis, *American Sphinx*, 121: "The Constitution, in short, did not resolve the long-standing political disagreements that existed within the revolutionary generation so much as establish a fresh and more stable context within which they could be argued out." Richard Ellis has similarly observed that "the Constitution as written and ratified was only a frame of government; actual policies still had to be formulated and implemented" (*The Jeffersonian Crisis*, 271). See also the words of Benjamin Rush in 1786: "we have only finished the first act of the great drama. We have changed our forms of government, but it remains yet to effect a Revolution in our principles, opinions, and manners to accommodate them to the forms of government we have adopted" (quoted in ibid., 268). Finally, Robert Wiebe uses a similar metaphor in describing how, by the 1840s, the democratic revolution had left "almost nothing of the revolutionary gentry's venture except the shell of their Constitution" (*Opening of American Society*, xii).

20. Banning, *Jeffersonian Persuasion*, 202.

21. See Michael McGerr, *The Decline of Popular Politics*, chap. 2. Indeed, one may properly wonder whose view of the Constitution got ratified when the Constitution was approved by the states. For example, several states did not ratify the Constitution until they had been assured that the document would promptly be amended to include a Bill of Rights, a prominent demand of the Antifederalists. Does that mean that the Antifederalists' interpretation of the Constitution was dominant in those ratifying states?

22. Tulis, *Rhetorical Presidency*, 26; Bessette, *Mild Voice of Reason*, 2. Cf., Main, *Antifederalists*, 117 ("The Constitution did not, therefore, represent the views or the influence even of the moderate Antifederalists"). Saul Cornell makes this argument in the title of his outstanding study of the impact of the Antifederalist movement on American political thought from 1788 to 1828: *The Other Founders*. For a brilliant discussion of the idea (or perhaps more accurately, ideal) of Constitutional Originalism, see Rakove, *Original Meanings*, chap. 11. See also, Albert Furtwangler, *The Authority of Publius: A Reading of the Federalist Papers*, 84–85.

23. Siemers, "It Is Natural to Care," 407; Rakove, *Original Meanings*, 339–40.

24. Wood, *Radicalism of the American Revolution*, 32; cf., Bernard Bailyn, *The Ideological Origins of the American Revolution*, 331: "The identity between antifederalist thought and that of the most fervent ideologists of '76 is at times astonishing." The discussion of Antifederalist thought presented here focuses on one of the two major elements of that thought, direct democratic control of the government. The other major element not discussed here was the desirability of a weak central government. The two elements are connected in that concentrated power was thought to lead to aristocracy and diffused power to democratic rule. See Main, *Antifederalists*, xiv, 130. The discussion here also focuses on what Saul Cornell calls populist Antifederalism, as distinguished from elite Antifederalism, which shared the Federalists' elitist notions of class and a "natural aristocracy" whose members were the only ones fit to govern in a republican society. See Cornell, *Other Founders*, chap. 2.

25. Kerber, *Federalists in Dissent*, ix.

26. Appleby, *Capitalism and a New Social Order*, 9; Wood, *Radicalism of the American Revolution*, 27, 25; David Hackett Fischer, *The Revolution of American Conservatism*, 37; Appleby, *Capitalism and a New Social Order*, 12, 68, 21; Richard Hofstadter, "The Founding Fathers: An Age of Realism," in *Moral Foundations of the American Republic*, ed. Horwitz, 113; Bailyn, *Ideological Origins*, 318; Hofstadter, "Founding Fathers," 67. See also Main, *Antifederalists*, 4; J. G. A. Pocock, *The Machiavellian Moment*, 531.

27. Wood, *Radicalism of the American Revolution*, 58, 103–108. Wood, citing Edmund Burke's description of the English Parliament: "Parliament is a *deliberative* assembly of *one* nation, with *one* interest, that of the whole, where, not local purposes, not local prejudices ought to guide, but the general good, resulting from the general reason of the whole" (*Creation of the American Republic*, 175). Some upward mobility into the upper class "gentleman" rank was possible for a few especially talented individuals (ibid., 180). See also Appleby, *Capitalism and a New Social Order*, 59; Elkins and McKitrick, *Age of Federalism*, 750, Main, *Antifederalists*, 3.

28. Fischer, *Revolution of American Conservatism*, 151–52. It is instructive that one of the more popular pseudonyms used by Federalists was "Phocion," the name of an Athenian statesman who, according to Plutarch, was famous for his prudence and rectitude and was reelected forty-five times despite always being absent for the election and never saying anything to win the people's favor (see Kerber, *Federalists in Dissent*, 9). Cotton Mather's 1702 dismissive reference to the "crime of popularity" conveys a similar sense of the classic attitude toward the general public (Hofstadter, "Founding Fathers," 186).

29. Wood, *Radicalism of the American Revolution*, 175, 372–83; Appleby, *Capitalism and a New Social Order*, 63, 70, 73; Wiebe, *Opening of American Society*, 38; Fischer, *Revolution of American Conservatism*, 4 (representatives to be a "'speaking Aristocracy in the face of a silent Democracy'"), 134, 227 ("After

the French Revolution, older Federalists rarely disguised their contempt for democracy, political parties, popular opinion, and all the paraphernalia of Jeffersonian politics. Younger Federalists sought to use Jeffersonian ideas and innovations for their own elitist purposes—partisanship, popular rhetoric, libertarian ideology, the ideal of minimal government.")

30. Appleby, *Capitalism and a New Social Order,* 97; Wood, "Interests and Disinterestedness," 83, and *Radicalism of the American Revolution,* 256.

31. Wood, "Interests and Disinterestedness," 100–101, and *Radicalism of the American Revolution,* 294, 363–64. See ibid., 255–59, for Wood's account of the debate on this point in the Pennsylvania Assembly in 1786, which he describes as perhaps the "crucial moment in the history of America politics."

32. Wood, "Interests and Disinterestedness," 83, 102, 109; Richard Beeman, "Beyond Confederation: Introduction," in *Beyond Confederation,* ed. Beeman et al., 10; Cornell, *Other Founders,* 81, 111, 115.

33. Jefferson to William Say, Feb. 1, 1804, quoted in Appleby, *Capitalism and a New Social Order,* 97; Main, *Antifederalists,* 11; Wood, *Radicalism of the American Revolution,* 259, 364, 371. See also idem., "The Democratization of Mind in the American Revolution," in *Moral Foundations of the American Republic,* ed. Horwitz, 133. For discussions of the evolving radicalness of the meaning of "popular sovereignty" in America in the 1770s, see Bailyn, *Ideological Origins,* chap. 6, and Wood, *Creation of the American Republic,* chap. 9.

34. W. B. Allen and Gordon Lloyd, eds., *The Essential Antifederalist,* 138.

35. Kerber, *Federalists in Dissent,* ix; Main, *Antifederalists,* 105; Elkins and McKitrick, *Age of Federalism,* 11; Wood, "Democratization of Mind," 120–24, and "Interests and Disinterestedness," 76–77. See also Kerber, *Federalists in Dissent,* 179–81.

36. Wood, *Creation of the American Republic,* chap. 9; Morgan, *Inventing the People,* 267 (With the "remedy" of the U.S. Constitution, "Madison was inventing a sovereign people to overcome the sovereign states."); Joyce Appleby, "The Constitution and the Culture of Constitutionalism," in *Understanding the United States Constitution,* 1–13; Main, *Antifederalists,* 105–106. See also Wood, "Interests and Disinterestedness," 72–81; Hofstadter, "Founding Fathers," 63–65; and the excellent set of essays by Wood, Ann Stuart Diamond, Michael, Walter Berns, Wilson Carey McWilliams, Joseph M. Bessette, and Alfred F. Young in Robert A. Goldwin and William A. Schambra, eds., *How Democratic Is the Constitution?*

37. Wood, *Creation of the American Republic,* 476.

38. Wood, *Radicalism of the American Revolution,* 254–55, 261, 512–14. See also idem., *Creation of the American Republic,* chap. 12; Ceaser, *Presidential Selection,* 48–49.

39. Edmund S. Morgan, *The Birth of the Republic, 1763–89,* 148; Morgan, *Inventing the People,* 277–79; McDonald, *Novus Ordo Seclorum,* 209; Banning, *Jeffersonian Persuasion,* 103. Elkins and McKitrick provide an excellent overview of current scholarship on the intellectual history of the Constitution

(*Age of Federalism*, 3–29). For a magisterial exposition of the centuries of political thought underpinning the English political system, see Pocock, *Machiavellian Moment*. In chapter 15, Pocock discusses how this tradition was
translated from classic republicanism into a "new paradigm of democratic
politics" in America (ibid., 517). Appleby notes that "Federalists insisted that
American institutions were but improvements upon old forms, particularly
those of England," while Antifederalists and then Democratic-Republicans
"exaggerated the unparalled novelty of American constitutions and used
that novelty as proof of the possibility of dramatic social change" (*Capitalism
and a New Social Order*, 86).

40. Wood, *Radicalism of the American Revolution*, 255; Morgan, *Inventing the
People*, 277, 338 (Patrick Henry's condemnation of representation under
the new Constitution as nothing more than the English system of "virtual
representation" rejected in the American Revolution), 348; Cornell, *Other
Founders*, 101; Allen and Lloyd, *Essential Antifederalist*, 139 (proposed Constitution a threat to popular sovereignty unless presidents and senators made
more responsible to the people or the people's immediate representatives);
Banning, *Jeffersonian Persuasion*, 193. See also Wood, "Interests and Disinterestedness," 93–101, "Democratization of Mind," 122–23 (Federalists at Constitutional Convention anticipate attacks on Constitution based on its alleged
aristocratic nature); Cornell, *Other Founders*, 40–41, 107; Main,
Antifederalists, 132–34.

41. Wood, *Creation of the American Republic*, 516.

42. Ceaser, *Presidential Selection*, 51, 59.

43. See Main, *Antifederalists*, chaps. 9–11; Morgan, *Birth of the Republic*, chap. 11;
and Rakove, *Original Meanings*, chap. 5, for excellent state-by-state overviews
of the ratification machinations. For a map illustrating the wide variation
across the United States in support for the proposed Constitution, see Cornell,
Other Founders, 23. See Main, *Antifederalists*, chaps. 2 and 3, for a survey of
divisions in the states before the new Constitution was proposed. In the
battle, the Federalists strategically outmatched the Antifederalists. The Federalists made numerous clever moves, some of which merit mention here.
First, in providing that the proposed Constitution would take effect upon ratification by nine out of the thirteen states, the Federalists ignored the provi-
sion in the Articles of Confederation that the national system of government
agreed to by the states could only be changed unanimously (Ackerman, *We the
People*, 2:34, 53). They also, of course, ignored their basic charge to meet and
develop proposed *amendments* to the Articles of Confederation (Main,
Antifederalists, 126; Ackerman, *We the People*, 2:35). Second, the Federalists
chose specially called state conventions as the mechanism for ratification, with
delegates to be elected in elections that the Federalists could influence, rather
than the existing state legislatures, which had large numbers of Antifederalist
representatives (Morgan, *Birth of the Republic*, 143; Ackerman, *We the People*,
2:57–58, 160). Third, the Federalists exaggerated the economic and social

problems in the young nation so as to make it appear that conditions were so desperate that only drastic, speedy alterations in the government would suffice (Main, *Antifederalists*, 177–79, 187–89, 251 [for Federalist "disinformation" efforts]). Finally, Federalists worked—most famously through the *Federalist Papers*—to get their proratification articles published in newspapers throughout the country while at the same time suppressing the publication of Antifederalist writings (Cornell, *Other Founders*, 46, 104; Morgan, *Birth of the Republic*, 151; Main, *Antifederalists*, 188–89, 198–99, 201, 209 n 64, 210, 217, 221, 236, 250 [Antifederalist complaints about delays in delivery of newspapers]).

44. Wood, *Radicalism of the American Revolution*, 259.

45. Richard Loss, *The Modern Theory of Presidential Power*, 24–25. However, another scholar asserts the *Federalist Papers* "actually had little value as propaganda" because there were too many of them and they were too hard to understand (Linda Grant De Pauw, *The Eleventh Pillar*, 114). Elbridge Gerry dismissed the *Federalist Papers* as a work of "political heresy, calculated to lull the conscience of those who differed in opinion with him at that time; and having accomplished his object, he is probably desirous that it may die with the opposition itself" (Cornell, *Other Founders*, 189).

46. Tulis, *Rhetorical Presidency*, 19, 26–27; Jefferson quoted in De Pauw, *Eleventh Pillar*, 66. See also Ceaser, Thurow, Tulis, and Bissette, "Rise of the Rhetorical Presidency."

47. Furtwangler, *Authority of Publius*, 35. See ibid., 42–43, for a similar argument.

48. Elkins and McKitrick, *Age of Federalism*, 23.

49. *Federalist Paper no. 49*, in *The Federalist Papers*, ed. Clinton Rossiter.

50. Ibid., 313.

51. See *Federalist Paper no. 43*, ibid., 276.

52. *Federalist Paper no. 1*, ibid., 35.

53. *Federalist Paper no. 10*, ibid., 79–80, 82.

54. *Federalist Paper no. 63*, ibid., 384.

55. *Federalist Paper no. 71*, ibid., 432.

56. *Federalist Paper no. 85*, ibid., 527.

57. *Federalist Paper no. 58*, ibid., 360; Ceaser et al., "Rise of the Rhetorical Presidency," 161 n 12.

58. Ceaser, in his discussion of *Federalist Papers* 59 and 48, does acknowledge that the references to leadership in those papers do not occur "in the context of a direct reference to the presidency" (*Presidential Selection*, 60).

59. Tulis, *Rhetorical Presidency*, 30; Ceaser, *Presidential Selection*, 56–57.

60. *Federalist Paper no. 71*, in *Federalist Papers*, ed. Rossiter, 434.

61. For a thorough discussion by Hamilton of this point, see *Federalist Paper no. 71*.

62. See Furtwangler, *Authority of Publius*, 23–33; Rakove, *Original Meanings*, 287, 350.

63. De Pauw, *Eleventh Pillar*, 109; Furtwangler, *Authority of Publius*, 86–87 (emphasis in original).

64. Cf., Rakove, *Original Meanings*, 283, referring to Hamilton's "exploitation of the ambiguity of Article II" of the Constitution in his "ambivalent" Federalist Papers on the executive.

65. Elkins and McKitrick view the *Federalist Papers* as representing "in aggregate the outer bounds as well as the central substance of what their authors conceived was the claim they could make—the object being above all persuasion—on their readers experience, aspirations, and habits of thought" (*Age of Federalism*, 22).

66. Madison to Jefferson, Feb. 8, 1825, quoted in Furtwangler, *Authority of Publius*, 38.

67. Rakove, *Original Meanings*, 280. Determining who can properly be called the partisan forebears of today's Democratic and Republican Parties can get quite confusing if one focuses on particular individuals or state and local party organizations. However, if the focus is on ideology, the lineage of the two parties becomes quite clear, as John Gerring has shown in *Party Ideologies in America*. Cf., Mark A. Graber, "Federalist or Friends of Adams: The Marshall Court and Party Politics," *Studies in American Political Development* 12, no. 2 (fall, 1998): 229–66; Jeffrey A. Jenkins, "Why No Parties? Investigating the Disappearance of Democrat-Whig Divisions in the Confederacy," *Studies in American Political Development* 13, no. 2 (fall, 1999): 245–62.

68. See Wood, *Radicalism of the American Revolution*, 262–70; Cornell, *Other Founders*, 147–53; Banning, *Jeffersonian Persuasion*, 153–59, 165.

69. Cornell, *Other Founders*, 191, and chap. 6; Banning, *Jeffersonian Persuasion*, 114 n 45; Ellis, *Jeffersonian Crisis*, 274, 342 n 20; Siemers, "It Is Natural to Care," 409–10. Governor George Clinton of New York, a leader of the state's Antifederalists in their battle against the ratification of the Constitution, wound up as the Jeffersonian-Republicans nominee for vice president against the Federalists' John Adams in 1792. The Federalists made much of this Antifederalist association in the campaign (James Roger Sharp, *American Politics in the Early Republic: The New Nation in Crisis*, 57–58). Madison, in an essay published in 1792 in the *National Gazette*, traced Republicanism back to Antifederalism (Elkins and McKitrick, *Age of Federalism*, 269).

70. Fischer, *Revolution of American Conservatism*, 160 and note 42; Cornell, *Other Founders*, 190 (discussing Madison's evolution). Perhaps most notably, as James Roger Sharp has pointed out, Madison's view of the role of public opinion in governmental affairs seems to have moved quite a bit toward the Antifederalist view. In *Federalist Paper* no. 49, Madison had warned that frequent appeals to the public on constitutional matters was undesirable, but by early 1792, he was arguing—in the pages of the *National Gazette*—that "enlightened public sentiment" was critical to keeping the national government on its proper course (Sharp, *American Politics in the Early Republic*, 45).

71. David Waldstreicher, "Federalism, the Styles of Politics, and the Politics of Style," in *Federalists Reconsidered*, ed. Doron Ben-Atar and Barbara B. Oberg, 105; Donald H. Stewart, *The Opposition Press of the Federalist Period*, 6, 431

(Republicans were convinced that "the judgment of many was in the long run infinitely superior to the caprice of the single individual," 438 (faith in the "ultimate wisdom of the masses"); Appleby, *Capitalism and a New Social Order*, chap. 4; Sharp, *American Politics in the Early Republic*, 66.

72. Andrew Siegel, "The Defense of Federalism in Connecticut," in *Federalists Reconsidered*, ed. Ben-Atar and Oberg, 205; Kerber, *Federalists in Dissent*, 175–81, 194; Stewart, *Opposition Press*, 425–26; Elkins and McKitrick, *Age of Federalism*, 456; Main, *Antifederalists*, 170. See Fischer, *Revolution of American Conservatism*, 34; Cornell, *Other Founders*, chap. 6. On the wide variation in meanings of, and attitudes toward, the word "democracy," see Main, *Antifederalists*, 169–70.

73. Appleby, *Capitalism and a New Social Order*, 4, 6, 22, 58, 74; Elkins and McKitrick, *Age of Federalism*, 456; Fischer, *Revolution of American Conservatism*, 160; Cornell, *Other Founders*, 173.

74. Appleby, *Capitalism and a New Social Order*, 56; James Jasinski, "Rhetoric and Judgment in the Constitutional Ratification Debates of 1787–1788," *Quarterly Journal of Speech* 78, no. 2 (May, 1992): 197–218. Outstanding examples of how Federalists thought that, due to their elevated status in the natural order of society, they were "above" personal electioneering can be found in Alan Taylor, "From Fathers to Friends of the People: Political Personae in the Early Republic," in *Federalists Reconsidered*, ed. Ben-Atar and Oberg, 237–39. In one, from 1792, a Federalist judge says to a man who refused the Federalist ballot handed to him, "What, then young man, you will not vote as I would have you. You are a fool, young man, for you cannot know how to vote as well as I can direct you, for I am a man in public office."

75. Elkins and McKitrick, *Age of Federalism*, 750. The partisan composition of the House of Representatives changed dramatically in the 1800 election. The 1799 House was Federalist by a 63–43 margin, whereas the Democratic-Republicans had a 65–41 edge in the 1801 House.

76. Letter to Spencer Roane, Sept. 6, 1819, in Ford, ed., *Works of Thomas Jefferson*, 12:136. This letter is quoted and discussed in Wood, *Radicalism of the American Revolution*, 328. The defeated Federalists saw their loss in equally stark terms: the *Gazette of the United States* announced the election results in a black-bordered issue with the headline, "ALL IS LOST" (Kerber, *Federalists in Dissent*, 163).

77. Letter to William Short, Jan. 8, 1824, in Ford, ed., *Works of Thomas Jefferson*, 12:396. See Fischer, *Revolution of American Conservatism*, 182–87, 197; Kerber, *Federalists in Dissent*, 161.

78. Wood, "Democratization of Mind," 132. See also idem., *Radicalism of the American Revolution*, 363.

79. Walsh, *Intellectual Origins*, 47. For a similar analysis that employs the terms "egalitarian republicanism" and "republicanism," see ibid., 12–15, 46–61. Looking back on what he had wrought, Thomas Jefferson in 1816 said: "the introduction of this new principle of representative democracy has rendered

useless almost everything written before on the structure of government, and in a great measure relieves our regret, if the political writings of Aristotle, or of any other ancient have been lost" (quoted in Appleby, *Capitalism and a New Social Order,* 84).

80. Quoted in Richard J. Ellis, *American Political Cultures,* 67. Such an approach may seem unrealistically simplistic by current standards as a way for dealing with the plethora of complicated and detailed policy decisions that must be made at the national level, and certainly contrasts with the involved national legislative process as it exists today. See, e.g., John W. Kingdon, *Agendas, Alternatives, and Public Policies.* However, especially when a president's or party's agenda is largely negative, as it was for Democrats vis-à-vis the federal government in the nineteenth century, further debate at the national level would indeed seem pointless (see Gerring, *Party Ideologies in America,* 171). Even now, many Americans probably feel that, for some issues at least (such as abortion), debate in Washington accomplishes very little.

81. Fischer, *Revolution of American Conservatism,* 198; quotes in Gerring, *Party Ideologies in America,* 178. See also ibid., 86.

82. Marcus Cunliffe, *American Presidents and the Presidency,* 141–57; Howe, *Political Culture,* 30–31, 76, 89; Schlesinger, *Age of Jackson,* 38, 275; Gerring, *Party Ideologies in America,* 86, 179 (quoting 1868 Democratic party platform's warning against the "usurpations of Congress."); Johnstone, *Jefferson and the Presidency,* 40–57; Richard J. Ellis, "Introduction," in *Speaking to the People,* ed. Richard J. Ellis, 13; Binkley, *President and Congress,* preface; Ford, *Works of Thomas Jefferson,* 1:134. Active in determining war policy, Lincoln was often quite deferential to Congress in other policy areas (see Sandburg, *Abraham Lincoln,* 4:561; Holt, *Political Parties,* 331; Cunliffe, *Presidency,* 153).

83. Ellis, *American Political Cultures,* 67.

84. Gerring, *Party Ideologies in America,* 121. By 1815, Federalists in Pennsylvania had become "Federal Republicans" (Rosemarie Zagarri, "Gender and the First Party System," in *Federalists Reconsidered,* Ben-Atar and Oberg, 118). After 1800, Federalists felt their original party name had been so discredited that they began casting about for a new name (Fischer, *Revolution of American Conservatism,* 34). The topic of "Federalists in Opposition" after the triumph of the Jeffersonian Republicans in 1800 has been the subject of some excellent scholarly study. See, in general, Fischer, *Revolution of American Conservatism,* and Ben-Atar and Oberg, eds., *Federalists Reconsidered.*

85. Ceaser, *Presidential Selection,* 165–66; Gerring, *Party Ideologies in America,* 109, 120; E. Malcolm Carroll, *Origins of the Whig Party,* 3, 197–99, 202, 204–208 (citing de Tocqueville); Binkley, *American Political Parties,* chap. 7; Daniel Walker Howe, *The Political Culture of the American Whigs.* It should be noted that until the early 1820s, even most Federalists identified themselves as Republicans. Factionalism split the Republicans into what eventually were to become the Whig and Democratic Parties (Binkley, *American Political Parties,* 98–99, 216; Jenkins, "Why No Parties?" 247). In 1816, Monroe wrote a letter

to Andrew Jackson explaining that he was excluding Federalists from appointive positions in his administration because some of them still "entertained principles unfriendly to our system" (quoted in Ketcham, *Presidents Above Party*, 126). In his diary, James K. Polk refers to Whigs as the "federal party" (Cunliffe, *Presidency*, 101).

86. Morgan, *Inventing the People*, 103; Siegel, "Steady Habits under Siege," in *Federalists Reconsidered*, ed. Ben-Atar and Oberg, 219.

87. Gerring, *Party Ideologies in America*, 57, 82–83 (Federalist influence), 86–87.

88. Ibid., 87. The elements of presidential election rhetoric studied by Gerring were "speeches, party platforms, and other campaign tracts disseminated by party leaders during presidential campaigns." Ralph Ketcham notes that some delegates to the Constitutional Convention extensively discussed such "Whiggish views" of legislative superiority (*Presidents Above Party*, 114–15, 120).

89. Morgan, *Inventing the People*, 120, 224, 267; David K. Nichols, *The Myth of the Modern Presidency*, 147–48; Albert Furtwangler, *American Silhouettes*, 41; Wilfred E. Binkley, *President and Congress*, 171; Leonard D. White, *The Jacksonians*, 6–7, 22, 27–28; Gerring, *Party Ideologies in America*, 87–88.

90. Quoted in Binkley, *President and Congress*, 125 (emphasis added).

91. Ford, ed., *Works of Thomas Jefferson*, 1:134; quoted in Binkley, *President and Congress*, 126. Active in determining war policy, Lincoln was often quite deferential to Congress in other policy areas. See Michael F. Holt, *Political Parties and American Political Development*, 331; Cunliffe, *Presidency*, 84–85, 153; Howe, *Political Culture*, 274–75.

92. Gerring, *Party Ideologies in America*, 92; Milkis and Nelson, *American Presidency*, 131. The fundamental disagreements between Whigs and Democrats over several aspects of the presidency, including the veto power and the president's status as the direct representative of the people, are discussed in White, *Jacksonians*, chap. 2.

93. Quoted in White, *Jacksonians*, 21.

94. Binkley, *American Political Parties*, 169, 173. On the evolution of the parties in general, see Ellis, *Jeffersonian Crisis*, 283–84 and the works cited there. On the ideological continuity of the Federalist-Whig-Republican and Antifederalist–Jeffersonian Republican–Democratic Parties, see Gerring, *Party Ideologies in America*, and Ronald P. Formisano, *The Transformation of Political Culture*, chap. 12. On the Whig-Republican connection, see Howe, *Political Culture*; Edgar E. Robinson, *The Evolution of American Political Parties*, 156; Jenkins, "Why No Parties?" 248–49. Richard Beeman notes that the same debates over strict versus broad construction of the Constitution divided not only Federalists and Republicans but, later, Democrats and Whigs ("Beyond Confederation: Introduction," 16). Gerring makes the same point (*Party Ideologies in America*, 12, 170).

95. See Morgan, *Inventing the People*, 259–60; Pocock, *Machiavellian Moment*, 518–19; and Ketcham, *Presidents Above Party*, chaps. 3–4, 8, and pp. 207–

208, for the intellectual history of this concept. For an illuminating exposition based on the writings of Cicero, see Robert Hariman, *Political Style*, chap. 4. See also Glen E. Thurow, "Dimensions of Presidential Character," in *Beyond the Rhetorical Presidency*, ed. Medhurst, 15–29; James Jasinski, "Rhetoric and Judgment in the Constitutional Ratification Debate of 1787–1788: An Exploration of the Relationship Between Theory and Critical Practice," *Quarterly Journal of Speech* 78 (1992): 197–218; idem., "The Forms and Limits of Prudence in Henry Clay's (1850) Defense of the Compromise Measures," *Quarterly Journal of Speech* 81 (1995): 454–78.

96. Ketcham, *Presidents Above Party*, 89; Bailyn, *Ideological Origins*, 44–54; Wood, *Radicalism of the American Revolution*, 103–109; Furtwangler, *American Silhouettes*, 78.

97. Robert A. Ferguson, *Laws and Letters in American Culture*, 74; Cicero, *De Officiis*, 1.124, quoted in Hariman, *Political Style*, 117; Cicero, *Orator*, 71, quoted in ibid., 106.

98. Hariman, *Political Style*, 96, 102, 107, 110–11, 117, 121, 122, 123–24. See also Howe, *Political Culture*, 27. For an illuminating discussion of the profound influence of the classic Ciceronian hero Cato on Washington and many other Americans during the revolutionary times, see Furtwangler, *American Silhouettes*, 64–84.

99. Appleby, *Capitalism and a New Social Order*, 70. Stephen E. Lucas employs this terminology in *Portents of Rebellion*, 254–62.

Chapter 2. The Presidential Newspaper: The Forgotten Way of Going Public

1. Alexis de Tocqueville, *Democracy in America*, vol. 2, pt. 2, p. 517.

2. Bleyer, *Main Currents*, 105.

3. The 1850 census identified only five percent of the papers in the country as "neutral" or "independent." Mott, *American Journalism*, 216.

4. William T. Laprade, "The Power of the English Press in the Eighteenth Century," in *Highlights in the History of the American Press*, ed. Edwin H. Ford and Edwin Emery, 38–39. France has the same tradition; Richelieu, Louis XIII, Guizot, and Napoleon all wrote for French papers (Hudson, *Journalism in the United States*, xxxviii).

5. Arthur Aspinal, *Politics and the Press c. 1780–1850*, 5.

6. Ibid., 24–27.

7. Thomas C. Leonard, *News for All*, 7. One newspaper found that 506 persons in 107 families were reading the twenty-two issues of the paper being sent to one post office regularly (ibid., 15).

8. Mott, *American Journalism*, 59, 63, 71, 107 (quotation), 108.

9. Stewart, *Opposition Press*, 13, 16, 19, 20, 630 (Nemours quotation). Newspapers of the time achieved their popularity despite their modest appearance: "nearly all were somber 'single sheets,' folded but once and thus limited to four pages. Paper was scarce and of uneven quality; of durable rag content,

it was usually rough, inevitably costly, and frequently had a grayish or even bluish cast. Type, set by the individual printer, ran to a variety of sizes, some of which were appreciably smaller than that used in today's classified advertising. Sheepskin bags, or 'ink balls,' dipped in home-mixed ink were used to spread the fluid as evenly as possible on the set type after it was locked in place; the actual printing was accomplished by placing a sheet of paper on the type, protecting it with a layer of cloth, and using a long handle to force a large wood block down upon the cloth" (ibid., 14–15).

10. Cooke, *Alexander Hamilton*, 110; Mott, *American Journalism*, 122; Rubin, *Press, Party, and Presidency*, 10.

11. Tebbel and Watts, *Press and the Presidency*, 10; Payne, *History of Journalism*, 155; Smith, *Press, Politics, and Patronage*, 13, 14; Rubin, *Press, Party, and Presidency*, 12; Cooke, *Alexander Hamilton*, 119; Hamilton to Theodore Sedgwick, Feb. 2, 1799, in *The Works of Alexander Hamilton*, ed. Henry Cabot Lodge, 10:340. See also Claude G. Bowers, *Jefferson and Hamilton*, 154.

12. Thomas Jefferson to Van Buren, June 29, 1824, quoted in Martin Van Buren, *Inquiry into the Origin and Course of Political Parties*, 430.

13. Ford, ed, *Works of Thomas Jefferson*, 5:336. See Bleyer, *Main Currents*, 109.

14. Payne, *History of Journalism*, 161; Stewart, *Opposition Press*, 16; quoted in Smith, *Press, Politics, and Patronage*, 15; Bleyer, *Main Currents*, 109; Elkins and McKitrick, *Age of Federalism*, 285–86 (citing Jefferson to Washington, Sept. 9, 1792). Jefferson also denied any connection with the attacks on administration policy that began appearing in the paper (Wiebe, *Opening of American Society*, 102).

15. *Independent Chronicle*, Sept. 12, 1792, quoted in Bowers, *Jefferson and Hamilton*, 155.

16. Smith, *Press, Politics, and Patronage*, 15–16; Stewart, *Opposition Press*, 613–14.

17. Cooke, *Alexander Hamilton*, 119 (first quote); James Thomas Flexner, *George Washington: Anguish and Farewell*, 382; Broadus Mitchell, *Alexander Hamilton*, 212 (second quote). Although he earlier in life had denied it under oath, the editor of the Philadelphia *National Gazette* late in life asserted that Jefferson had been responsible for some of the fiercest Antifederalist articles in that newspaper (Tebbel and Watts, *Press and the Presidency*, 11). For an exhaustive survey of the evidence on Jefferson, see Stewart, *Opposition Press*, 8, and 853 n 28.

18. Cooke, *Alexander Hamilton*, 128; Rossiter, *Alexander Hamilton*, 85, 292 n 79. See Frisch, "Executive Power," 287–88.

19. Ford, ed., *Works of Thomas Jefferson*, 6:338; Pollard, *Presidents and Press*, 61.

20. Cooke, *Alexander Hamilton*, 129. Madison argued that the legislature had to at least be an "integral and preeminent" part of making foreign policy, and that "in foreign as in domestic matters . . . republican government required that the president's power be confined to the execution of laws." See also Banning, *Jeffersonian Persuasion*, 166 n 9; Elkins and McKitrick, *Age of Federalism*, 266–70; and Mitchell, *Alexander Hamilton*, 234–35.

21. John C. Fitzpatrick, ed., *Writings of George Washington,* 31:189. See also Flexner, *George Washington: Anguish and Farewell,* 382.

22. Ford, ed., *Works of Thomas Jefferson,* 12:176; Mitchell, *Alexander Hamilton,* 215; Banning, *Jeffersonian Persuasion,* 172–75.

23. Mitchell, *Alexander Hamilton,* 216. For an excerpt from the *Gazette* that conveys the full flavor of the monarchist charges levied against the Federalists by the Jeffersonians, see Hudson, *Journalism in the United States,* 186.

24. Ford, ed., *Works of Thomas Jefferson,* 1:231; Pollard, *Presidents and Press,* 15; Flexner, *George Washington: Anguish and Farewell,* 36. Jefferson's somewhat implausible explanation of the circumstances under which Freneau came to be employed in the State Department is quoted at length in James Melvin Lee, *History of American Journalism,* 149–50.

25. Mitchell, *Alexander Hamilton,* 243; Ford, ed., *Works of Thomas Jefferson,* 1:252–54; Banning, *Jeffersonian Persuasion,* 218; Payne, *History of Journalism,* 164–67. In addition to the articles Hamilton wrote defending the Neutrality Proclamation, he produced more than thirty others covering a wide range of subjects. The subjects included: attacking the behavior in 1793 of the new French ambassador Genet; arguing against a proposed anti-British trade policy in 1794; defending the administration's actions in putting down the Whiskey Rebellion in 1794, and in 1795 defending the proposed treaty with Great Britain (Cooke, *Alexander Hamilton,* 128, 130–31, 136, 162; Hecht, *Odd Destiny,* 299). Other Democratic-Republican newspapers also viciously attacked Washington in 1795 (Banning, *Jeffersonian Persuasion,* 242–43). On the problems Genet's visit caused the Washington administration and the administration's response, see Sharp, *American Politics in the Early Republic,* 78–84.

26. Rubin, *Press, Party, and Presidency,* 13; Smith, *Press, Politics, and Patronage,* 19.

27. Cunliffe, *George Washington,* 165.

28. Mott, *American Journalism,* 54. See also ibid., 47, 65, 89–91(use of pseudonyms by notables such as Thomas Paine and John Dickinson, author of "Letters from a Farmer in Pennsylvania to the Inhabitants of the British Colonies"), 103 (in 1765–83 period, "opinion was still expressed mainly by letters signed by pen-names").

29. Wiebe, *Opening of American Society,* 100–101; Cornell, *Other Founders,* 36–38, 105–106; Wood, "Democratization of Mind," 126. For an account of how the possibility of prosecution under the Sedition Act was behind one pseudonym, see Hudson, *Journalism in the United States,* 161.

30. Payne, *History of Journalism,* 137–38; 141, 144, 156 (Hamilton's "expressed belief that government was best conducted when it was not too much subject to the direct control of the people" was seen by Samuel Adams and others as a "lack of faith in the people"), 191 (Jefferson's belief in the masses, and in a government resting on a broad popular appeal").

31. Wiebe, *Opening of American Society,* 101–103.

32. Ketcham, *Presidents Above Party*, 89–93.

33. Flexner, *George Washington and the New Nation*, 174–75, 195, 196; Milkis and Nelson, *American Presidency*, 71.

34. John R. Alden, *George Washington*, 247; Michael P. Riccards, *A Republic, If You Can Keep It*, 102; Glenn A. Phelps, "George Washington and the Paradox of Party," *Presidential Studies Quarterly* 19 (1989), 738; Flexner, *George Washington: Anguish and Farewell*, 269. One political scientist asserts that these tours contradict the assertion that the role of the president as a popular leader only appeared later in our history (see Abbott, "Do Presidents Talk too Much?" 353 n).

35. Stephen E. Lucas and Susan Zaeske, "George Washington (1732–1799)," in *U.S. Presidents as Orators*, ed. Halford Ryan, 7. See also Tulis, *Rhetorical Presidency*, 69. On page 64, Tulis provides a table listing all the speeches, formal or informal, given by the first twenty-four presidents. While clearly in light of the cumulative statistics this makes little difference, it should be noted that there are some discrepancies in some of the speech counts. Washington is listed as having given a total of twenty-five speeches in eight years. Of those, twenty were made on two of his tours of the country. However, as Tulis himself indicates, Washington gave annual addresses to Congress as well as two inaugural addresses. This adds up to more than the five additional speeches with which he credits Washington. Tulis also lists Washington as having made only two trips instead of the three he actually made; the total number of "tour speeches" Washington is credited with is therefore too low by twenty-three. Similarly, the table lists Jefferson as having given a total of only three speeches in his eight years in office, yet puts his average number of speeches per year at five.

36. The speeches can be found in Dorothy Twohig, ed., *The Papers of George Washington*.

37. Lucas and Zaeske, "George Washington," 7. Tulis, in *Rhetorical Presidency*, 67, appears to indicate incorrectly that Washington delivered all of his replies in writing.

38. Lucas and Zaeske, "George Washington," 11; Elkins and McKitrick, *Age of Federalism*, 290 (consulted by Washington, Madison recommends a direct message to the people, delivered via the newspapers, over a message to Congress), 489–90.

39. Ketcham, *Presidents Above Party*, 98–99; Page Smith, *John Adams*, 951.

40. See, e.g., Adams addresses of May 2, 8, 10, and 27, 1798 in *Life and Works of John Adams*, ed. Charles Francis Adams; Waldstreicher, "Federalism," 111–13; David Farrell, "John Adams (1735–1826)," in *U.S. Presidents as Orators*, ed. Ryan, 22; Sharp, *American Politics in the Early Republic*, 179.

41. Madison to Jefferson, May 20, 1798 in *The Writings of James Madison*, ed. Gaillard Hunt, 6:320–22; Farrell, "John Adams," 22. See also Sharp, *American Politics in the Early Republic*, 179.

42. Quoted in Stewart, *Opposition Press*, 11.

43. Stewart, *Opposition Press*, 10, 611 (quotation); John Tebbel, *The Compact History of the American Newspaper*, 68.

44. Stewart, *Opposition Press*, 633; Pollard, *Presidents and the Press*, 62.

45. Frank Luther Mott, *Jefferson and the Press*, 47; Payne, *History of Journalism*, 181. This is definitely a case of biased perspective. A Boston Federalist paper wrote: "Should the Infidel Jefferson be elected to the Presidency, the *seal of death* is that moment set on our holy religion, our churches will be prostrated, and some infamous prostitute, under the title of the Goddess of Reason, will preside in the Sanctuaries now devoted to the Most High" (quoted in Mott, *Jefferson and the Press*, 169).

46. Quoted in Stewart, *Opposition Press*, 637.

47. Payne, *History of Journalism*, 181; William E. Ames, *A History of the National Intelligencer*, 31.

48. Smith, *Press, Politics, and Patronage*, 24. In 1811, Jefferson wrote that the *Aurora* had "unquestionably rendered incalculable services to republicanism through all its struggles with the federalists, and has been the rallying point for the orthodoxy of the whole Union" (Jefferson to William Wirt, Mar. 30, 1811, in Ford, ed., *Works of Thomas Jefferson*, 9:316–17. See also Stewart, *Opposition Press*, 634).

49. Smith, *Press, Politics, and Patronage*, 27; Daniel Ross Chandler, "Thomas Jefferson (1743–1826), in *U.S. Presidents as Orators*, ed. Halford Ryan, 31; Ketcham, *Presidents Above Party*, 106. Ellis, *American Sphinx*, 180–81, notes this would have allowed the audience to follow Jefferson's speech "despite the poor projection of his voice."

50. Ames, *History of the National Intelligencer*, 21, 38, 39 (quotation), 55.

51. Mott, *Jefferson and the Press*, 177.

52. Ames, *History of the National Intelligencer*, 30; Smith, *Press, Politics, and Patronage*, 28.

53. Noble E. Cunningham Jr., *The Process of Government Under Jefferson*, 32; idem., *The Jeffersonian Republicans in Power*, 261, 262; Ames, *History of the National Intelligencer*, 39; Robert M. Johnstone Jr., *Jefferson and the Presidency*, 270. Tulis states without further discussion that many of Jefferson's "private communications" were "of course . . . leaked to the press" (*Rhetorical Presidency*, 70 n 9). Pollard describes another apparent instance in which Jefferson himself wrote a newspaper article responding to some criticism of a special message he had sent to Congress in 1807 on gunboats (*Presidents and the Press*, 78).

54. Cunningham, *Jeffersonian Republicans*, 256.

55. Johnstone, *Jefferson and the Presidency*, 249.

56. Manasseh Cutler to Dr. Torrey, Dec. 8, 1801, quoted in Johnstone, *Jefferson and the Presidency*, 249.

57. Merrill D. Peterson, *Thomas Jefferson and the New Nation*, 684–85; Ryan, ed., *U.S. Presidents as Orators*, 60; Milkis and Nelson, *American Presidency*, 105; Tulis, *Rhetorical Presidency*, 56; Cunliffe, *Presidency*, 45.

58. Cunningham, *Jeffersonian Republicans*, 258, 261 (quotation).

59. Ibid., 263.

60. Ames, *History of the National Intelligencer,* 40.

61. Cunningham, *Jeffersonian Republicans,* 263, 257.

62. Ford, ed., *Works of Thomas Jefferson,* 8:361. In "Decline of the Official Press in Washington," in *Journalism Quarterly* 33 (summer, 1956): 335–41, Frederick B. Marbut reported he had found several *National Intelligencer* articles whose language was "practically identical" to the language of letters Jefferson sent to Smith.

63. Ames, *History of the National Intelligencer,* 40.

64. Ackerman, *We the People,* 1:73; Banning, *Jeffersonian Persuasion,* 280. According to James Sterling Young, "[T]o be involved in a collusive relationship with the White House in any circumstances was to run a continuous risk of social stigmatization for sycophancy" (*The Washington Community, 1800–1828,* 165). See also Skowronek, *Politics Presidents Make,* 73–74, for a discussion of how Jefferson dominated the Congress, leaving little room for any real deliberative process; and Gary King and Lyn Ragsdale, *The Elusive Executive,* 19.

65. Merrill D. Peterson, *Thomas Jefferson and the New Nation,* 690–91; Binkley, *American Political Parties,* 88; Ketcham, *Presidents Above Party,* 109; Johnstone, *Jefferson and the Presidency,* chap. 5.

66. Aug. 23, 1803 letter to Gallatin quoted in Johnstone, *Jefferson and the Presidency,* 73 (emphasis added).

67. Skowronek, *Politics Presidents Make,* 74.

68. Johnstone, *Jefferson and the Presidency,* 237.

69. Pollard, *Presidents and the Press,* 107, 116, 125; Ralph Ketcham, *James Madison,* 536; Ketcham, *Presidents Above Party,* 123.

70. Ketcham, *Presidents Above Party,* 121; James D. Richardson, ed., *A Compilation of the Messages and Papers of the Presidents,* 2:484. See also James L. Sundquist, *The Decline and Resurgence of Congress,* 23.

71. Cunningham, *Presidency of James Monroe,* 30–40, 71–75, 83–83; Harry Ammon, *James Monroe,* 372–79; Tulis, *Rhetorical Presidency,* 71.

72. Compare the negative assessments of Sundquist (*Decline and Resurgence of Congress,* 23) and Ketcham (*Presidents Above Party,* 124–29) with the very positive assessments of Ammon (*James Monroe,* 382, 645 n 8) and Cunningham (*Presidency of James Monroe,* chaps. 7 and 9). See also ibid., 45.

73. Charles Jared Ingersoll to Monroe, Aug. 10, 1819, quoted in ibid., 62.

74. Ibid., 61; Pollard, *Presidents and the Press,* 116, 118–24, 125.

75. Pollard, *Presidents and the Press,* 132 (quotation); Ceaser, *Presidential Selection,* 150–51; Ketcham, *Presidents Above Party,* 139. Monroe did encourage his son-in-law, George Hay, to write a series of anonymous newspaper essays regarding slavery and the issue of whether Congress could prohibit slavery in new states when it admitted them to the Union (Cunningham, *Presidency of James Monroe,* 93–96).

76. Ceaser, *Presidential Selection,* 150–51; Ketcham, *Presidents Above Party,* 139; Mary W. M. Hargreaves, *The Presidency of John Quincy Adams,* 253–55.

77. Pollard, *Presidents and the Press*, 128; Smith, *Press, Politics, and Patronage*, 6, 9. A few years later, during the Jackson presidency, Adams made the acute observation that "in our Presidential canvassing an editor has become as essential an appendage to a candidate as in the days of chivalry a 'squire' was to a knight" (Pollard, *Presidents and the Press*, 142).

78. Formisano, *Transformation of Political Culture*, 16 (quotation); Richard R. John, *Spreading the News*, 112. This growth rate far exceeded that of the U.S. population, which roughly tripled during the same period.

79. Quoted in John, *Spreading the News*, 10.

80. Letter to Edward Carrington, Jan. 16, 1787, quoted in Richard D. Brown, *Knowledge Is Power*, 242. For similar statements from around the same time by Elbridge Gerry, Benjamin Rush, and former Minuteman William Manning, see Michael Warner, *The Letters of the Republic*, 127–30.

81. Brown, *Knowledge Is Power*, 13, 230; Smith, *Press, Politics, and Patronage*, 6, 9; Stewart, *Opposition Press*, 16; John, *Spreading the News*, 4. See also Richard Kielbowicz, *News in the Mail.* James Madison, Jefferson, and other prominent Americans argued strenuously in the early 1790s that newspapers should either be able to be sent free or at extremely low rates through the mails (see Richard D. Brown, *The Strength of a People*, 67, 90–91; Warner, *Letters of the Republic*, 127; John, *Spreading the News*, 60–61).

82. Brown, *Knowledge Is Power*, 13–15, 219; John, *Spreading the News*, 17–18; Tebbel and Watts, *Press and the Presidency*, 75; Richard Davis, *The Press and American Politics*, 55; de Tocqueville, *Democracy in America*, ed. Mayer, vol. 1, pt. 2, 185 (quotation). The telegraph did not come into use until the 1840s.

83. Tebbel and Watts, *Press and the Presidency*, 79; Rubin, *Press, Party, and Presidency*, 30; Walsh, *Intellectual Origins*, 23.

84. Stewart, *Opposition Press*, 19. See also Rubin, *Press, Party, and Presidency*, 26, 31–32. See Wiebe, *Opening of American Society*, 206–207, on the sharp populist character of Jackson's candidacy.

85. See Robert V. Remini, *The Election of Andrew Jackson*, 76–86. On the massive extent of franking, see John, *Spreading the News*, 58–59.

86. Smith, *Press, Politics, and Patronage*, 61–62; Bleyer, *Main Currents*, 151; Rubin, *Press, Party, and Presidency*, 33; Pollard, *Presidents and the Press*, 148.

87. Tebbel and Watts, *Press and the Presidency*, 72. See also Davis, *Press and American Politics*, 57.

88. Remini, *Election of Andrew Jackson*, 62.

89. Ibid., 62, 63 (quotation).

90. Smith, *Press, Politics, and Patronage*, 90, 114–15, 140; Pollard, *Presidents and the Press*, 154, 161; Tebbel and Watts, *Press and the Presidency*, 85.

91. June 1830 letter to Major Lewis quoted in John Niven, *Martin Van Buren*, 262. See Gerald J. Baldasty, *The Press and Politics in the Age of Jackson*, 8.

92. Smith, *Press, Politics, and Patronage*, 122.

93. Marquis James, *Andrew Jackson*, 268; Baldasty, *Press and Politics*, 10; Pollard, *Presidents and the Press*, 155–57; Leonard, *News for All*, 13. Leonard notes that

in the early republic, members of Congress also often knew who was subscribing to a newspaper, because constituents would send subscription requests for newspapers to their representatives. See John, *Spreading the News*, chap. 6, on the Jacksonians' transformation of the postal system "from the central administrative apparatus of the American state into a wellspring of the mass party." Blair claimed that, as a result of the paper's attacks against the U.S. Bank, circulation had grown to 12,100, an increase of 6,724 just since December (*Washington Globe*, Jan. 1, 1834).

94. Pollard, *Presidents and the Press*, 156; *Washington Globe*, Jan. 18, 1834.

95. Donald B. Cole, *Martin Van Buren and the American Political System*, 227.

96. Cunliffe, *Presidency*, 75, 78; "Protest" of Andrew Jackson to the Senate, Apr. 15, 1834, in Remini, ed., *Age of Jackson*, 115. See also Ketcham, *Presidents Above Party*, 153. For a vivid account of the collision between these two conceptions of representative democracy during Jackson's presidency, see Robert V. Remini, *Andrew Jackson*, 3:149–60.

97. Jackson to Van Buren, Sept. 8, 1833, in Robert V. Remini, *The Life of Andrew Jackson*, 262. See also Remini, *Andrew Jackson*, 3:93. Viewed by Jeffersonians and Antifederalists as a potential "aristocratic engine," the idea of a national bank had been the source of heated partisan controversy since first proposed by Alexander Hamilton in 1790 (see Banning, *Jeffersonian Persuasion*, 147–50; Wiebe, *Opening of American Society*, 218–21).

98. Jackson to Van Buren, Sept. 22, 1833, in Pollard, *Presidents and the Press*, 167. At the request of some of his cabinet members, Jackson also used the *Globe* to announce publicly that the decision to remove the bank deposits had been his personally, and should not be considered a "cabinet measure" (Remini, *Andrew Jackson*, 3:104).

99. *Washington Globe*, Sept. 23, 1833, 2 (emphasis added).

100. Tulis, *Rhetorical Presidency*, 55, 58–59.

101. The texts of Jackson's letter to the Senate and Clay's speech are found in the *Washington Globe*, Dec. 13, 1833, 2.

102. Quoted in Smith, *Press, Politics, and Patronage*, 134 (1st quote; emphasis added); 135.

103. Remini, *Life of Andrew Jackson*, 264, 274–75.

104. Excerpts from five or more other papers were carried in the following issues of the *Globe*: Oct. 1, 4, 7, 8, 12, 21, and Dec. 21, 1833; Jan. 3, 7, 15, 27, and 29, Feb. 1, 3, 8, 18, 21, 22, 26, and 27, and Mar. 20, 21, and 28, 1834. Letters can be found in almost every issue from February 1 to March 15, 1834. Resolutions of support, often purportedly the result of special conventions attended by thousands, began appearing in late January, 1834 (see January 27 for the first, from Philadelphia); twenty were published in the month of March. See Appendix B. Direct popular actions, ranging from group petitions to the formation of local committees to mob action, were common occurrences in the late eighteenth and early nineteenth centuries in America (Morgan, *Inventing the People*, 229–30, 257–58; Kerber, *Federalists in Dissent*,

181–85; Wiebe, *Opening of American Society*, 22; Binkley, *American Political Parties*, 67). The local support actions for Jackson's war against the Bank that were reported in the *Globe* may well have been carried out and reported in this same tradition to demonstrate Jackson's popular support on this issue.

105. Smith, *Press, Politics, and Patronage*, 133.
106. Baldasty, *Press and Politics*, 21; Smith, *Press, Politics, and Patronage*, 133.
107. Quoted in Wiebe, *Opening of American Society*, 239.
108. Hudson, *Journalism in the United States*, 249.
109. William Ernest Smith, *The Francis Preston Blair Family in Politics*, 117; Pollard, *Presidents and the Press*, 160; William Ernest Smith, "Francis P. Blair, Pen-Executive of Andrew Jackson," in *Highlights in the History of the American Press*, ed. Ford and Emery, 145.
110. Smith, *Press, Politics, and Patronage*, 131, 135. See also Lee, *History of American Journalism*, 149–50; W. Smith, *Francis Preston Blair Family*, 46.
111. Smith, *Press, Politics, and Patronage*, 139.
112. Tebbel, *Compact History*, 87; Pollard, *Presidents and the Press*, 158.
113. See Robert V. Remini, ed., *The Age of Jackson*, intro, xxiii.
114. Quoted in Smith, *Press, Politics, and Patronage*, 97.
115. Ibid., 135. For an account of how Jackson and his advisors valued the "purity, intelligence, and patriotism of the people" over a resolution passed overwhelmingly by the House of Representatives during the Bank Deposits removal turmoil, see Richard J. Ellis and Stephen Kirk, "Jefferson, Jackson, and the Origins of the Presidential Mandate," in *Speaking to the People*, ed. Richard J. Ellis, 53.
116. Arthur M. Schlesinger Jr., *The Age of Jackson*, 52.
117. Rubin, *Press, Party, and Presidency*, 53; de Tocqueville, *Democracy in America*, ed. Mayer, vol.1, pt. 2, 186. For an extreme view of the power of the political press to mold public opinion, see the 1855 *Toledo Blade* commentary quoted in William E. Gienapp, *The Origins of the Republican Party, 1852–1856*, 9.

Chapter 3. The Presidential Newspaper, 1836–60: The Rest of the Story

1. Martin Van Buren to Rufus King, May 31, 1822, quoted in Niven, *Martin Van Buren*, 127 (epigraph quotation).
2. Robert V. Remini, *Martin Van Buren and the Making of the Democratic Party*. The impetus for Van Buren's party work was his trip to Washington as a senator in 1821. He was "horrified at what he and his friends termed 'the Monroe heresy . . . of amalgamation' of the parties, and he frankly avowed his intention to 'revive the old contest between federals and anti-federals'" (Ketcham, *Presidents Above Party*, 144–45).
3. Hudson, *Journalism in the United States*, 277.
4. Tebbel and Watts, *Press and the Presidency*, 91.
5. Jackson to Major Lewis, June, 1830, quoted in Niven, *Martin Van Buren*, 262.
6. Ibid., 265–66.

7. Cole, *Martin Van Buren*, 262. See also Pollard, *Presidents and the Press*, 184.

8. This is the generally accepted view. See Pollard, *Presidents and the Press*, 188; Tebbel and Watts, *Press and the Presidency*, 96; and Smith, *Francis Preston Blair Family*, 130. For the view that "As the Democratic party's chief propagandist, Blair would support Van Buren with the same loyalty and dedication he had previously reserved only for Jackson," see Elbert B. Smith, *Francis Preston Blair*, 128.

9. Smith, *Francis Preston Blair Family*, 127.

10. Tebbel and Watts, *Press and the Presidency*, 95. See also Major L. Wilson, *The Presidency of Martin Van Buren*, 47; and Norma Lois Peterson, *The Presidencies of William Henry Harrison and John Tyler*, 15.

11. Cole, *Martin Van Buren*, 292–93, 296.

12. Wilson, *Presidency of Martin Van Buren*, 68, 100, 101. But note also New Yorker Thomas Olcott's Sept. 19, 1837 letter to Van Buren complaining about the "ultra" and "harsh and offensive course of the *Globe*" on the independent treasury issue (ibid., 313).

13. See ibid., chap. 7.

14. Ibid., 113.

15. Smith, *Francis Preston Blair Family*, 127; *Washington Globe*, June 4, 1838.

16. Tebbel and Watts, *Press and the Presidency*, 102; Smith, *Francis Preston Blair*, 133–37.

17. Smith, *Francis Preston Blair*, 138–39.

18. Tebbel and Watts, *Press and the Presidency*, 96–97, 103; Peterson, *Presidencies of Harrison and Tyler*, 31–36. However, Harrison was reported to have made a campaign speech in Dayton, Ohio, to over a hundred thousand people (Binkley, *American Political Parties*, 176).

19. Quoted in Peterson, *Presidencies of Harrison and Tyler*, 36. For similar statements made by Harrison during the campaign, see ibid., 28.

20. Ibid., 26–27, 52–53.

21. Ibid., 19, 53.

22. Pollard, *Presidents and the Press*, 213; Richard A. Bland, "Politics, Propaganda, and the Public Printing: The Administration Organs, 1829–1849" (Ph.D. diss., University of Kentucky, 1975), 92.

23. Peterson, *Presidencies of Harrison and Tyler*, 64.

24. Tebbel and Watts, *Press and the Presidency*, 106.

25. Webster explained why he did not resign in a letter to the *National Intelligencer* published on September 14 (Peterson, *Presidencies of Harrison and Tyler*, 86). Tyler himself composed a statement responding to the criticism over his vetoes and the cabinet resignations, but it was not published in the *Madisonian* until after he left office. He explained that he had not released the statement at the time of the incidents

> because I felt that it would be unbecoming the individual who, by the regular forms of the Constitution, has been inducted into

the presidential office, to enter into a personal controversy with
retiring cabinet officers or others, who thought proper to indulge in
vituperation and abuse, either from mistaken or corrupt motives.
There was something due to the executive office itself; there was
much more due to the country, which forbade the president from
entering into a mere newspaper controversy, which, whatever
might be the result, could not fail to diminish the respect entertained for the United States and their political institutions, in the
estimation of all foreign governments. But these considerations no
longer exist. (Quoted in Pollard, *Presidents and the Press*, 220).

This statement shows how a president like Tyler, who went public via his
newspaper, was able to preserve a "dignified" public image.

26. Peterson, *Presidencies of Harrison and Tyler*, 89; White, *Jacksonians*, 30; Tulis,
    Rhetorical Presidency, 58.
27. Tyler to Webster, quoted in *The Letters of Daniel Webster*, ed. Claude H. Van
    Tyne, 231.
28. Tyler to Wise, Sept. 27, 1841, quoted in Lyon G. Tyler, ed., "Original Letters,"
    William and Mary Quarterly 20, 1st series (July, 1911), 7.
29. Wilson, *Presidency of Martin Van Buren*, 64; Smith, *Francis Preston Blair*, 122
    (quotation; emphasis in original); Bland, "Politics, Propaganda, and the Pub-
    lic Printing," 94.
30. Bland, "Politics, Propaganda, and the Public Printing," 95–96.
31. Pollard, *Presidents and the Press*, 214.
32. Bland, "Politics, Propaganda, and the Public Printing," 100.
33. Charles G. Sellers, *James K. Polk, Continentalist, 1843–46*, 135. After Polk de-
    feated Clay, Tyler's nemesis, Tyler ordered Jones to "Leave off abusing Mr.
    Clay altogether. He is dead and let him rest" (quoted in Robert Seager II, *And
    Tyler Too*, 242).
34. Bland, "Politics, Propaganda, and the Public Printing," 99–102.
35. Ibid., 95; *Madisonian*, Nov. 6, 7, and 9, 1842.
36. *National Intelligencer*, Dec. 3, 1842.
37. *Congressional Globe*, 27 Cong., 2 sess., 303. Jones himself later complained
    that Congress had denied the president the "power of bestowing on a press
    which supported his Administration the little Executive printing in this city"
    (*Madisonian*, Dec. 8, 1843). These congressional efforts were just part of the
    bipartisan war against Tyler. For most of Tyler's term, Congress refused to
    appropriate any funds to pay for the expense of heating, lighting, and main-
    taining the White House, or for any presidential entertainment expenses.
    Tyler paid these himself (Peterson, *Presidencies of Harrison and Tyler*, 56).
38. Seager, *And Tyler Too*, 233.
39. Pollard, *Presidents and the Press*, 216.
40. Bland, "Politics, Propaganda, and the Public Printing," 119–21; Paul H.
    Bergeron, *The Presidency of James K. Polk*, 18.

41. Polk, fourth annual message to Congress, quoted in Richardson, ed., *Compilation of the Messages and Papers*, 4:664–65. See Charles A. McCoy, *Polk and the Presidency*, 145, for a discussion of the clash between Polk and the Whigs, whose victory in the 1848 election prompted Polk to explain his conception of the presidency in his last annual message.

42. Bergeron, *Presidency of James K. Polk*, 172.

43. Pollard, *Presidents and the Press*, 229–30.

44. Quoted in Pollard, *Presidents and the Press*, 235. Some understanding of the intensity of the political environment Polk was operating in can be gleaned from the 1844 diary entries of Calvin Fletcher in Indianapolis, Indiana. In July of that year he noted that "nearly every house had a pole erected—Ash is Whig—Hickory Democrat or Polk." By the fall, "evry child we met would hollow for Polk & Dallas or Clay & Frelinghyson. . . . Every wagoner & at evry cabin from men women & childrin I received the salute as I have in all my travels this fall—Huza for Clay or huza for Polk. Teamsters have it written on the wagon covers. . . . Evryman has his mind made up yes evry woman & child" (quoted in Brown, *Knowledge Is Power*, 237).

45. Polk to Jackson, Mar. 26, 1845, quoted in Pollard, *Presidents and the Press*, 237. See also Jackson's Feb. 28, 1845, letter quoted ibid., 235.

46. Polk to Jackson, Mar. 17, 1845, quoted in Pollard, *Presidents and the Press*, 235–36.

47. Pollard, *Presidents and the Press*, 239; Bergeron, *Presidency of James K. Polk*, 174; Bland, "Politics, Propaganda, and the Public Printing," 119–23. In his farewell editorial, Blair stated that "The *Globe* had its origin in the will of General Jackson, and owes to him and Mr. Van Buren, and their political friends, the success which has attended it. . . . It has been the misfortune of the *Globe*, in sustaining the strong administration of Gen. Jackson, the uncompromising administration of Mr. Van Buren, and in opposing the abuses of Mr. Tyler's administration, to make enemies of some who united with the democracy in its last struggle" (Apr. 14, 1845, quoted in Bland, "Politics, Propaganda, and the Public Printing," 145).

48. See Pollard, *Presidents and the Press*, 230–35; Bland, "Politics, Propaganda, and the Public Printing," 119–23.

49. Bergeron, *Presidency of James K. Polk*, 175; Bland, "Politics, Propaganda, and the Public Printing," 144, 146 (quotation).

50. Bland, "Politics, Propaganda, and the Public Printing," 146–47.

51. Bergeron, *Presidency of James K. Polk*, 176–77. Polk wrote in his diary that this was the "second or third time since I have been President that I have sketched an article for the paper" (Allan Nevins, ed., *Polk: The Diary of a President*, 76–77).

52. Bland, "Politics, Propaganda, and the Public Printing," 154.

53. Pollard, *Presidents and the Press*, 244–45; Bergeron, *Presidency of James K. Polk*, 177 (first quotation); Bland, "Politics, Propaganda, and the Public Printing," 154–55, 208–209 (second quotation).

54. This account is taken from Bland, "Politics, Propaganda, and the Public Printing," 208–14.

55. Bergeron, *Presidency of James K. Polk*, 178; McCoy, *Polk and the Presidency*, 190–91; Pollard, *Presidents and the Press*, 246–47; Tebbel and Watts, *Press and the Presidency*, 124–25.

56. Quoted in Bergeron, *Presidency of James K. Polk*, 98.

57. Ibid., 122, 182; Pollard, *Presidents and the Press*, 245–46.

58. Nevins, *Polk*, 369–70.

59. See Pollard, *Presidents and the Press*, 241; Bland, "Politics, Propaganda, and the Public Printing," 158; Bergeron, *Presidency of James K. Polk*, 177–78.

60. Nevins, *Polk*, 77n 18.

61. Quoted in Bergeron, *Presidency of James K. Polk*, 180. For protestations by Ritchie, see Pollard, *Presidents and the Press*, 241–42; and Bland, "Politics, Propaganda, and the Public Printing," 151–52, who both dismiss them.

62. Bland, "Politics, Propaganda, and the Public Printing," 152 (quotation); Bergeron, *Presidency of James K. Polk*, 175–76.

63. Bergeron, *Presidency of James K. Polk*, 175; Bland, "Politics, Propaganda, and the Public Printing," 162, 215. For another discussion of Polk's use of his newspaper, see McCoy, *Polk and the Presidency*, 185–91.

64. Nevins, *Polk*, 353.

65. For reports of such incidents, albeit isolated, in the Grant and Benjamin Harrison presidencies, see Robert C. Hilderbrand, *Power and the People*, 25, 53.

66. See, e.g., Tulis, *Rhetorical Presidency*, 46.

67. Bergeron, *Presidency of James K. Polk*, 252; Tebbel and Watts, *Press and the Presidency*, 130; Elbert B. Smith, *The Presidencies of Zachary Taylor and Millard Fillmore*, 143. Nevertheless, the *Intelligencer* was a strong supporter of Taylor. According to Smith, the paper "defended with equal ardor the traditional Whig attitude" and Taylor's presidency against those who wanted him to more actively pursue the Whig agenda.

68. Pollard, *Presidents and the Press*, 264 (quotation), 265; see also Tebbel and Watts, *Press and the Presidency*, 134. Just four months after Taylor's inauguration, Kentucky governor John Crittenden, one of the few politicians Taylor knew personally, asked a Taylor aide to tell the editor of the *Republic* that the paper needed to be more aggressive in its attacks on the opponents of "Old Zach." A few weeks later, Crittenden advised the editor that, now that the paper had been gotten up to "the right temperature, he must keep it as hot as a furnace till the *Union* is purged in 'liquid fire'" (quoted in Pollard, *Presidents and the Press*, 265).

69. *Republic*, Feb. 16, 1850; emphasis in original.

70. Tebbel and Watts, *Press and the Presidency*, 136; Hamilton, *Zachary Taylor*, 322 (quotation), 334, 337.

71. Smith, *Presidencies of Taylor and Fillmore*, 119–20; Hamilton, *Zachary Taylor*, 322–23.

72. Hamilton, *Zachary Taylor*, 334–35.

73. Smith, *Presidencies of Taylor and Fillmore,* 141. For yet another example of Taylor's use of the *Republic,* see Hamilton's account of the paper defending Taylor against the allegations in a Senate speech during the Texas territory dispute in *Zachary Taylor,* 379.

74. Hamilton, *Zachary Taylor,* 222–29.

75. Smith, *Presidencies of Taylor and Fillmore,* 165.

76. Ibid., 143.

77. Quoted in Pollard, *Presidents and the Press,* 269.

78. Tebbel and Watts, *Press and the Presidency,* 142 (quotation), 143.

79. Ibid.; Smith, *Presidencies of Taylor and Fillmore,* 163; Pollard, *Presidents and the Press,* 275.

80. Pollard, *Presidents and the Press,* 268; Tebbel and Watts, *Press and the Presidency,* 143; Smith, *Presidencies of Taylor and Fillmore,* 189 (quotation).

81. Tebbel and Watts, *Press and the Presidency,* 144. Tebbel and Watts rather unconvincingly describe Fillmore's action as an attempt to gain the confidence of both sides on the slavery question, for which he was desperately seeking a compromise, by taking a hands-off approach to the press. In 1850, Fillmore spoke despairingly of how, "in times like this, the telegraph in the hands of irresponsible and designing men is a tremendous engine for mischief, aided as it is in many places by a mercenary and prostituted press" (quoted in Pollard, *Presidents and the Press,* 273).

82. See Tebbel and Watts, *Press and the Presidency,* 146, 149, 155.

83. See White, *Jacksonians,* chap. 15; Smith, *Press, Politics, and Patronage.*

84. Larry Gara, *The Presidency of Franklin Pierce,* 52, 69, 91, 94, 182; Pollard, *Presidents and the Press,* 282, 287–88, 289.

85. Pollard, *Presidents and the Press,* 285, 290; Tebbel and Watts, *Press and the Presidency,* 153–54, 156; Gara, *Presidency of Franklin Pierce,* 52, 81, 182; Pollard, *Presidents and the Press,* 289.

86. Pollard, *Presidents and the Press,* 252; Tebbel and Watts, *Press and the Presidency,* 157. See also Elbert B. Smith, *The Presidency of James Buchanan,* 88.

87. Tebbel and Watts, *Press and the Presidency,* 159.

88. Pollard, *Presidents and the Press,* 293.

89. Quoted in Tebbel and Watts, *Press and the Presidency,* 162.

90. Pollard, *Presidents and the Press,* 295; Tebbel and Watts, *Press and the Presidency,* 162.

91. Dec. 20, 1860, quoted in Pollard, *Presidents and the Press,* 298.

92. Bland, "Politics, Propaganda, and the Public Printing," 218.

93. Smith, *Press, Politics, and Patronage,* 230.

94. Smith, *Presidency of James Buchanan,* 148–50; Pollard, *Presidents and the Press,* 299 (quotation), 310n 62.

95. See Tebbel and Watts, *Press and the Presidency,* 98–99, 157, 208–209; Payne, *History of Journalism,* 237–39.

96. Sources for the foregoing description of congressional attempts to alter the government printing process are: Smith, *Press, Politics, and Patronage,* 230–

31, 234–35; Tebbel and Watts, *Press and the Presidency*, 98–99, 157, 208–209; White, *Jacksonians*, chap. 15; and Payne, *History of Journalism*, 237–39.

97. House Report 249, 36th Cong., 1st sess. (Mar. 26, 1860), 28.
98. Hudson, *Journalism in the United States*, 258–59.

Chapter 4. The Old Norm against Going Public: Constitutional Principle or Partisan Fancy?

1. During the four years and forty-three days he served as president, Lincoln made seventy-eight speeches, according to Tulis. Because Lincoln served part of a fifth year, his average number of speeches is sixteen per year in Tulis's compilation of the average number of speeches given by all presidents in the nineteenth century. Adjusting for the drastically shortened fifth year of his presidency, the actual average for Lincoln is over nineteen (see Tulis, *Rhetorical Presidency*, 64).

2. Ibid., 61, 79.
3. Ibid., 79–80.
4. Ibid., 81.
5. Even if one is inclined to accept Tulis's interpretation of the speech, how can we be sure that Lincoln was publicly giving his honest reason(s) for declining to speak on specific matters? After all, Lincoln, like virtually all politicians and other human beings, was capable of prevaricating a little now and then, especially to achieve a "greater good." He admitted as much when responding to a newspaper editor who had complained to him that the Lincolns had canceled their subscription to a new Springfield paper in 1857. Lincoln explained that when his wife complained to him that he had subscribed to yet "another worthless paper," he had "said to her evasively, 'I have not directed the paper to be left.'" This resulted in Mrs. Lincoln canceling the paper without his knowledge, to Lincoln's subsequent embarrassment (Pollard, *Presidents and the Press*, 332).
6. Pollard, *Presidents and the Press*, 347.
7. Letter to Henry J. Raymond, Nov. 28, 1860, quoted in ibid.
8. *Abraham Lincoln: Speeches and Writings, 1859–1865*, ed. Don E. Fehrenbacher, 205.
9. Ibid., 375.
10. Pollard, *Presidents and the Press*, 312.
11. Ibid., 313; A. J. Beveridge, *Abraham Lincoln*, 1:212–18, 291, and 2:5–7, 56.
12. Pollard, *Presidents and the Press*, 320; T. A. Levy, *Lincoln the Politician*, 177. See also Lincoln's use in 1860 of a short newspaper note he wrote anonymously to contradict a prior claim in the paper that after his nomination for the presidency he had declined an invitation to visit Kentucky out of a fear that it was a "trap laid by some designing person to inveigle him into a slave state for the purpose of doing violence to his person" (Pollard, *Presidents and the Press*, 338).

13. Beveridge, *Abraham Lincoln*, 2:215.

14. Sandburg, *Abraham Lincoln*, 2:142.

15. Quoted in Pollard, *Presidents and the Press*, 332–33.

16. Account of Attorney General Bates, quoted in ibid., 391 n 44.

17. Sandburg, *Abraham Lincoln*, 2:306.

18. Roy P. Basler, ed., *The Collected Works of Abraham Lincoln*, 5:388–89.

19. Quoted in Pollard, *Presidents and the Press*, 372.

20. Ibid., 356–62, 364, 366, 367, 375–76; Sandburg, *Abraham Lincoln*, 4:502.

21. On the general point of multiple rhetorical audiences, see Medhurst, "Introduction," xviii–xix.

22. See Mario M. Cuomo and Harold Holzer, eds., *Lincoln on Democracy*, 277.

23. Fehrenbacher, ed., *Abraham Lincoln*, 229–31 (Virginia letter, Apr. 13, 1861); 454–63 (Albany letter, June 12, 1863); 465–70 (Ohio letter, June 29, 1863); 522–27 (Missouri letter, Oct. 5, 1863).

24. Aug. 26, 1863, in *Abraham Lincoln*, ed. Fehrenbacher, 495–99; Sandburg, *Abraham Lincoln*, 4:380–81. Lincoln seriously considered traveling to Springfield to deliver the speech himself (Sandburg, *Abraham Lincoln*, 4:380), but instead asked Conkling to read the letter aloud "very slowly" (Cuomo and Holzer, *Lincoln on Democracy*, 288).

25. See Sandburg, *Abraham Lincoln*, 4:380–87.

26. Ibid., 4:386.

27. Fehrenbacher, ed., *Abraham Lincoln*, 333 (June 24, 1862); 350–51 (Aug. 6, 1862); 353–57 (Aug. 22, 1862); 361–67; 441–42 (Mar. 27, 1863); 600–601 (June 16, 1864); 635–36 (Oct. 19, 1864).

28. Ibid., 589–91 (Apr. 18, 1864).

29. Ibid., 697–701.

30. Pollard, *Presidents and the Press*, 350.

31. Quoted in ibid., 389 (emphasis added).

32. Quoted in ibid.

33. See Fred I. Greenstein, *The Hidden-Hand Presidency*.

34. Tulis, *Rhetorical Presidency*, 87–93. Ceaser et al., in "The Rise of the Rhetorical Presidency," 159, state that Johnson's speaking tour "was considered highly irregular."

35. Holt, *Political Parties*, 339.

36. Ibid., 351.

37. Eric L. McKitrick, "Andrew Johnson, Outsider," in *Andrew Johnson: A Profile*, ed. Eric L. McKitrick, 70–74. As Michael Holt points out, Johnson must have helped the ticket, because Lincoln received about 340,000 more votes in the election, with 146,000 of those votes coming from the border states, where he won Maryland, Missouri, and West Virginia (*Political Parties*, 351).

38. Kenneth M. Stampp, "Andrew Johnson: The Last Jacksonian," in *Andrew Johnson*, ed. McKitrick, 116.

39. McKitrick, "Andrew Johnson," 71.

40. Albert Castel, *The Presidency of Andrew Johnson*, 5.

41. Joseph G. Baldwin, *Party Leaders* (1855), quoted in Cunliffe, *Presidency*, 73.

42. Stampp, "Andrew Johnson," 121–24; Pollard, *Presidents and the Press*, 403.

43. Pollard, *Presidents and the Press*, 72.

44. George Fort Milton, *The Age of Hate*, 359, 362.

45. Ibid., 362–67.

46. Pollard, *Presidents and the Press*, 402. See also Milton, *Age of Hate*, 367.

47. Quoted in Pollard, *Presidents and the Press*, 407.

48. George Milton says, "It was doubtful if the words of any President of the United States have ever been so distorted, deliberately misquoted and misconstrued as were Johnson's words on this tour" (*Age of Hate*, 366).

49. Quoted in Tulis, *Rhetorical Presidency*, 91. See also Milkis and Nelson, *American Presidency*, 177. Ackerman offers a recent reexamination of Johnson's impeachment by a noted constitutional law scholar; the absence of any mention of this part of article ten suggests that Ackerman too sees no substance in that part of the charge (*We the People*, 2:223).

50. Binkley, *President and Congress*, 166. In a veto message, for example, Johnson pointed out: "The President of the United States stands toward the country in a somewhat different attitude from that of any member of Congress. Each member of Congress is chosen from a single district or State; the President is chosen by the people of all the States" (Feb. 19, 1866, message vetoing the Freedmen's Bureau Bill, quoted in Ackerman, *We the People*, 2:171).

51. The vote was 128–47 (Hans L. Trefousse, *Andrew Johnson*, 315). See also Howard P. Nash Jr., *Andrew Johnson*, 151–52. Some sense of the fervor of the Republican attack on Johnson is conveyed by Milton's report that, when the planned House impeachment vote had to be adjourned from the anniversary of Washington's birthday on Saturday, February 22, to the following Monday, the House leaders "set back the clock of the House in order that Monday should appear on the House journal as Saturday, February 22" (Milton, *Age of Hate*, 511).

52. Michael Les Benedict, *The Impeachment and Trial of Andrew Johnson*, 104; Binkley, *President and Congress*, 172–77. In his opening address to the Senate, Butler also asserted that an impeachable offense was not necessarily a crime but could be anything that was "in its nature or consequence subversive of some fundamental or essential principle of government" (quoted in Binkley, *President and Congress*, 172–73).

53. Milton, *Age of Hate*, 518; Benedict, *Impeachment and Trial of Andrew Johnson*, 113, 114. Even some who did vote in favor of Article 10 or any of the other articles may have done so for less than intellectual reasons. A few days after the impeachment vote, a House member told Secretary of War Gideon Wells "'he regretted that he was compelled to vote for it under party command. . . . It would have been death for him to have resisted'" (quoted in Milton, *Age of Hate*, 525).

54. Letter to John A. Logan, Mar. 6, 1868, quoted in Milton, *Age of Hate*, 518.

55. Ibid., 624; Benedict, *Impeachment and Trial of Andrew Johnson*, 170, 183; Binkley, *President and Congress*, 172–77.

56. Binkley, *President and Congress*, 172–77. Tulis, without citation, says that no one "expressly disagreed" with the premise of Article 10 that Johnson's conduct was "improper," and that many of those who opposed Article 10 did so for "strategic considerations (whether the defense could delay the trial) rather than upon a judgment that the charge was improper" (*Rhetorical Presidency*, 91–92). The absence of any recorded disagreement with a claim does not necessarily indicate agreement with it. In general, conclusions about motives of actors are notoriously difficult to prove. Whether these particular conclusions are justified is impossible to evaluate since no basis for them is given.

57. Castel, *Presidency of Andrew Johnson*, 186.

58. Milton, *Age of Hate*, 528, 546, 552.

59. Pollard, *Presidents and the Press*, 434 (quotation), 435.

60. Binkley, *President and Congress*, 177, 181.

61. Quoted in Cunliffe, *American Presidents*, 183; Milkis and Nelson, *American Presidency*, 179.

62. Quoted in Binkley, *President and Congress*, 184.

63. Ibid., 184. The closest Grant came to what could be called an appeal to the public was sending a special message to Congress in June, 1870, that argued against armed intervention in Cuba. According to one historian, Grant "expected his words to have as much impact on the public as on his critics at the east end of Pennsylvania Avenue" (Hilderbrand, *Power and the People*, 25). Such efforts were extremely rare, however, and "most of the time . . . [Grant's] administration paid scant attention to public opinion" (ibid., 41).

Chapter 5. Presidents and Public Communication in the Late Nineteenth Century

1. Woodrow Wilson, *Congressional Government*, 181.

2. Justus D. Doenecke, *The Presidencies of James A. Garfield and Chester A. Arthur*, 10, 16.

3. Quotes and account are from Henry Jones Ford, *The Cleveland Era*, 71–72. Cleveland's battle with the Senate ended when it approved his new nominee for the district attorney position, establishing definitively his right to make removals and appointments at his own discretion (ibid., 75).

4. Kenneth E. Davison, *The Presidency of Rutherford B. Hayes*, 6, 156–57, 162–63. See also Ari Hoogenboom, *The Presidency of Rutherford B. Hayes*, 59, 96–97.

5. Davison, *Presidency of Rutherford B. Hayes*, 11; Pollard, *Presidents and the Press*, 457.

6. Davison, *Presidency of Rutherford B. Hayes*, xv.

7. T. Harry Williams, ed., *Hayes: The Diary of a President 1875–1881*, 273 (emphasis in original); Pollard, *Presidents and the Press*, 463.

8. Williams, ed., *Hayes*, 125–26; Hoogenboom, *Presidency of Rutherford B. Hayes*, 259. Hayes also managed to antagonize Washington reporters,

known as members of the "Newspaper Row," in various ways. In one incident, reporters were inadvertently omitted from the guest list for a White
House reception for the diplomatic corps. This, Hayes wrote, caused "great
irritation" among the reporters who sent out accounts of the affair "corresponding with the feelings of the writers." He went on to observe of the reporters that, while "strictly they are not officials, . . . their connection with
Congress is so intimate and important that they might properly be included
with the officers of Congress" (Pollard, *Presidents and the Press*, 465).

9. Davison, *Presidency of Rutherford B. Hayes*, 210.

10. Tulis, *Rhetorical Presidency*, 84. There is no compilation of Hayes's speeches,
    and Tulis is apparently relying on Charles Richards Williams's *The Life of Ru-
    therford Birchard Hayes* for this judgment. Gerald Gamm and Renee M. Smith
    reached a similar conclusion based on some of Hayes's statements ("Presi-
    dents, Parties, and the Public: Evolving Patterns of Interaction, 1877–1929,"
    in *Speaking to the People*, ed. Ellis). For a speech in which Hayes took a stand in
    favor of helping Native Americans survive as a people, see Davison, *Presi-
    dency of Rutherford B. Hayes*, 218–19.

11. Williams, *Life of Rutherford Birchard Hayes*, 293–94.

12. Quoted in Davison, *Presidency of Rutherford B. Hayes*, 218–19.

13. Quoted in Williams, *Life of Rutherford Birchard Hayes*, 294. Williams also
    mentions Hayes's belief that "on public occasions, in which men of every
    political faith were participating, political topics were to be avoided" (ibid.,
    242). Tulis cites this work and page number but does not mention this state-
    ment (*Rhetorical Presidency*, 84). Hayes was "obsessed" with the idea of
    "nonpartisanship" (see Harry Bainard, *Rutherford B. Hayes and His America*).

14. Doenecke, *Presidencies of Garfield and Arthur*, 38.

15. Ibid., 182; Pollard, *Presidents and the Press*, 485–86.

16. Pollard, *Presidents and the Press*, 491; Doenecke, *Presidencies of Garfield and
    Arthur*, 76, 80.

17. Doenecke, *Presidencies of Garfield and Arthur*, 80, 181; Pollard, *Presidents and
    the Press*, 495.

18. Richard E. Welch Jr., *The Presidencies of Grover Cleveland*, 9, 11. Nonetheless,
    Cleveland's conception of presidential authority evolved (ibid., 147). See also
    Allan Nevins, *Grover Cleveland*, 271.

19. Welch, *Presidencies of Grover Cleveland*, 18, 35, 106. However, by the end of
    his second term Cleveland seemed to be trying to command rather than per-
    suade (ibid., 222).

20. Ibid., 56, 205, 218 (2d quotation); Woodrow Wilson, "Mr. Cleveland's Cabi-
    net," *Review of Reviews*, Apr., 1893, 289.

21. Welch, *Presidencies of Grover Cleveland*, 55. See also Nevins, *Grover Cleveland*,
    641, for a description of the waves of "warlike enthusiasm" and the "imperi-
    alist sentiment" that swept the country after Cleveland's December 17, 1895,
    special message to Congress on America's disagreement with Britain over
    Venezuela's border dispute with British Guiana.

22. Pollard, *Presidents and the Press*, 500–501.

23. Ibid., 513–14.

24. This account and the quotes are taken from Nevins, *Grover Cleveland*, 270–71. The interviews appeared in the *New York Herald* and *World*, and the Louisville *Courier-Journal* on January 5 and 6, 1886.

25. Nevins, *Grover Cleveland*, 270–71. See also Welch, *Presidencies of Grover Cleveland*, 147.

26. Nevins, *Grover Cleveland*, 685–87.

27. David S. Barry, "News-Getting at the Capital," *Chautauquan* 26 (Dec., 1897): 282–86.

28. Ibid., 282–83.

29. See Pollard, *Presidents and the Press*, 528. See also letters dated Oct. 27, 1885, Apr. 7, 1895, and June 16, 1896, in Allan Nevins, ed., *Letters of Grover Cleveland*.

30. George F. Parker, *Recollections of Grover Cleveland*, 361–62. See also Pollard, *Presidents and the Press*, 515–16.

31. Welch, *Presidencies of Grover Cleveland*, 104. See also Tulis's perhaps related but undocumented statement that Cleveland published "collections of his correspondence year by year in an effort to foster a climate favorable to his party's policies" (*Rhetorical Presidency*, 85).

32. Pollard, *Presidents and the Press*, 502, 503, 507, 515, 518. Parker also recalled that, "in the one or two cases when he had been drawn into giving an interview" with one reporter, Cleveland would arrange with Parker for the news to be shared with reporters from other papers to "keep the news from becoming exclusive" (Parker, *Recollections of Grover Cleveland*, 362).

33. Dec. 12, 1885, Nevins, *Letters of Grover Cleveland*. Cleveland himself was not above that time-honored political technique of, to use the polite term, dissembling. A few months after his second term began in 1893, the president discovered a growth in his mouth. Physicians determined it was cancerous and should be removed. The operation was performed in secrecy on the presidential yacht, and resulted in the removal of most of Cleveland's upper left jaw. Not until sixty days after the operation did a newspaper run a story claiming the operation had occurred, and even then the administration promptly denied the report. As Cleveland himself explained in a letter to Ambassador Thomas F. Bayard, "the policy here has been to deny and discredit" the story. The stonewalling worked; Cleveland finished his presidency with the news of the serious operation kept from the public (Pollard, *Presidents and the Press*, 523–25).

34. Homer E. Socolofsky and Allan B. Spetter, *The Presidency of Benjamin Harrison*, 11, 16.

35. Ibid., 47. See also Ford, *Cleveland Era*, 150; Gerring, *Party Ideologies in America*, 120n 252.

36. Oct. 13, 1890, in Charles Hedges, ed., *Speeches of Benjamin Harrison*, 285.

37. Ibid., 183; Socolofsky and Spetter, *Presidency of Benjamin Harrison*, 170 and chap. 9 generally; Tulis, *Rhetorical Presidency*, 64, 440; Hedges, ed., *Speeches of Benjamin Harrison*, 361, 484, 488.

38. Socolofsky and Spetter, *Presidency of Benjamin Harrison*, 170, 173–74, 176, 239 (*New York Times* editorial of Apr. 24, 1891 criticizing Harrison's support of subsidies); Hedges, ed., *Speeches of Benjamin Harrison*, 324, 327, 409, 559. Harrison also wrote a public letter to the Western States Commercial Congress in 1891 stating his support for a bimetallic currency policy (Socolofsky and Spetter, *Presidency of Benjamin Harrison*, 59).

39. On the subject of time, for example, this is the entire text of what Harrison had to say as he was leaving Philipsburg, Pennsylvania, where the "entire population of the town" had welcomed him, according to Hedges: "Citizens of Philipsburg—I thank you for this very cordial expression of your esteem. You must excuse my not addressing you at any length because of the very limited time at our disposal. I again thank you" (*Speeches of Benjamin Harrison*, 234). See also, e.g., ibid., 252, 266, 322, 347. On his voice, see, e.g., ibid., 251, 265, 283, 446. With regard to his "duties," there are several references. At the dedication (attended by a hundred thousand people) of the Soldiers' and Sailors' Monument August 22, 1889, in his hometown of Indianapolis, Harrison began his short address by saying: "I did not expect to make any address on this occasion. It would have been pleasant, if I could have found leisure to make suitable preparation, to have accepted the invitation of the committee having these exercises in charge to deliver an oration .... Public duties, however, prevented the acceptance of the invitation, and I could only promise to be present with you today" (ibid., 214). Similarly, on April 30, 1889, Harrison began his two paragraphs of remarks in New York at the massive, lengthy celebration of the hundredth anniversary of George Washington's inauguration by saying: "Official duty of a very exacting character has made it quite impossible that I should deliver an address on this occasion. Foreseeing this, I early notified your committee that the programme must not contain any address by me. The selection of Mr. [Chauncey M.] Depew as the orator of this occasion makes further speech not only difficult, but superfluous" (ibid., 207).

40. In individual encounters, Harrison was usually cold and distant. One friend speculated that this coldness came from Harrison's conception of the office of the presidency (Socolofsky and Spetter, *Presidency of Benjamin Harrison*, 78). Another said Harrison was "not a practical politician" (ibid, 160).

41. Tulis, *Rhetorical Presidency*, 86.

42. Both quoted in ibid., 86 (emphasis added).

43. Hedges, ed., *Speeches of Benjamin Harrison*, 469. See also another speech ibid., 520.

44. Quoted in Tulis, *Rhetorical Presidency*, 86.

45. Hedges, ed., *Speeches of Benjamin Harrison*, 495.

46. Harrison also alluded to his nonpartisan ideal in his inaugural speech when, referring to his goal of civil service reform, he said: "We shall not, however, I am sure, be able to put our civil service upon a non-partisan basis until we have secured an incumbence that fair minded men of the opposition will

approve for impartiality and integrity" (Hedges, ed., *Speeches of Benjamin Harrison*, 201).

47. Speech in Johnson City, Tennessee, Apr. 14, 1891, ibid., 293. See also speech of Apr. 22, 1891, ibid., 347. An echo of this attitude is found in William McKinley's statement after his reelection in 1900: "I can no longer be called the President of a party; I am now the President of the whole people" (quoted in H. Wayne Morgan, *William McKinley and His America*, 508). For a similar statement, see Pollard, *Presidents and the Press*, 563. McKinley nevertheless did not shirk from controversial policy pronouncements.

48. Speech in Tuscola, Illinois, May 14, 1891, in Hedges, ed., *Speeches of Benjamin Harrison*, 478. See also ibid., 347.

49. Quoted in Tulis, *Rhetorical Presidency*, 87. See also Milkis and Nelson, *American Presidency*, 184.

50. Morgan, *William McKinley*, 513, 517, 518–19; Lewis L. Gould, *The Presidency of William McKinley*, 244, 250, 251. To get elected, McKinley gave over three hundred speeches to more than 750,000 people who visited his home in Canton, Ohio, and even was filmed for a campaign movie. Newspapers were stuffed with campaign inserts about him (Gould, *Presidency of William McKinley*, 11). In the 1900 campaign, workers sent out 2 million copies of campaign material every week to some five thousand newspapers (ibid., 228).

51. Morton Keller, *Affairs of State*, 592–93.

52. William McKinley, *Speeches and Addresses of William McKinley*, 185–91. See Morgan's description of this speech as a "noble dream and a forceful speech, a major utterance in McKinley's presidency, and many who had derided him as weak and without character took fresh note" (*William McKinley*, 423).

53. McKinley, *Speeches and Addresses*, 213. Morgan calls this McKinley's "blunt . . . answer to the anti-imperialists" (*William McKinley*, 436). McKinley followed up this speech with a demand in his annual message to Congress in December that he control American policy in the Philippines (ibid., 437). He rejected an adviser's suggestion that a special session of Congress be convened to determine the precise legal rights to be enjoyed by Philippine residents as inhabitants of a U.S. possession, preferring instead to "present a plan for Congress simply to ratify" (ibid., 440).

54. Gould, *Presidency of William McKinley*, 214.

55. See Morgan, William McKinley, 407; Gould, *Presidency of William McKinley*, 127–28; Hilderbrand, *Power and the People*, 135–42. The tour was novel as a thinly disguised presidential campaign trip. One opposition newspaper criticized it as an "'electioneering enterprise'" that raised questions about the "'good taste, if not the propriety, of the action taken'" (Gould, *Presidency of William McKinley*, 207).

56. McKinley, *Speeches and Addresses*, 105; Gould, *Presidency of William McKinley*, 136. All of McKinley's appearances were carefully arranged, with the president writing out most of his speeches ahead of time (Gould, *Presidency of*

William McKinley, 7). Morgan writes that "McKinley's public speech-making was accompanied by a fanfare that to many seemed almost royal, so dignified was the guest of honor and so deferentially did his prosperous fellow countrymen receive him" (*William McKinley,* 324).

57. McKinley, *Speeches and Addresses,* 164, 175; Margaret Leech, *In the Days of McKinley,* 575. On the southern tour generally, see Gould, *Presidency of William McKinley,* 143. Gould writes that these tours constituted attempts by McKinley to "lead popular opinion to his position in a way that no president had done before him" (ibid., viii).

58. Gould, *Presidency of William McKinley,* 475–80; McKinley, *Speeches and Addresses,* 365; Leech, *In the Days of McKinley,* 487.

59. Morgan, *William McKinley,* 339, 340. See also ibid., 354, 357, 375. As the crisis deepened, the president's silence began to strain the patience of his supporters. A proadministration Boston newspaper said in early March, 1898: "We all owe a debt of gratitude to the President, and we shall be under obligation to him whatever may be the outcome of the [investigation of] the *Maine* disaster, for should worse come to worse his devotion to the duty of silence will have gained us time from the enemy" (quoted in ibid., 362). In Virginia, a mob burned an effigy of McKinley, and his picture was "hissed in theaters and torn from walls in some cities" (ibid., 367).

60. Ibid., 375. McKinley maintained that same inscrutability during the controversy over ratification of the treaty ending the war, and the silence has been criticized as having hindered the ratification effort and perhaps encouraged the rebellion by the Filipinos in early 1899 (ibid., 421). See also Gould, *Presidency of William McKinley,* 213.

61. McKinley, *Speeches and Addresses,* 65. See also the speech McKinley gave three weeks after his reelection, in which he declared the election results were a vote of confidence of the American people in his policies (Gould, *Presidency of William McKinley,* 231). References to many more of McKinley's speeches can be found in the Library of Congress *Index to the William McKinley Papers.*

62. Gould, *Presidency of William McKinley,* 38, 137; Pollard, *Presidents and the Press,* 557–58. Regarding the interviews, one failed disastrously, while the other, given during House debate on the Puerto Rico tariff bill, had a great influence on wavering legislators because it conveyed the president's satisfaction with a compromise proposal (Gould, *Presidency of William McKinley,* 210; Leech, *In the Days of McKinley,* 489).

63. Gould, *Presidency of William McKinley,* 87, 98, 99, 134, 167 (magazine article partly written by McKinley that defended administration's civil service policy), 210, 238; Morgan, *William McKinley,* 322. See also Stephen Ponder, *Managing the Press,* 1–15.

64. See generally Gould, *Presidency of William McKinley,* 204. Quotes are found in ibid., 243. In 1900, Adm. George Dewey's presidential hopes collapsed amid public derision over his statement that the presidency was not a difficult job because all the president had to do was carry out the laws passed

by Congress (Gould, *Presidency of William McKinley*, 214; Morgan, *William McKinley*, 486). There were, however, other voices. In 1897, at the end of Cleveland's administration, the *Richmond Times* editorialized: "The truth is, all this idea of prerogative in the President is wholly out of place in our Constitution" (quoted in Gould, *Presidency of William McKinley*, 2). In December, 1900, the *New York Times*, in dismissing the London *Times*'s suggestion that McKinley appeal "boldly from the Senate to the people" regarding ratification of the Hay-Pauncefote Treaty, stated: "Congress, so far as the President is concerned, is the people, and to it his appeals of one sort and another will be addressed" (quoted in Gerald Gamm and Renee M. Smith, "Presidents, Parties, and the Public: Evolving Patterns of Interaction, 1877–1929," in *Speaking to the People*, ed. Ellis, 97). In light of the speechmaking McKinley had already done by this time, the *Times*'s attitude is hard to understand. As is the wont of editorial writers, the author(s) of this editorial speak as if they were referring to a universal truth, instead of the decidedly Whiggish notion of the presidency that McKinley himself had clearly not been following. Even the *Times*, a different paper in the nineteenth century than it is today, has not always accurately conveyed the sense of all Americans. For example, in 1878 the *Times* editorialized that all Americans had "to be sure, the right to good government, but not the right to take part, either immediately or indirectly, in the management of the state" (quoted in Michael McGerr, *The Decline of Popular Politics*, 47).

65. Based on a sample of nine days of *New York Times* editions out of the almost four and one-half years that McKinley served as president, one study concluded that McKinley rarely gave policy-oriented speeches (see Gamm and Smith, "Presidents, Parties, and the Public"). The sampling appears to have drawn days that were not within the times of McKinley's speaking tours and so produced no mention of these activities.

Chapter 6. The Evolution of Going Public

1. Tulis, *Rhetorical Presidency*, 61.
2. By the time he ran for reelection in 1864, as discussed in connection with the presidency of Andrew Johnson, Lincoln had moved himself and the Republican Party, he hoped, into a new party: the National Union Party. For an excellent account of Lincoln's plan, see the chapter titled "Abraham Lincoln and the Politics of Union" in Michael Holt's *Political Parties*.
3. Madison and Monroe are classified as Democrats even though (1) their party, the Democratic-Republicans, for a while in the early 1800s encompassed virtually the whole spectrum of partisan ideologies that would later split into the Democratic and Whig/Republican Parties, and (2) their conceptions of the presidency were decidedly Classicist, not Democratist. The source of the presidential party designations is Skowronek, *Politics Presidents Make*, 2. As suggested in the text here, the designations of Lincoln as a Republican and

Madison and Monroe as Democrats are somewhat debatable, but those are issues that are not necessary to pursue for my purposes here. Classifying them otherwise would of course (fairly) invite criticism, and I believe that the partisan character of going public can be demonstrated even if, in effect, these three presidencies are arguably coded against their "true" partisan affiliations.

4. In his study of the evolution of the presidential nomination acceptance message, Richard Ellis finds similarly that "one remarkable pattern stands out: virtually every innovation came from the Democratic side" ("Accepting the Nomination: From Martin Van Buren to Franklin Delano Roosevelt," in *Speaking to the People*, ed. Ellis, 132).

5. See Milkis and Nelson, *American Presidency*.

6. See McGerr, *Decline of Popular Politics*, chap. 2.

7. Ibid., chaps. 3–4.

8. See Sundquist, *Decline and Resurgence of Congress*, 25, and chap. 2 in general.

9. Socolofsky and Spetter, *Presidency of Benjamin Harrison*, 48.

10. Wilson, *Congressional Government*, 32.

11. George F. Hoar, *Autobiography of Seventy Years*, 2:46; Wilson, *Congressional Government*, 181.

12. Lucas and Zaeske, "George Washington," 11.

13. Milton, *Age of Hate*, 511.

14. Michael Kammen, *A Season of Youth*, 252.

15. Wilson, *Congressional Government*, 56.

16. McGerr, *Decline of Popular Politics*, chap. 6.

17. See, e.g., Tulis, *Rhetorical Presidency*; Fishkin, *Democracy and Deliberation*, 46–49.

18. As conceptualized by Jurgen Habermas, the public sphere in the modern political world is primarily a discourse carried on by a reading public (see *The Structural Transformation of the Public Sphere*). For intriguing applications of the concept to early American political development, see Michael Warner, *Letters of the Republic*, and Cornell, *Other Founders*. The term "public sphere" is Habermas's; Warner uses "public arena" (*Letters of the Republic*, xiii).

19. See Tulis, *Rhetorical Presidency*, 55, 59, 61, 93.

20. For an intriguing analysis of different "genres" of rhetorical efforts by presidents, see Karlyn Kohrs Campbell and Kathleen Hall Jamieson, *Deeds Done in Words*. For "reasons of space and because they are the products of historical change and modern technology," however, their study does not consider "the press conference, the fireside chat and direct popular appeals to the citizenry" (ibid., 223).

21. Pollard, *Presidents and the Press*, 128.

22. Cf., Johnstone, *Jefferson and the Presidency*, 78; Ketcham, *Presidents Above Party*, xi and 187 (early presidents were in a "time of transition").

23. Note, however, that the *New York Times* reporter present when Lincoln delivered the Gettysburg Address wrote: "President Lincoln's address was delivered

in a clear loud tone of voice, which could be distinctly heard at the extreme limits of the large assemblage" (quoted in Sandburg, *Abraham Lincoln*, 4:470).

24. Jay Heinrichs, "How Harvard Destroyed Rhetoric," *Harvard Magazine*, July–Aug. 1995, 36–43.

25. Wilson, *Congressional Government*, 181, and *Constitutional Government in the United States*, 73.

26. Wilson, *Constitutional Government*, 54, 56.

27. Ibid., 70, 72.

28. Ibid., 68, 73.

29. Ford, *Works of Thomas Jefferson*, 8:26.

30. Wilson, *Constitutional Government*, 54, 56, 57, 59, 60.

31. Ibid., 60, 69, 74. For helpful historical perspective on the evolution in Wilson's thinking, see Terri Bimes and Stephen Skowronek, "Wilson's Critique of Popular Leadership: Reassessing the Modern-Traditional Divide in Presidential History," in *Speaking to the People*, ed. Ellis.

32. Walter Lippman, *Public Opinion*, 30; Ponder, *Managing the Press*, 77–125. For an examination of other public initiatives by Wilson during his presidency, see Daniel Stid, "Rhetorical Leadership and 'Common Counsel' in the Presidency of Woodrow Wilson," in *Speaking to the People*, ed. Ellis. For a comprehensive treatment of Wilson's thought and his presidency, see Daniel Stid, *The President as Statesman*.

33. On the other hand, *Congressional Government* had gone through fifteen printings by 1900 (Bimes and Skowronek, "Wilson's Critique of Popular Leadership," 137).

34. See the discussion in chapter 2 and, in particular, Edward S. Corwin, *The President*, 10–16; Ketcham, *Presidents Above Party*, 106; Johnstone, *Jefferson and the Presidency*, 41–57.

35. Tebbel and Watts, *Press and the Presidency*, 79; Wiebe, *Opening of American Society*, chap. 8. An additional factor was the adoption by most states of winner-take-all rules for the selection of presidential electors (Holt, *Political Parties*, 41).

36. Gamm and Smith argue that change in the institution of the presidency arose out of a "conflict among elites that gave rise to new styles of campaigning and, later, governing" ("Presidents, Parties, and the Public," 29). See also Milkis and Nelson, *American Presidency*, 126.

37. Wiebe, *Opening of American Society*, 156; Robert A. Dahl, "On Removing Certain Impediments in the United States," in *Moral Foundations of the American Republic*, ed. Horwitz, 236; Milkis and Nelson, *American Presidency*, 124–25; White, *Jacksonians*, 23–28.

38. As Joyce Appleby has also noted, there is quite a bit of irony in the fact that many aspects of the constitutional order created by the Framers were then utilized by others in quite different and unexpected ways, often *against* what the Framers had intended (*Capitalism and a New Social Order*, 76).

39. See James W. Davis, "The Public Presidency: Press, Media, and Public Approval," in *Understanding the Presidency*, ed. Pfiffner and Davidson, 122–23, for a comparison of the limited power of presidents as party and legislative leaders with the broad powers of prime ministers in parliamentary systems. Davis argues that presidents compensate for their limited powers by depending heavily on public support, personal magnetism, and the ability to work with congressional leaders.

40. Neustadt, *Presidential Power*, 73.

41. de Tocqueville, *Democracy in America*, 122.

42. Quoted in White, *Jacksonians*, 32.

43. Lowi, *Personal President*, 34–35.

44. See Corwin, *President*, 20–23.

45. See John W. Kingdon, *Congressmen's Voting Decisions*, and David R. Mayhew, *Congress*.

46. It should be noted that a president who believed that the federal government was too powerful or intrusive might still utilize this technique as a way of marshalling support for his efforts to cut the government back. One example is Andrew Jackson, who has been described as a "forceful Chief Executive" who did "not approve of a forceful federal government" (Cunliffe, *Presidency*, 72). Another more recent example is Ronald Reagan, who devoted a great part of his efforts at going public to justifying his attempts to downsize parts of the federal government. The irony here is that those wishing to reduce the role of the federal government have realized that first capturing control of the government would make their work much easier. And both a presidency with enhanced powers and the strengthened national government itself might actually be useful weapons in the dismantlement effort. Cf., Binkley, *American Political Parties*, ix, 93.

Chapter 7. The Legitimacy of Going Public

1. Kernell, *Going Public*, 9.

2. Ibid., 13, 14, 20, 28.

3. Tulis, *Rhetorical Presidency*, 33, 34, 188.

4. Fishkin, *Democracy and Deliberation*, 18.

5. Herbert J. Storing, *What the Anti-Federalists Were For*, 17.

6. Fishkin, *Democracy and Deliberation*, 18. See also Wood's judgment that although "the Anti-Federalists lost the battle over the ratification of the Constitution," they "did not lose the war over the kind of government the United States would have" (*Radicalism of the American Revolution*, 259).

7. Ackerman, *We the People*, vol. 1, *Foundations*.

8. Kernell, *Going Public*, 11.

9. See, e.g., Tulis, "Two Constitutional Presidencies," 93–94.

10. See, e.g., Richard Fenno, *Home Style*, 161; R. Douglas Arnold, *The Logic of Congressional Action*; Kingdon, *Congressmen's Voting Decisions*, chap. 2.

11. E. E. Schattschneider, *The Semi-Sovereign People.*

12. For an excellent account of the bargaining that underlay one of Ronald Reagan's greatest achievements, see Marc Bodnick, "'Going Public' Reconsidered: Reagan's 1981 Tax and Budget Cuts, and Revisionist Theories of Presidential Power," *Congress and the Presidency* 17 (spring, 1990): 13–28.

13. See Peter W. Sperlich, "Bargaining and Overload: An Essay on Presidential Power," in *The Presidency,* ed. Aaron Wildavsky, 406–30.

14. Kernell, *Going Public,* 254. In the early stages of a labor contract dispute between a union and a business, acrimony and hyperbole can often be found in abundant quantities in the statements of both sides. Yet most such disputes eventually get settled. An excellent example of how rhetoric is not allowed to get in the way of a deal is the settlement of the strike in 1998 by UAW workers over planned production changes at a GM plant in Flint, Michigan that had shutdown GM operations nationwide (see Keith Bradsher, "Bit of Progress in Talks to End Strikes at G.M.," *New York Times,* July 4, 1998, B1, and "At G.M., Can't They Get Along?" *New York Times,* July 29, 1998, C1).

15. Kernell, *Going Public,* 21.

16. See Kingdon, *Congressmen's Voting Decisions,* esp. chap. 2.

17. See Mark A. Peterson, *Legislating Together.*

18. "Gingrich to Clinton: We're Here, We Sneer, Get Used to It," *Ann Arbor News,* Dec. 6, 1994, A4.

19. Alison Mitchell, "Clinton Applies '94 Lesson to Fight G.O.P. on Budget," *New York Times,* Oct. 13, 1995.

20. Ibid.

21. Frank Bruni and Alison Mitchell, "Bush Pushes Hard to Woo Democrats Over to Tax Plan," *New York Times,* Mar. 5, 2001. See also Frank Bruni, "Bush Takes His Tax Proposal on Tour," *New York Times,* Mar. 1, 2001, and "Bush Takes Tax-Cut Drive Back on the Road," *New York Times,* Mar. 27, 2001. Explaining his view of how members of Congress should respond to messages from constituents, Bush said at another stop, "I know that when it comes to doing the right thing, they'll listen to the people of Nebraska" (Feb. 28, 2001, rally as reported on CNN).

22. Tulis, "Two Constitutional Presidencies," 116; Tulis, "Revising the Rhetorical Presidency," in *Beyond the Rhetorical Presidency,* ed. Medhurst, 5.

23. On this last point, see Medhurst, "Introduction," xix–xx.

24. For a discussion of the deliberative quality of "modern American democracy," see Bessette, *Mild Voice of Reason.*

25. Indeed, Congress for a good part of its history seems to have been a body where, no matter what might be said in debates on the floor, control over legislation has rested in the hands of political leaders such as the president and the speaker and committee chairs (see Sundquist, *Decline and Resurgence of Congress,* chap. 7). Moreover, the modern proliferation of committees and staffs would seem capable most of the time of offsetting any deleterious effects on the deliberative process caused by modern presidential

attempts to sway legislation through public appeals (cf., Bessette, *Mild Voice of Reason*, chap. 6).

26. Tulis, *Rhetorical Presidency*, 35.
27. Ibid., 174 and chaps. 2 and 5. See also Tulis's essays, "Two Constitutional Presidencies," 116, and "Revising the Rhetorical Presidency," 5.
28. Sundquist, *Decline and Resurgence of Congress*, 19n 5.
29. King and Ragsdale, *Elusive Executive*, 21.

BIBLIOGRAPHY

Abbott, Philip. "Do Presidents Talk Too Much? The Rhetorical Presidency and its Alternative." *Presidential Studies Quarterly* 18, no. 2 (spring, 1988): 347–62.

Ackerman, Bruce. *We the People.* 2 vols. Cambridge: Harvard University Press, 1991, 1998.

Adams, Charles Francis, ed. *Life and Works of John Adams.* 10 vols. Boston: Little, Brown, 1850–56.

Alden, John R. *George Washington: A Biography.* Baton Rouge: Louisiana State University Press, 1984.

Allen, W. B., and Gordon Lloyd, eds. *The Essential Antifederalist.* New York: University Press of America, 1985.

Ames, William E. *A History of the National Intelligencer.* Chapel Hill: University of North Carolina Press, 1972.

Ammon, Harry. *James Monroe: The Quest for National Identity.* New York: McGraw-Hill, 1971.

Arnold, R. Douglas. *The Logic of Congressional Action.* New Haven, Conn.: Yale University Press, 1990.

Appleby, Joyce. *Capitalism and a New Social Order: The Republican Vision of the 1790s.* New York: New York University Press, 1984.

———. "The Constitution and the Culture of Constitutionalism." In *Understanding the United States Constitution, 1787–1987 Bicentennial Lectures.* Colorado College Studies no. 24. Colorado Springs: Colorado College, 1988.

Aspinal, Arthur. *Politics and the Press c. 1780–1850.* London: Home and Van Thal, 1949.

Axelrad, Jacob. *Philip Freneau: Champion of Democracy.* Austin: University of Texas Press, 1967.

Bailyn, Bernard. *The Ideological Origins of the American Revolution.* Enlarged ed. Cambridge, Mass.: Belknap Press, 1992.

Bainard, Harry. *Rutherford B. Hayes and His America.* Indianapolis: Bobbs-Merrill, 1954.

Baldasty, Gerald J. *The Press and Politics in the Age of Jackson.* Columbia, S.C.: Association for Education in Journalism and Mass Communications, 1984.

Banning, Lance. *The Jeffersonian Persuasion: Evolution of a Party Ideology*. Ithaca, N.Y.: Cornell University Press, 1978.

Barber, James David. *The Presidential Character: Predicting Performance in the White House*. 4th ed. Englewood Cliffs, N.J.: Prentice Hall, 1992.

Barry, David S. "News-Getting at the Capital." *Chautauquan* 26 (December, 1897): 282–86.

Basler, Roy P., ed. *The Collected Works of Abraham Lincoln*. 8 vols. New Brunswick, N.J.: Rutgers University Press, 1953–55.

Beeman, Richard, Stephen Botein, and Edward C. Carter II, eds. *Beyond Confederation: Origins of the Constitution and American National Identity*. Williamsburg: University of North Carolina Press, 1987.

Ben-Atar, Doron, and Barbara B. Oberg, eds., *Federalists Reconsidered*. Charlottesville: University Press of Virginia, 1998.

Benedict, Michael Les. *The Impeachment and Trial of Andrew Johnson*. New York: W. W. Norton, 1973.

Bergeron, Paul H. *The Presidency of James K. Polk*. Lawrence: University Press of Kansas, 1987.

Bessette, Joseph M. *The Mild Voice of Reason: Deliberative Democracy and American National Government*. Chicago: University of Chicago Press, 1994.

———, and Jeffrey Tulis, eds. *The Presidency in the Constitutional Order*. Baton Rouge: Louisiana State University Press, 1981.

Beveridge, Albert J. *Abraham Lincoln*. 2 vols. New York: Houghton Mifflin, 1928. Reprint, St. Clair Shores, Mich.: Scholarly Press, 1971.

Bimes, Terri, and Stephen Skowronek. "Wilson's Critique of Popular Leadership: Reassessing the Modern-Traditional Divide in Presidential History." In *Speaking to the People: The Rhetorical Presidency in Historical Perspective*, edited by Richard J. Ellis. Amherst: University of Massachusetts Press, 1998.

Binkley, Wilfred E. *President and Congress*. 3d ed. New York: Vintage Books, 1962.

———. *American Political Parties: Their Natural History*. 4th ed. New York: Alfred A. Knopf, 1971.

Bland, Richard A. "Politics, Propaganda, and the Public Printing: The Administration Organs, 1829–1849." Ph.D. diss., University of Kentucky, 1975.

Bleyer, Willard G. *Main Currents in the History of American Journalism*. Boston: Houghton Mifflin, 1927.

Blumenthal, Sidney. "Marketing the President." *New York Times Magazine*, September 13, 1981.

Bodnick, Marc. "'Going Public' Reconsidered: Reagan's 1981 Tax and Budget Cuts, and Revisionist Theories of Presidential Power." *Congress and the Presidency* 17, no. 1 (spring, 1990): 13–28.

Bowers, Claude G. *Jefferson and Hamilton: the Struggle for Democracy in America*. Boston: Houghton Mifflin, 1925.

Bradsher, Keith. "Bit of Progress in Talks to End Strikes at G.M." *New York Times*, July 4, 1998, B1.

———. "At G.M., Can't They Get Along?" *New York Times*, July 29, 1998, C1.

Brown, Richard D. *The Strength of a People: The Idea of an Informed Citizenry in America, 1650–1870.* Chapel Hill: The University of North Carolina Press, 1996.

———. *Knowledge Is Power: The Diffusion of Information in Early America, 1700–1865.* New York: Oxford University Press, 1989.

Burns, James MacGregor. *Presidential Government: The Crucible of Leadership.* Boston: Houghton Mifflin, 1973.

Campbell, Karlyn Kohrs, and Kathleen Hall Jamieson. *Deeds Done in Words: Presidential Rhetoric and the Genres of Governance.* Chicago: University of Chicago Press, 1990.

Carroll, E. Malcolm. *Origins of the Whig Party.* New York: Da Capo, 1970.

Castel, Albert. *The Presidency of Andrew Johnson.* Lawrence: University Press of Kansas, 1979.

Ceaser, James W. *Presidential Selection: Theory and Development.* Princeton: Princeton University Press, 1979.

———. "The Rhetorical Presidency Revisited." In *Modern Presidents and the Presidency,* edited by Marc Landy. Lexington, Mass.: D. C. Heath, 1985.

———, Glen E. Thurow, Jeffrey Tulis, and Joseph M. Bessette. "The Rise of the Rhetorical Presidency." *Presidential Studies Quarterly* 11, no. 2 (spring, 1981): 158–71.

Chambers, William Nisbet. "Election of 1840." In *History of American Presidential Elections, 1789–1968,* edited by Arthur M. Schlesinger Jr. New York: Chelsea House, 1971.

Cicero. *De Officiis.* Trans. Harry G. Edinger. Indianapolis: Bobbs-Merrill, 1974.

Cole, Donald B. *Martin Van Buren and the American Political System.* Princeton, N.J.: Princeton University Press, 1984.

Cooke, Jacob Ernest. *Alexander Hamilton.* New York: Charles Scribner's Sons: 1982.

Cornell, Saul. *The Other Founders: Anti-Federalism and the Dissenting Tradition in America, 1788–1828.* Chapel Hill: University of North Carolina Press, 1999.

Cornwell, Elmer E. Jr. *Presidential Leadership of Public Opinion.* Bloomington: Indiana University Press, 1965.

Corwin, Edwin S. *The President: Office and Powers, 1787–1957.* 4th rev. ed. New York: New York University Press, 1957.

Crockett, David. *The Life of Martin Van Buren: Heir-Apparent to the "Government," and the Appointed Successor of General Andrew Jackson.* New York: Nafish and Cornish, 1845.

Cronin, Thomas E. *Rethinking the Presidency.* Boston: Little, Brown, 1982.

Cuomo, Mario M., and Harold Holzer, eds. *Lincoln on Democracy.* New York: Harper Collins, 1990.

Cunliffe, Marcus. *The Presidency.* 3d. ed. Boston: Houghton Mifflin, 1987.

———. *American Presidents and the Presidency.* 2d. ed. New York: McGraw-Hill, 1972.

———. *George Washington, Man and Monument.* Boston: Little, Brown, 1958.

Cunningham, Noble E. Jr. *The Presidency of James Monroe.* Lawrence: University Press of Kansas, 1996.

————. *The Process of Government Under Jefferson.* Princeton, N.J.: Princeton University Press, 1978.

————. *The Jeffersonian Republicans in Power: Party Operations, 1801–1809.* Chapel Hill: University of North Carolina Press, 1963.

Dahl, Robert A. "On Removing Certain Impediments in the United States." In *The Moral Foundations of the American Republic,* edited by Robert H. Horwitz. 3d ed. Charlottesville: University Press of Virginia, 1986.

Davis, James W. "The Public Presidency: Press, Media, and Public Approval." In *Understanding the American Presidency,* edited by James P. Pfiffner and Roger H. Davidson. 3d ed. New York: Longman, 2000.

Davis, Richard. *The Press and American Politics.* New York: Longman, 1992.

Davison, Kenneth E. *The Presidency of Rutherford B. Hayes.* Westport, Conn.: Greenwood Press, 1972.

De Pauw, Linda Grant. *The Eleventh Pillar: New York State and the Federal Constitution.* Ithaca, N.Y.: Cornell University Press.

de Tocqueville, Alexis. *Democracy in America.* Edited by J. P. Mayer. New York: HarperCollins/Perennial, 2000.

Dickinson, Matthew J. *Bitter Harvest: FDR, Presidential Power and the Growth of the Presidential Branch.* Cambridge: Cambridge University Press, 1997.

Doenecke, Justus D. *The Presidencies of James A. Garfield and Chester A. Arthur.* Lawrence: Regents Press of Kansas, 1981.

Edwards, George C. III. *The Public Presidency: The Pursuit of Popular Support.* New York: St. Martin's, 1983.

Elkins, Stanley, and Eric McKitrick. *The Age of Federalism.* New York: Oxford University Press, 1993.

Ellis, Joseph J. *American Sphinx: The Character of Thomas Jefferson.* New York: Alfred A. Knopf, 1997.

Ellis, Richard J. *American Political Cultures.* New York: Oxford University Press, 1993.

————. *The Jeffersonian Crisis: Courts and Politics in the Young Republic.* New York: W. W. Norton, 1971.

————, ed. *Speaking to the People: The Rhetorical Presidency in Historical Perspective.* Amherst: University of Massachusetts Press, 1998.

Ellis, Richard J., and Stephen Kirk. "Jefferson, Jackson, and the Origins of the Presidential Mandate." In *Speaking to the People: The Rhetorical Presidency in Historical Perspective,* edited by Richard J. Ellis. Amherst: University of Massachusetts Press, 1998.

Emery, Edwin, and Michael Emery. *The Press and America: An Interpretive History of the Mass Media.* 4th ed. Englewood Cliffs, N.J.: Prentice-Hall, 1978.

Fehrenbacher, Don E., ed. *Abraham Lincoln: Speeches and Writings, 1859–1865.* Library of America: 1989.

Fenno, Richard. *Home Style.* Boston: Little, Brown, 1978.

Ferguson, Robert A. *Laws and Letters in American Culture.* Cambridge, Mass.: Harvard University Press, 1984.

Fischer, David Hackett. *The Revolution of American Conservatism: The Federalist Party in the Era of Jeffersonian Democracy.* New York: Harper and Row, 1965.

Fishkin, James S. *Democracy and Deliberation.* New Haven, Conn.: Yale University Press, 1991.

Fitzpatrick, John C., ed. *Writings of George Washington.* 39 vols. Washington, D.C.: GPO, 1931–44.

Flexner, James Thomas. *George Washington and the New Nation, 1783–1793.* Boston: Little, Brown, 1969.

———. *George Washington: Anguish and Farewell, 1793–99.* Boston: Little, Brown, 1969.

Ford, Henry Jones. *The Cleveland Era: A Chronicle of the New Order in Politics.* New Haven, Conn.: Yale University Press, 1921.

Ford, Paul L., ed. *The Works of Thomas Jefferson.* 12 vols. New York: G. P. Putnam's Sons, 1904–1905.

Forman, Samuel E. *The Political Activities of Philip Freneau.* Baltimore: Johns Hopkins Press, 1902.

Formisano, Ronald P. *The Transformation of Political Culture: Massachusetts Parties, 1790s–1840s.* New York: Oxford University Press, 1983.

Frisch, Morton J. "Executive Power and Representative Government—1787." *Presidential Studies Quarterly* 17, no. 2 (spring, 1987): 281–91.

Furtwangler, Albert. *American Silhouettes: Rhetorical Identities of the Founders.* New Haven, Conn.: Yale University Press, 1987.

———. *The Authority of Publius: A Reading of the Federalist Papers.* Ithaca, N.Y.: Cornell University Press, 1984.

Gamm, Gerald, and Renee M. Smith. "Presidents, Parties, and the Public: Evolving Patterns of Interaction, 1877–1929." In *Speaking to the People: The Rhetorical Presidency in Historical Perspective,* edited by Richard J. Ellis. Amherst: University of Massachusetts Press, 1998.

Gara, Larry. *The Presidency of Franklin Pierce.* Lawrence: University Press of Kansas, 1991.

Gerring, John. *Party Ideologies in America, 1828–1996.* Cambridge: Cambridge University Press, 1998.

———. "Party Ideology in America: The National Republican Chapter, 1828–1924." *Studies in American Political Development* 11, no. 1 (spring, 1997): 44–108.

Gienapp, William E. *The Origins of the Republican Party, 1852–1856.* New York: Oxford University Press, 1987.

"Gingrich to Clinton: We're Here, We Sneer, Get Used to It." *Ann Arbor News,* December 6, 1994, A4.

Goldwin, Robert A., and William A. Schambra, eds. *How Democratic Is the Constitution?* Washington, D.C.: American Enterprise Institute for Public Policy Research, 1980.

———, ed. *Political Parties, U.S.A.* Chicago: Rand McNally, 1964.

Gould, Lewis L. *The Presidency of William McKinley.* Lawrence: Regents Press of Kansas, 1980.

Graber, Mark A. "Federalist or Friends of Adams: The Marshall Court and Party Politics." *Studies in American Political Development* 12, no. 2 (fall, 1998): 229–66.

Greenstein, Fred I. *The Hidden-Hand Presidency: Eisenhower as Leader.* New York: Basic Books, 1982.

———. "Eisenhower's Presidential Leadership." In *Modern Presidents and the Presidency,* edited by Marc Landy. Lexington, Mass.: D. C. Heath, 1985.

Habermas, Jurgen. *The Structural Transformation of the Public Sphere.* Trans. Thomas Burger. Cambridge: Massachusetts Institute of Technology Press, 1989.

Hamilton, Hamilton. *Zachary Taylor: Soldier in the White House.* New York: Bobbs-Merrill, 1951.

Hargreaves, Mary M. *The Presidency of John Quincy Adams.* Lawrence: University Press of Kansas, 1985.

Hariman, Robert. *Political Style: The Artistry of Power (New Practices of Inquiry).* Chicago: University of Chicago Press, 1995.

Hart, Roderick P. *The Sound of Leadership: Presidential Communication in the Modern Age.* Chicago: University of Chicago Press, 1987.

Hecht, Marie B. *Odd Destiny: The Life of Alexander Hamilton.* New York: Macmillan, 1982.

Hedges, Charles, ed. *Speeches of Benjamin Harrison.* New York: United States Book, 1892.

Heinrichs, Jay. "How Harvard Destroyed Rhetoric." *Harvard Magazine,* July–August, 1995, 37–42.

Hilderbrand, Robert Clinton. *Power and the People: Executive Management of Public Opinion in Foreign Affairs, 1869–1921.* Chapel Hill: University of North Carolina Press, 1981.

Hinckley, Barbara. *The Symbolic Presidency: How Presidents Portray Themselves.* New York: Routledge, 1990.

Hoar, George F. *Autobiography of Seventy Years.* 2 vols. New York: Scribner's, 1903.

Hofstadter, Richard. "The Founding Fathers: An Age of Realism." In *The Moral Foundations of the American Republic,* edited by Robert H. Horwitz. 3d. ed. Charlottesville: University Press of Virginia, 1986.

———. *The Idea of a Party System: the Rise of Legitimate Opposition in the United States, 1780–1840.* Berkeley: University of California Press, 1972.

Hoge, Warren. "Responding to Britain's Sorrow, Queen Will Address the Nation." *New York Times.* September 5, 1997, 1.

Holt, Michael F. *Political Parties and American Political Development: From the Age of Jackson to the Age of Lincoln.* Baton Rouge: Louisiana State University Press, 1992.

Hoogenboom, Ari. *The Presidency of Rutherford B. Hayes.* Lawrence: University Press of Kansas, 1988.

Horwitz, Robert H., ed. *The Moral Foundations of the American Republic.* 3d ed. Charlottesville: University Press of Virginia, 1986.

Howe, Daniel Walker. *The Political Culture of the American Whigs.* Chicago: University of Chicago Press, 1979.

Hudson, Frederic. *Journalism in the United States From 1690 to 1872.* 1873. Reprint, Grosse Pointe, Mich.: Scholarly Press, 1968.

Hunt, Gaillard, ed. *The Writings of James Madison.* 9 vols. New York: G. P. Putnam's
Sons, 1900–10.

Jaffa, Harry. "The Nature and Origin of the American Party System." In *Political
Parties, U.S.A.*, edited by Robert Goldwin. Chicago: Rand McNally, 1964.

James, Marquis. *Andrew Jackson: Portrait of a President.* Indianapolis: Bobbs Merrill,
1937.

Jasinski, James. "Rhetoric and Judgment in the Constitutional Ratification Debate
of 1787–1788: An Exploration of the Relationship Between Theory and Critical
Practice." *Quarterly Journal of Speech* 78, no. 2 (May, 1992): 197–218.

————. "The Forms and Limits of Prudence in Henry Clay's (1850) Defense of the
Compromise Measures." *Quarterly Journal of Speech* 81, no. 4 (November, 1995):
454–78.

Jenkins, Jeffrey A. "Why No Parties?: Investigating the Disappearance of Democrat-
Whig Divisions in the Confederacy." *Studies in American Political Development* 13,
no. 2 (fall, 1999): 245–62.

John, Richard R. *Spreading the News: The American Postal System from Franklin to
Morse.* Cambridge, Mass.: Harvard University Press, 1995.

Johnstone, Robert M. Jr. *Jefferson and the Presidency: Leadership in the Young Republic.*
Ithaca, N.Y.: Cornell University Press, 1978.

Kammen, Michael. *A Season of Youth: The American Revolution and the Historical
Imagination.* Ithaca, N.Y.: Cornell University Press, 1978.

Keller, Morton. *Affairs of State: Public Life in Late Nineteenth Century America.*
Cambridge, Mass.: Harvard University Press, 1977.

Kerber, Linda K. *Federalists in Dissent: Imagery and Ideology in Jeffersonian America.*
Ithaca, N.Y.: Cornell University Press, 1970.

Kernell, Samuel. *Going Public: New Strategies of Presidential Leadership.* 3d ed.
Washington, D.C.: Congressional Quarterly Press, 1997.

Ketcham, Ralph. *Presidents above Party: The First American Presidency, 1789–1829.*
Chapel Hill: University of North Carolina Press, 1984.

————. *James Madison.* New York: Macmillan, 1971.

————. "Executive Leadership, Citizenship and Good Government." *Presidential
Studies Quarterly* 17, no. 2 (spring, 1987): 267–79.

Kielbowicz, Richard. *News in the Mail: The Press, Post Office, and Public Information,
1700–1860s.* New York: Greenwood Press, 1989.

Kiewe, Amos, ed. *The Modern Presidency and Crisis Rhetoric.* Westport, Conn.:
Praeger, 1994.

King, Gary, and Lyn Ragsdale. *The Elusive Executive.* Washington, D.C.: CQ Press,
1988.

Kingdon, John W. *Agendas, Alternatives, and Public Policies.* 2d ed. New York:
Longman, 1995.

————. *Congressmen's Voting Decisions.* New York: Harper and Row, 1981.

Landy, Marc., ed. *Modern Presidents and the Presidency.* Lexington, Mass.: D. C.
Heath, 1985.

Laprade, William T. "The Power of the English Press in the Eighteenth Century." In

Highlights in the History of the American Press, edited by Edwin H. Ford and Edwin Emery. Minneapolis: University of Minnesota Press, 1954.

Lawler, Peter Augustine. "The Federalists' Hostility to Leadership and the Crisis of the Contemporary Presidency." *Presidential Studies Quarterly* 17, no. 4 (fall, 1987): 711–23.

Lee, James Melvin. *History of American Journalism.* Boston: Houghton Mifflin, 1917.

Leech, Margaret. *In the Days of McKinley.* New York: Harper and Brothers, 1959.

Leonard, Thomas C. *News For All: America's Coming-of-Age with the Press.* New York: Oxford University Press, 1995.

Levy, T. A. *Lincoln the Politician.* Baton Rouge: R.G. Badger, 1918.

Library of Congress. *Index to the William McKinley Papers.* Washington, D.C.: GPO, 1963

Lippman, Walter. *Public Opinion.* 1922. Reprint, New York: Free Press, 1965.

Lodge, Henry Cabot, ed. *The Works of Alexander Hamilton.* 12 vols. New York: Putnam's, 1903.

Loss, Richard. *The Modern Theory of Presidential Power: Alexander Hamilton and the Corwin Thesis.* New York: Greenwood, 1990.

Lowi, Theodore J. *The Personal Presidency: Power Invested, Promise Unfulfilled.* Ithaca, N.Y.: Cornell University Press, 1985.

Lucas, Stephen E. *Portents of Rebellion: Rhetoric and Revolution in Philadelphia, 1765–76.* Philadelphia: Temple University Press, 1976.

———, and Susan Zaeske, "George Washington (1732–1799)." In *U.S. Presidents as Orators: A Bio-Critical Sourcebook,* edited by Halford Ryan. Westport, Conn.: Greenwood Press, 1995.

Macy, Jesse. *Political Parties in the United States 1846–1861.* 1900. Reprint, New York: Arno, 1974.

Main, Jackson Turner. *The Antifederalists: Critics of the Constitution, 1781–1788.* Chapel Hill: University of North Carolina Press, 1961.

Maltese, John Anthony. *Spin Control.* Chapel Hill: University of North Carolina Press, 1992.

Marbut, Frederick B. "Decline of the Official Press in Washington." *Journalism Quarterly* 33, no. 3 (summer, 1956): 335–41.

Mayhew, David R. *Congress: The Electoral Connection.* New Haven, Conn.: Yale University Press, 1974.

McCoy, Charles A. *Polk and the Presidency.* Austin: University of Texas Press, 1960.

McDonald, Forrest. *Novus Ordo Seclorum: The Intellectual Origins of the Constitution.* Lawrence: University Press of Kansas, 1985.

———. *The Presidency of Thomas Jefferson.* Lawrence: University Press of Kansas, 1976.

McGerr, Michael E. *The Decline of Popular Politics.* New York: Oxford University Press, 1986.

McKinley, William. *Speeches and Addresses of William McKinley.* New York: Doubleday and McClure, 1900.

McKitrick, Eric L., ed. *Andrew Johnson: A Profile.* New York: Hill and Wang, 1969.

Medhurst, Martin J., ed. *Beyond the Rhetorical Presidency.* College Station: Texas A&M University Press, 1996.

Milkis, Sidney M. and Nelson, Michael. *The American Presidency: Origins and Development, 1776–1993.* 2d ed. Washington, D.C.: CQ Press, 1994.

Miller, John C. *The Federalist Era, 1789–1801.* New York: Harper and Brothers, 1960.

Milton, George Fort. *The Age of Hate: Andrew Johnson and the Radicals.* 1930. Reprint, Hamden, Conn.: Archon Books, 1965.

Miroff, Bruce. "The Presidency and the Public: Leadership as Spectacle." In *The President and the Political System,* edited by Michael Nelson. 6th ed. Washington: CQ Press, 2000.

Mitchell, Broadus. *Alexander Hamilton: The National Adventure, 1788–1804.* New York: MacMillan, 1962.

Morgan, Edmund S. *The Birth of the Republic, 1763–89.* 3d ed. Chicago: University of Chicago Press, 1992.

———. *Inventing the People: The Rise of Popular Sovereignty in England and America.* New York: W. W. Norton, 1988.

Morgan, H. Wayne. *William McKinley and His America.* Syracuse, N.Y.: Syracuse University Press, 1963.

Morrisey, Will. "The Moral Foundations of the American Republic: An Introduction." In *The Moral Foundations of the American Republic,* edited by Robert H. Horwitz. 3d ed. Charlottesville: University Press of Virginia, 1986.

Mott, Frank Luther. *American Journalism: A History of Newspapers in the United States Through 260 Years: 1690 to 1950.* New York: Macmillan, 1950.

———. *Jefferson and the Press.* Baton Rouge: Louisiana State University Press, 1943.

Nash, Howard P. Jr. *Andrew Johnson: Congress and Reconstruction.* Rutherford, N.J.: Farleigh Dickinson University Press, 1972.

Nelson, Michael, ed. *The President and the Political System.* 6th ed. Washington: CQ Press, 2000.

Neustadt, Richard E. *Presidential Power and the Modern Presidents.* New York: Free Press, 1990.

Nevins, Allan. *Grover Cleveland: A Study in Courage.* New York: Dodd, Mead, 1932.

———, ed. *Polk: The Diary of a President, 1845–1849.* London, New York: Longmans, Green, 1929.

———, ed. *Letters of Grover Cleveland.* New York: Houghton Mifflin, 1933. Reprint, New York: Da Capo, 1970.

Nichols, David K. *The Myth of the Modern Presidency.* University Park: Pennsylvania State University Press, 1994.

Nicolay, John G., and John Hay. *The Complete Works of Abraham Lincoln.* 2 vols. New York: Century, 1894).

Niven, John. *Martin Van Buren: The Romantic Age of American Politics.* New York: Oxford University Press, 1983.

Parker, George F. *Recollections of Grover Cleveland.* New York: Appleton-Century, 1909.

Payne, George Henry. *History of Journalism in the United States.* New York: D. Appleton, 1920.

Peterson, Mark A. *Legislating Together: The White House and Capitol Hill from Eisenhower to Reagan.* Cambridge, Mass.: Harvard University Press, 1990.

Peterson, Merrill D. *Thomas Jefferson and the New Nation.* London: Oxford University Press, 1970.

Peterson, Norma Lois. *The Presidencies of William Henry Harrison and John Tyler.* Lawrence: University Press of Kansas, 1989.

Pfiffner, James P. and Roger H. Davidson, eds. *Understanding the American Presidency.* 3d ed. New York: Longman, 2000.

Phelps, Glenn A. "George Washington and the Paradox of Party." *Presidential Studies Quarterly* 19, no. 4 (fall, 1989): 733–45.

———. "George Washington and the Founding of the Presidency." *Presidential Studies Quarterly* 17, no. 2 (spring, 1987): 345–63.

———. "George Washington and the Building of the Constitution: Presidential Interpretation and Constitutional Development." *Congress and the Presidency* 12, no. 2 (autumn, 1985): 95–109.

Pocock, J. G. A. *The Machiavellian Moment: Florentine Political Thought and the Atlantic Republican Tradition.* Princeton, N.J.: Princeton University Press, 1975.

Polk, James K. *The Diary of James K. Polk during His Presidency, 1845 to 1849.* Edited by Milo M. Quaife. 4 vols. Chicago: A. C. McClurg, 1910.

Pollard, James E. *The Presidents and the Press.* New York: Macmillan, 1947.

Ponder, Stephen. *Managing the Press: Origins of the Media Presidency, 1897–1933.* New York: St. Martin's, 1998.

Quirk, Paul J. "Presidential Competence." In *The President and the Political System,* edited by Michael Nelson. 6th ed. Washington: CQ Press, 2000.

Rakove, Jack N. *Original Meanings: Politics and Ideas in the Making of the Constitution.* New York: Vintage Books: 1997.

Remini, Robert V. *The Life of Andrew Jackson.* New York: Harper and Row, 1988.

———. *Andrew Jackson.* Vol. 3, *The Course of American Democracy, 1833–1845.* Baltimore: Johns Hopkins University Press, 1984.

———. *The Election of Andrew Jackson.* 1963. Reprint, Westport, Conn.: Greenwood Press, 1980.

———. *Martin Van Buren and the Making of the Democratic Party.* New York: Columbia University Press, 1959.

———, ed. *The Age of Jackson.* Columbia: University of South Carolina Press, 1972.

Riccards, Michael P. *A Republic, If You Can Keep It: The Foundation of the American Presidency, 1700–1800.* New York: Greenwood Press, 1987.

Richardson, James D., ed. *A Compilation of the Messages and Papers of the Presidents, 1789–1897.* 10 vols. Washington, D.C.: Government Printing Office, 1897.

Robinson, Edgar E. *The Evolution of American Political Parties: A Sketch of Party Development.* (New York: Harcourt, Brace, and Company, 1924. Reprint edited by Richard H. Leach. Johnson Reprint Corporation for *Reprints in Government and Political Science,* 1970.

Rockman, Bert A. *The Leadership Question: The Presidency and the American System* New York: Praeger Publishers, 1984.

Rossiter, Clinton. *Alexander Hamilton and the Constitution.* New York: Harcourt, Brace and World, 1964.

Rossiter, Clinton, ed. *The Federalist Papers.* New York: The New American Library, 1961.

Rubin, Richard L. *Press, Party, and Presidency.* New York: W. W. Norton, 1981.

Rutland, Robert Allen. *The Presidency of James Madison.* Lawrence: University Press of Kansas, 1990.

Sandburg, Carl. *Abraham Lincoln.* 6 vols. Sangamon Edition. New York: Scribner's, 1939.

Schattschneider, E. E. *The Semi-Sovereign People: A Realist's View of Democracy in America.* New York: Holt, Rinehart, and Winston, 1960.

Schlesinger, Arthur M. Jr. *The Age of Jackson.* Boston: Little, Brown, 1950.

Seager, Robert II. *And Tyler Too: A Biography of John and Julia Gardiner Tyler.* New York: McGraw Hill, 1963.

Sedgwick, Jeffrey Leigh. "Executive Leadership and Administration: Founding Versus Progressive Views." *Administration and Society* 17, no. 4 (February, 1986): 411–32.

Sellers, Charles G. *James K. Polk, Continentalist, 1843–46.* Princeton, N.J.: Princeton University Press, 1966.

Sharp, James Roger. *American Politics in the Early Republic: The New Nation in Crisis.* New Haven, Conn.: Yale University Press, 1993.

Siemers, David J. "It is Natural to Care for the Crazy Machine: The Antifederalists' Post-Ratification Acquiescence." *Studies in American Political Development* 12, no. 2 (fall, 1998): 383–410.

Skowronek, Stephen. *The Politics Presidents Make: Leadership from John Adams to Bill Clinton.* Cambridge, Mass.: Belknap Press, 1997.

Smith, Craig Allen, and Kathy B. *The White House Speaks: Presidential Leadership as Persuasion.* Westport, Conn.: Praeger, 1994.

Smith, Culver H. *The Press, Politics, and Patronage: The American Government's Use of Newspapers 1789–1875.* Athens: University of Georgia Press, 1977.

Smith, Elbert B. *The Presidencies of Zachary Taylor and Millard Fillmore.* Lawrence: University Press of Kansas, 1988.

———. *Francis Preston Blair.* New York: Free Press, 1980.

———. *The Presidency of James Buchanan.* Lawrence: University Press of Kansas, 1975.

Smith, Page. *John Adams: 1784–1826.* Garden City, N.Y.: Doubleday, 1962.

Smith, William E. *The Francis Preston Blair Family in Politics.* New York: Macmillan, 1933.

———. "Francis P. Blair, Pen-Executive of Andrew Jackson." In *Highlights in the History of the American Press,* edited by Edwin H. Ford and Edwin Emery. Minneapolis: University of Minnesota Press, 1954.

Socolofsky, Homer E., and Allan B. Spetter. *The Presidency of Benjamin Harrison.* Lawrence: University Press of Kansas, 1987.

Sperlich, Peter W. "Bargaining and Overload: An Essay on Presidential Power." In *The Presidency,* edited by Aaron Wildavsky. Boston: Little, Brown, 1969.

Stampp, Kenneth M. "Andrew Johnson: The Last Jacksonian." In *Andrew Johnson: A Profile,* edited by Eric McKitrick. New York: Hill and Wang, 1969.

Stein, Herbert. *Presidential Economics: The Making of Economic Policy from Roosevelt to Reagan and Beyond.* 2d ed. Washington, D.C.: American Enterprise Institute for Public Policy Research, 1988.

Stewart, Donald H. *The Opposition Press of the Federalist Period.* Albany: State University of New York Press, 1969.

Stewart, Robert K. "Jacksonians Discipline a Party Editor: Economic Leverage and Political Exile." *Journalism Quarterly* 66, no. 3 (1989): 591–99.

Stid, Daniel. *The President as Statesman: Woodrow Wilson and the Constitution.* Lawrence: University Press of Kansas Press, 1998.

———. "Rhetorical Leadership and 'Common Counsel' in the Presidency of Woodrow Wilson." In *Speaking to the People: The Rhetorical Presidency in Historical Perspective,* edited by Richard J. Ellis. Amherst: University of Massachusetts Press, 1998.

Storing, Herbert J. *What the Anti-Federalists Were For.* Chicago: University of Chicago Press, 1981.

Sundquist, James L. *The Decline and Resurgence of Congress.* Washington D.C.: Brookings, 1981.

Syrett, H.C., ed. *The Papers of Alexander Hamilton.* New York, 1975.

Tebbel, John. *The Compact History of the American Newspaper.* New York: Hawthorn Books, 1969.

———, and Sarah Miles Watts. *The Press and the Presidency from George Washington to Ronald Reagan.* New York: Oxford University Press, 1985.

Thach, Charles. *The Creation of the American Presidency: 1775–1789.* Baltimore: Johns Hopkins University Press, 1922.

Thomas, Norman, Joseph Pika, and Richard Watson. *The Politics of the Presidency.* 3d ed. Washington: CQ Press, 1994.

Thurow, Glen E. "Dimensions of Presidential Character." In *Beyond the Rhetorical Presidency,* edited by Martin J. Medhurst. College Station: Texas A&M University Press, 1996.

Trefousse, Hans L. *Andrew Johnson: A Biography.* New York: W. W. Norton, 1989.

Tulis, Jeffrey K. *The Rhetorical Presidency,* (Princeton, N.J.: Princeton University Press, 1987).

———. "The Two Constitutional Presidencies." In *The Presidency and the Political System,* edited by Michael Nelson. 6th ed. Washington D.C.: Congressional Quarterly Press, 2000.

———. "Revising the Rhetorical Presidency." In *Beyond the Rhetorical Presidency,* edited by Martin J. Medhurst. College Station: Texas A&M University Press, 1996.

Twohig, Dorothy, ed. *The Papers of George Washington: Presidential Series.* 9 vols. Charlottesville: University Press of Virginia, 1987–2000.

Tyler, James. "Original Letters." Edited by Lyon G. Tyler. *William and Mary Quarterly* 20, 1st ser. (July, 1911): 1–15.

Van Buren, Martin. *Inquiry into the Origin and Course of Political Parties in the United States.* 1867. Reprint, New York: Augustus M. Kelley, 1967.

Van Tyne, Claude H., ed. *The Letters of Daniel Webster.* New York: McClure, Phillips, 1902.

Waldstreicher, David. "Federalism, the Styles of Politics, and the Politics of Style." In *Federalists Reconsidered,* edited by Doron Ben-Atar and Barbara B. Oberg. Charlottesville: University of Virginia Press, 1998.

Walsh, Julie M. *The Intellectual Origins of Mass Parties and Schools in the Jacksonian Period: Creating a Conformed Citizenry.* New York: Garland, 1998.

Warner, Michael. *The Letters of the Republic: Publication and the Public Sphere in Eighteenth-Century America.* Cambridge, Mass.: Harvard University Press, 1990.

Washington Globe, Washington, D.C., 1830–36.

Welch, Richard E. Jr. *The Presidencies of Grover Cleveland.* Lawrence: University Press of Kansas, 1988.

White, Leonard D. *The Jacksonians: A Study in Administrative History, 1829–1861.* New York: Macmillan, 1954.

Wiebe, Robert H. *The Opening of American Society: From the Adoption of the Constitution to the Eve of Disunion.* New York: Alfred A. Knopf, 1984.

Williams, Charles Richard. *The Life of Rutherford Birchard Hayes.* Boston: Houghton Mifflin, 1914.

Williams, T. Harry, ed. *Hayes: The Diary of a President, 1875–1881.* New York: David McKay, 1964.

Wills, Garry, ed. *The Federalist Papers.* New York: Bantam Books, 1982.

Wilson, Major L. *The Presidency of Martin Van Buren.* Lawrence: University Press of Kansas, 1984.

Wilson, Woodrow. *Congressional Government: A Study in American Politics.* 1885. Reprint, New York: Meridian Books, 1965.

———. *Constitutional Government in the United States.* 1908. Reprint, New York: Columbia University Press, 1947.

———. "Mr. Cleveland's Cabinet," *Review of Reviews,* April, 1893, 286–97.

Windt, Theodore and Beth Ingold, eds. *Essays in Presidential Rhetoric.* 2d ed. Dubuque, Iowa: Kendall Hunt, 1987.

Wood, Gordon S. *The Creation of the American Republic, 1776–1787.* 2d ed. Chapel Hill: University of North Carolina Press, 1998.

———. *The Radicalism of the American Revolution.* New York: Random House, 1991.

———. "Interests and Disinterestedness in the Making of the Constitution." In *Beyond Confederation: Origins of the Constitution and American National Identity,* edited by Richard Beeman, Stephen Botein, and Edward C. Carter II. Chapel Hill: University of North Carolina Press, 1987.

———. "The Democratization of Mind in the American Revolution." In *The Moral Foundations of the American Republic,* edited by Robert H. Horwitz. 3d. ed. Charlottesville: University Press of Virginia, 1986.

Young, James Sterling. *The Washington Community, 1800–1828.* New York: Columbia University Press, 1966.

Zagarri, Rosemary. "Gender and the First Party System." In *Federalists Reconsidered,* edited by Doron Ben-Atar and Barbara B. Oberg. Charlottesville: University Press of Virginia, 1998.

INDEX

Bergeron, Paul H., 86

Bessette, Joseph M., 3, 35, 197, 238n. 24, 239n. 25

Beveridge, Albert J., 137

Biddle, Nicolas, 85

Bill of Rights, 26, 202n. 21

Binkley, Wilfred, 118, 120, 121, 228n. 56, 237n. 46

Blair, Francis P.: circulation of *Washington Globe*, 181, 218n. 93; creation of *Washington Globe*, 69–70; defense of VanBuren, 81, 220n. 8; farewell editorial, 222n. 47; involvement with Polk, 87–88; support of Jackson, 73, 78–79

Bleyer, Willard, 47

Board of Visitors, 37

body politic, 27, 67

Booth, John Wilkes, 115

Boston Daily Globe, 176

Boston Morning Post, 74, 176, 182

Boy Scouts, 151

British Guiana, 229n. 21

British Parliament. *See* Parliament

British Whigs, 44. *See also* English Whig Party

Brooklyn Advocate, 176

Brougham, Henry, 47

Buchanan, James, 75, 77, 88, 90, 95–98, 140, 154, 155

bully pulpit, 10, 149

Burke, Edmund, 200n. 23, 203n. 27

Burr, Aaron, 59

Bush, George H. W., 163

Bush, George W., 143, 166, 168n. 21, 238n. 21

Butler, Benjamin F., 118–120, 227n. 52

Calhoun, John C., 67, 69, 78

Canisius, Theodore, 106–107

Capitol Hill, 63

Carolene, 80

Carnegie, Andrew, 134

Cato, 211n. 98

Catullus, 51

Ceaser, James W., 3, 31, 35, 148, 198n. 9, 206n. 58

Celebrator Model, 7, 65, 66, 136, 145, 148, 168. *See also* National Cheerleader Model

Central Committee, 68

Chase, Samuel, 29

Chesapeake, 62

Chicago, 110, 114

Chicago Tribune, 95, 114, 119, 120

Chief Magistrate, 44, 57, 116, 150

Cicero, 44, 211nn. 95, 98

Cincinnati Republican, 16, 27, 28, 29, 44, 45, 57, 122

Civil War, 77, 95, 98, 101, 110, 122, 142

classical republicanism, 16, 27, 28, 29, 44, 45, 57, 122

classicist philosophy: definition, 13, 42, 160, 166; Benjamin Harrison, 133; Hayes, 126; incorporation into Republican party, 14, 38, 41; influence on presidential behavior, 44, 45, 142, 147, 162; Johnson impeachment, 117, 119; Madison, 64, 234n. 3; Monroe, 234n. 3; Whig attitude toward Jackson, 70. *See also* Republican Party; Whig Party; Whig-Republicans

Clay, Henry, 43, 72, 79, 84, 91, 92, 179, 180, 181, 182, 190, 218n. 101, 221n. 33, 222n. 44

Cleveland, Grover: executive privilege, 122; newspaper editorial on presidential powers, 234n. 65; nominations, 228n. 3; reserved conception of presidency, 144, 148; presidency, 127–31, 139, 140, 229n. 19, 230nn. 31–33; presidential messages, 91, 123

Cleveland Leader, 116

Cleveland Plain Dealer, 115

Clinton, Bill, 68, 143, 165, 166, 168, 170

Clinton, George, 207

Cole, Donald, 79
Committee of Colored Men, 110
Committee of Detail, 24
Confederacy, 109
Confederate Virginia Assembly, 109
Congressional Government, 149. *See also* Woodrow Wilson
Conkling, James, 109, 226n. 24
Conkling, Roscoe, 126, 127, 226n. 24
Connecticut Courant, 58
Constitution: disagreements over meaning, 14, 16, 19–25, 38–39, 162; Federalists and Antifederalists disagreements, 25–31; Freneau, 52–53; Benjamin Harrison's interpretation, 131; evolution, 152–53, 160, 202n. 22; Lincoln, 102, 108; Radical Republican interpretation, 118; ratification battle,13, 49, 201n. 16, 202n. 21, 205nn. 40, 43, 237n. 6; Republican interpretation of presidency, 123; Taylor and slavery, 93; Tyler's interpretation, 86; vagueness, 15, 18, 200n. 2, 201n. 12, 202n. 19; Van Buren, 79; veto, 155; Washington, 56; Whig interpretation, 43, 81; Wilson, 150–52
Constitution, 96, 97. See also *Washington Union*
Constitutional Convention, 16, 21–25, 32, 33, 205nn. 40, 43, 210n. 88
Constitutional Government, 149, 151. *See also* Woodrow Wilson
constitutional order: absence of original, 91; alternative view, 168; evolution, 26; flawed conception, 159, 162; Lincoln and original, 101; "original," 9, 27, 117, 236n. 38; president's place, 4, 11
Cornell, Saul, 202n. 22, 203n. 23
Covode Committee, 98
Crittenden, John J., 90, 223n. 68
Cuba, 135, 137, 228
Cunliffe, Marcus, 53, 210, 237n. 46

Declaration of Independence, 13, 27
deliberation, 16, 29, 40, 43, 65, 71, 123, 167, 168, 169
Deliberator Model, 7, 57, 65, 66, 128, 145, 147, 148
demagogue (demagoguery), 27, 31, 33–35, 102, 115, 127
democracy, 47, 55; *Aurora*, 58; definition, 16, 208n. 72; demagogues, 33; differing conceptions, 13, 14, 17, 39, 41, 45, 63, 64, 159, 160, 199n. 21, 208n. 72; Federalists' view, 29, 204n. 29; *Globe* and Democratic Party, 222n. 47; populist view, 28, 162, 200n. 24; veto use, 154
Democratic coalition, 79
Democratic Party: 1840 platform, 41; first national convention, 70; *Globe* as party paper, 84; history, 207n. 67; Lincoln's attitude, 103–104; nineteenth century principles, 13, 14, 38; Pierce administration, 95; Taylor administration, 91; VanBuren, 78, 80
Democratic-Republicans, 9, 14, 38, 39, 52, 58, 153, 205n. 39, 208n. 75
Democracy in America, 46. *See also* Alexis de Tocqueville
Democratic Review, 40
democratist philosophy: definition,13, 40–41; incorporation into Democratic Party, 38, 41; influence on presidential behavior, 14, 45, 64, 162; Jackson, 70; president in public policy process, 117–18, 140; view of representation, 153, 160
De Nemours, Pierre Dupont, 49
Depew, Chauncey M., 231n. 39
de Tocqueville, Alexis *(Democracy in America)*, 46, 67, 76, 154
Dewey, Admiral George, 193, 233n. 65
Dickinson, John, 213n. 28
Divorce Bill, 80
Douglas, Stephen A., 106, 114

impeachment (*cont.*)
160–61, 198n. 13; Johnson's (Article 10), 116–21, 228n. 56; Johnson's (House vote), 144, 227nn. 51, 53; Tyler's attempted, 83

Indiana, 68, 82, 131, 137

interviews (presidential): Arthur, 127; as means of public communication, 12; Cleveland, 128–29, 230n. 32; Garfield, 126; Hayes, 124; Johnson, 120; Lincoln, 108; McKinley, 138, 233n. 63

Jackson, Andrew: activist conception of presidency, 15, 41, 117, 155, 160, 170, 237n. 46; attack by *Intelligencer,* 93; classification of presidency, 140, 142, 144; Democratic party, 40; general under Monroe, 65, 120; Polk, 87–88; government printing contracts, 97; presidential messages, 91, 128; presidential newspaper, 3, 47, 66–76, 90, 147, 175–92, 219n.104, 222n. 47; Senate censure, 83; Tulis, 197n. 8; Tyler, 82; VanBuren presidency, 77–80; veto, 154; Whig opposition, 43

Jacksonian Democrats, 41, 43, 67–69, 74, 78, 199, 218n. 93

Jacobinism, 58. *See also* Democratic Republicans; Jeffersonian Republican Party

Jaffa, Harry, 16

Jefferson, Thomas, 14, 57, 78, 97; clashes with Hamilton, 21–24, 31, 210n. 12; Democratic-Republicans, 37–40; Federalist Papers, 32–33; populist philosophy, 28, 200n. 25, 208n. 79, 212n. 30; presidency, 58–64, 150, 152, 170, 214n. 35; use of newspapers, 46, 48, 49–54, 67, 140, 160, 165, 212n. 17, 213n. 24, 215nn. 48, 53, 216n. 62, 217n. 81

Jeffersonian Republican Party, 9, 215n. 48; Antifederalist influence, 38–39, 207n. 69; evolution, 209n. 85, 210n. 94; influence on Democratic party, 14, 200n. 25; Jefferson administration, 58, 60; Washington administration, 50–51, 53. *See also* Democratic-Republicans; Jacobinism

Johnson, Andrew: activist view of presidency, 15, 142, 148, 160; battle with Congress, 143; going public, 139–40; impeachment, 17, 144, 161, 198n. 13, 227nn. 51–53, 228n. 56; Lincoln's running mate, 226n. 37, 234n. 2; presidency, 112–22

Jones, J. Beauchamp, 84–85, 221n. 37

Kansas-Nebraska Act, 96

Kendall, Amos, 69, 72, 177

Kentucky, 68, 69

Kerber, Linda, 27, 199n. 21

Kernell, Samuel (*Going Public: New Strategies of Presidential Leadership*) 4, 5, 7, 148, 158–59, 162–63, 197nn. 1, 8

Ketcham, Ralph, 20, 210n. 88, 219n. 2, 235n. 22

Lincoln, Abraham (*Letters of President Lincoln on Questions of National Policy*), 99, 225n. 5; Andrew Johnson, 113, 226n. 37, 234n. 2; approach to public communications, 115–16, 142, 144, 170, 225n. 12; Gettysburg Address, 235n. 23; presidency, 100–12; presidential messages, 91; use of letters in presidency, 85; Whig views of presidency, 43, 139, 140, 209n. 82, 210n. 91

Lee, Henry, 50

Lee, Robert E., 111

Leech, Margaret, 137

Letters. *See* Presidential Letters

86, 90; Taylor, 91, 93; Tulis, 197n.
8; Tyler, 82–86; VanBuren, 78
original intent, 5, 10, 158

Pacificus, 51
Paine, Thomas, 62, 213n. 28
Pan-American Exposition, 134
Panic of 1837, 79
Parker, George F., 130
Parliament: annual speech from throne,
62, 123, 201n. 7; Burke's descrip-
tion, 203n. 7; filter of public opinion,
16, 42
patriot-king or leader, 22, 44, 55, 57,
126, 134, 144
Patriot Press, 48
Payne, George, 54
Pennsylvania, 23, 56, 68, 87, 92; Anti-
federalist riot, 202n. 18; debate on
representation, 204n. 31; Federal-
ists, 209n. 84; Benjamin Harrison
speech, 231n. 39
Pennsylvania Assembly, 204n. 31
Peterson, Norma Lois, 83
Philadelphia, 32, 50, 59, 106
Philadelphia Aurora, 58, 59, 215n. 48
Philadelphia National Gazette, 212n. 17
Philadelphia Press, 126
Philadelphia Whig, 184
Philippines, 134–37, 193–96, 232n. 53
Phocion, 203n. 28
Pierce, Franklin, 95, 98, 140
plebiscitary presidency, 4, 197n. 4
Plutarch, 203n. 28
policy making process, 5, 6, 11, 82, 89,
140, 147, 166, 167, 168, 170
Polk, James, 8, 15, 47, 86–91, 140, 170
Politics Presidents Make, The, 10. *See also*
Stephen Skowronek
Pollard, James E., 86, 105, 111, 114,
115, 120, 199n. 17
popular rhetoric, 35, 204n. 29
postal system (mail), 66–69, 76, 94,
108, 162, 211n. 7, 218n. 93

Powell, Colin, 120
presidential bargaining. *See* bargaining
presidential letters, 5; John Adams, 57;
Lincoln, 104, 107, 109–10; Polk,
88–89; Tyler, 85
presidential messages, 12, 92, 143, 149;
Buchanan, 96, 155; Cleveland, 123,
128–30; John Adams, 57; Jackson,
71–73; Jefferson, 61–62; Lincoln,
109; Madison, 65; norm, 4; Polk,
90–91; Tyler, 82–82, 155; Van
Buren, 80
presidential newspaper. *See* Newspapers
press release, 12, 129, 130, 138, 151
printing. *See* government printing
protest message (Jackson), 71
pseudonyms, 49, 51, 53–55, 62, 63,
203n. 28, 213nn. 28–29
public affairs, 34, 54, 57, 133
public good, 13, 16, 27, 28, 42, 104
Publicola, 49
public opinion, 4, 36, 147, 167–68;
Antifederalists, 29; Buchanan, 95–
96; Democratists and Classicists
opposing conceptions, 39–42, 117;
Federalists, 31; Grant, 121, 228n.
63; Hayes, 126; Jackson, 72, 74–76;
Johnson, 198n. 13; Kernell's view,
163; Lincoln, 105; Madison, 207n.
70; presidential speaking tours, 12;
presidents, 153–54; use of newspapers to influence, 11, 47, 48, 53, 72–
76, 145, 219n. 117; Wilson, 150–51
Puerto Rico, 135
Puerto Rico Tariff Bill, 233n. 63
Pulitzer, Joseph, 129, 138

Queen Elizabeth, 201n. 7

Radical Republicans, 113, 115, 118,
119, 121, 161
Rakove, Jack, 26, 37
Raleigh Star, 176
Randolph, Edmund, 24, 51

Raymond, Henry J., 108
Reagan, Ronald, 168, 237n. 46, 238n. 12
Reconstruction, 113, 114, 161
Reconstruction Committee, 118
representation: different conceptions, 13, 14, 16, 17, 25, 30, 31, 169; "directed representation" vs. "representational deliberation," 169; implications for presidency, 14, 41, 153, 162; populist view, 17, 28, 29, 39, 205n. 40; reserved view, 16–17, 159; trustee vs. delegate, 17, 41
representative democracy: Antifederalists and Federalists, 25, 31; Classicist paradigm, 41–43; democratist paradigm, 40–41; 153, 162, 208n. 79; different views of, 13, 14, 17, 20, 38, 117, 166, 218n. 96
representative government, 20, 39
republic (concept of), 13, 15, 16, 18, 25, 27, 28, 30, 35, 36. See also Republicanism
Republic (Washington), 91, 92, 94, 224n. 73
Republican convention, 106
Republican government, 43, 212n. 20
Republicanism (classic concept of), 14, 16, 20, 27, 29, 160; Ciceronian rhetorical conventions and, 44, 45; evolution of, 200n. 25, 205n. 39, McKinley and, 134. See also Representative Democracy; Republic
Republicanism (Jeffersonian), 58, 215n. 48
Republican orthodoxy, 14, 15
Republican Party: Classicist philosophy, 117, 122, 142; ideological history, 207n. 67; impeachment of Johnson, 119; Lincoln and party paper, 106, 107; Lincoln's plan to replace, 112, 234n. 2; McKinley and 1896 platform; nineteenth century principles, 38, 41, 139, 143, 152;

presidential candidates avoid going public, 140; reserved conception of presidency, 43, 121, 138, 139, 140, 143, 152
Republican Press, 58, 115
Reserved Model, 57, 66, 169
Revolutionary War, 44
rhetoric: John Adams, 57; Ciceronian (Classicist), 44; definition of, 8; of *Federalist Papers*, 37; Federalists, 204n. 29; genres, 235n. 20; Benjamin Harrison's, 133; Johnson's, 112, 116; labor negotiations, 238, n. 14; Lincoln's, 101, 110; McKinley's, 134, 135; media, 167; nineteenth century, 149, 153; presidential, 4, 35, 42, 44, 147 210n. 88; Ciceronian (Classicist) form, 45; rhetorical presidency, 4, 20, 26, 168, 197n. 8, 198n. 13; Washington's, 55, 56. See also Rhetorical Presidency
rhetorical presidency, 3, 4, 12, 20, 26, 31, 35, 167, 168, 198n. 13
Rhetorical Presidency, The, 3, 7, 158, 198n. 13. See also Jeffrey Tulis
Rhode Island, 56
Richelieu, 211n. 4
Richmond Examiner, 62
Richmond Enquirer, 74, 80, 87, 175, 184
Richmond Times, 234n. 65
Rio Grande, 88
Ritchie, Thomas, 80, 87–90
Roane, Spencer, 208n. 76
Robertson, W.H., 126
Roosevelt, Franklin, 10, 18, 152
Roosevelt, Theodore, 10, 11, 18, 134, 149, 152, 168
Rubin, Richard L., 49, 76
Rush, Benjamin, 202n. 19, 217n. 80

Sandburg, Carl, 109
Sangamon Journal, 105
Schattschneider, E. E., 162
Scott, Winfield, 110

MELVIN C. LARACEY is an assistant professor of political science at the University of Texas at San Antonio. He earned his Ph.D. in political science from the University of Michigan, an M.P.A. from Harvard University's Kennedy School of Government, and a J.D. from the University of Michigan School of Law.